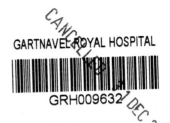

Practice leadership in mental health and intellectual disability nursing

Note

Healthcare practice and knowledge are constantly changing and developing
as new research and treatments, changes in procedures, drugs and equipment
become available.

The editors and publishers have, as far as is possible, taken care to confirm that
the information complies with the latest standards of practice and legislation.

Practice leadership in mental health and intellectual disability nursing

Edited by

Mark Jukes

QUAY
BOOKS

A division of MA Healthcare Ltd

Quay Books Division, MA Healthcare Ltd, St Jude's Church, Dulwich Road, London
SE24 0PB

British Library Cataloguing-in-Publication Data
A catalogue record is available for this book

© MA Healthcare Limited 2013

ISBN-10: 1-85642-506-1
ISBN-13: 978-1-85642-506-3

Edited by Jessica Anderson

Printed by Mimeo, Huntingdon, Cambridgeshire

Contents

List of contributors

Editor

Mark Jukes – Reader in Learning/Intellectual Disabilities, Faculty of Health, Department of Mental Health and Learning Disabilities, City South Campus, Birmingham City University.

Contributors

Paul Allen – Senior Lecturer in Public Health, Department of Public Health, Faculty of Health, Birmingham City University.

Carl Benton – Associate Lecturer/Practitioner for Medium Secure Forensics For People With Intellectual/Learning Disabilities, South Birmingham Mental Health Foundation Trust and Birmingham City University.

Jim Blair – Consultant Nurse in Intellectual/Learning Disabilities, St Georges Hospital, London.

Jonathan Beebee – Team Leader for the Intensive Support Team, Intellectual/ Learning Disabilities, Southampton.

Michael Brown – Nurse Consultant and Reader in Health and Social Care, Edinburgh Napier University, Edinburgh.

Tom Casey – Community Mental Health Nurse, Crisis Resolution and Home Treatment, Birmingham and Solihull Mental Health Foundation Trust.

Cheryl Chessum – Associate Lecturer/Practitioner, Birmingham Community Mental Health Trust and Birmingham City University.

Nicola Clarke – Senior Lecturer in Mental Health Nursing, Department of Mental Health and Learning Disabilities, Birmingham City University.

Vicky Clarke – Head of Department, Mental Health and Learning Disabilities, Birmingham City University.

Lorraine Conlon – Lead Nurse, Reaside Clinic, Specialist and Complex Care, Birmingham and Solihull Mental Health NHS Foundation Trust.

Stephen Conlon – Associate Lecturer/Practitioner in Solution Focused Practice, Birmingham City University and Longbridge Health and Community Centre, Birmingham.

Sophia Nuala Fletcher – Matron, Reaside Clinic, Specialist and Complex Care, Birmingham and Solihull Mental Health NHS Foundation Trust.

Rachael Garvey – Senior Community Forensic Nurse, Greenfields, Birmingham Community NHS Trust.

Helen Goulding – Lecturer in Learning Disabilities, Department of Mental Health and Learning Disabilities, Faculty of Health, Birmingham City University.

Stuart Guy – Matron, Reaside Clinic, Specialist and Complex Care, Birmingham and Solihull Mental Health NHS Foundation Trust.

Dean-David Holyoak – Senior Lecturer in Mental Health, University of Wolverhampton, West Midlands.

Paul Illingworth – Independent Nurse and Health, Social and Justice Sector Consultant, Targeted Health Integrated Solutions, Birmingham. Previously Head of School of Nursing, Faculty of Health, Birmingham City University.

Mike Jenkins – Clinical Nurse Specialist, Birmingham Child and Adolescent Mental Health Services.

Marion Johnson – Senior Lecturer in Mental Health, Department of Mental Health and Learning Disabilities, Faculty of Health, Birmingham City University.

Emma Lyall – Team Manager, Children's Services, Greenhill Lodge Children's Home, Worcester.

Josh Millwood – Patient Governor, Birmingham Childrens Hospital, Birmingham.

Paul Millwood – Senior Lecturer in Mental Health, Faculty of Health, Department of Mental Health and Learning Disabilities, Birmingham City University.

Premchunlall Mohabeersingh – Senior Academic, Faculty of Health, Department of Public Health, Birmingham City University.

Mervyn Morris – Professor of Mental Health, Director, Centre for Mental Health, Birmingham City University.

Karen Nankervis – Centre Director and Chair, Behaviour Support, Centre of Excellence for Behaviour Support, University of Queensland, Australia

Fred Ruddick – Senior Lecturer in Mental Health, Cumbria University, Carlisle

Jon Stringer – Nurse Consultant, Walsall Child and Adolescent Mental Health Services, Walsall, Birmingham.

Foreword

I am delighted to write this foreword as there has never been a better time to address leadership in mental health and learning disability nursing. The authors, all experts in their field, tackle this ambitious task by focusing on leadership in the delivery of personalised care, support, and the promotion of wider inclusion.

With nursing leadership under the spotlight, this book gives us the opportunity to identify why it is important to strengthen nursing leadership and to understand its influence in shaping practice and improving the quality of care. In an open and transparent culture staff members share and reflect on their experiences, they are encouraged to speak up when they have concerns, to seek support when needed and are helped to build emotional resilience. It helps us explore the relationships between effective leadership and improved outcomes for patients. The book is a valuable resource for educators, employers, and nurses working in practice, particularly those who are ready for change and improvement but are unsure how to go about making those changes.

Providing high quality personalised care can be a challenge for those working within mental health and learning disability services, but the principles of respect, participation, choice and control must always be applied. We have to get to grips with the failings identified in recent reports, listen to and involve the people we care for and their families, and make sure that high quality person-centred care is the norm. This book promotes investment and engagement to develop nurse leaders, illustrating how their skills can change service provision, engage service users in their care planning and embed patient-centred care across the health and social care system.

Mental health nursing and learning disability nursing offer valued, fulfilling and rewarding careers. It is important that we promote these fields of nursing, recognising and celebrating the contribution that they make. We need to enable role models to exert their influence across the whole nursing community and tackle the institutionalised discrimination towards these vulnerable groups.

Developing strong and influential leaders within mental health and learning disability services is an essential part of practice development. Mental health nurses and learning disability nurses are at the forefront of transforming services, service development and improvement. They lead new ways of working, wherever people need their care, creating a culture where good practice becomes common practice.

This book explores how to create and nurture practice leaders in mental health and learning disability services, and how this will improve people's experience of care. It offers a reminder of why most of us come into the nursing professions: to make a difference; to care for people when they are at their most vulnerable; to help people stay healthy or help them recover from illness; to promote well-being and support independence; and to ensure they experience high quality care and the best possible health outcomes.

Ben Thomas
Professional Nursing Adviser for Mental Health and
Learning Disability Nursing
Department of Health, England

Introduction

The landscape of services and support for people with mental health needs and for those with intellectual disabilities has changed considerably, particularly over the past 20 years since the introduction of the NHS and Community Care Act. Services continue to evolve around the personalisation and social inclusion agenda.

People with an intellectual disability also experience mental health distress and require treatment within acute primary, secondary or tertiary mental health settings. This text will help readers to acquire further insights and understanding into a broadened agenda for practice. Mental health and intellectual disabilities nurses share commonalities in terms of legislation, human rights, the deleterious effects of marginalisation and exclusion, and similar nursing practice issues towards the promotion of personalisation, inclusion and person-centred care.

The past decade has seen the arrival of personalisation in the UK, and the processes and outcomes of a traditional service-led approach have lead to people not receiving the right help at the right time. For some this has meant being excluded from mainstream services, such as transport, leisure, education, housing and health, and opportunities for employment regardless of age or disability (Allen et al, 2009; Department of Health, 2001, 2009).

So, the question that needs to be asked is, what are the leadership challenges in transforming mental health and intellectual disability services so as to deliver more personalised support, inclusion and care choices?

Several factors mitigate against engaging with personalisation, including traditional service model design and professional hierarchies. Nurses tend to resist letting go of established forms of assessments and methods of intervention.

Additionally, traditional forms of decision making culminate in an inability or reluctance to let go of professional power differentials, which are perceived as paternalistic and retain control over people.

Further challenges that personalisation offers for people with mental health needs and for people with intellectual disabilities are the opportunities to break down stigma and institutionalisation. This creates opportunities for integration through increasing self-determination, engaging with and promoting empowerment, independence, choice and control.

There are, however, additional challenges for professionals, where augmenting inclusion means managing particular types of risk and fluctuations in individuals' abilities to gain mental capacity. Professionals also need to be able to facilitate best interests and screen for and prevent deprivation of liberties – all issues that are embedded within the Equality Act 2010. Personalisation is about giving people more choice and control over their lives in all settings, including healthcare.

Personalisation implies a paradigm shift in thinking and practice at a personal/professional, political and developmental level, and therefore implies a radical agenda for change which ultimately will stretch present leadership norms and expectations.

Leadership challenges include driving a values-led service, and service transformation which sustains cultural change within and across organisations, all achieved within public spending restrictions.

This text is about practice leadership towards personalisation and person-centred care, and is grounded in relationship building, the development of shared values across services, the encouragement of creativity, the capacity to influence others and the ability to facilitate collective inputs and energies rather than "direct" them.

These human-based interactional qualities and competencies require practitioners to have a renewed, robust sense of confidence with strong person-centred values and leadership ethics, rather than a traditional paternalistic, authoritarian and hierarchical style of leadership.

We have recently witnessed the NHS at crisis point with the devastating results of the Mid-Staffordshire Inquiry (Francis, 2013). The Inquiry identified a lack of management and leadership capacity and that medical and nursing values and care had been breached, the outcome of which was the de-humanisation of patients.

Chapters within this text are about identifying concepts relative to leadership and about where the rightful place for practice leadership should be, which is at the sharp end of practice. Front-line mental health and intellectual disability nurses must work as effective role models in promoting leadership and managing change, and enable environments in which they work to become dynamic and palpable sources of positive growth and change.

References

Allen R, Gilbert P, Onyett S (2009) *Leadership for personalisation and social inclusion in mental health*. Social Care Institute for Excellence, London

Department of Health (2001) *Valuing people: A new strategy for people with learning disabilities in the 21st Century.* HMSO, London

Department of Health (2009) *Valuing people now.* HMSO, London

Francis R (2013) *Report of the Mid-Staffordshire NHS Trust Public Inquiry (The Francis Report).* HMSO, London

Note

The term practice leadership is used in this book rather than clinical leadership, as the latter tends to infer a medicalisation role and relationship. Practice leadership infers a collaborative process between practitioners and service users.

The term intellectual disability is now becoming more commonly used internationally and within the research literature, and so has been adopted here. However, it is also acknowledged that the term learning disability is still used in the UK and so both terms will be found within the book.

Mark Jukes
Birmingham City University

Chapter 1

Intellectual disability and mental health nursing in the 21st century

Mark Jukes and Vicky Clarke

Introduction

This chapter focuses initially on the policy development that enshrines both mental health and intellectual disability nursing. A focus on these two fields of nursing then identifies why there is a need for effective leadership in these most challenging areas of contemporary practice, within a context of a sea of ideological and health and social care policy changes.

The past 20 years, in particular, have brought a raft of legislation and policy changes that have impacted on both service users/carers and nurses in these fields.

Emphasis on and ways of thinking about management and leadership have been favoured at certain times in our history and currently, mostly in response to critical incidents that have stemmed from policy implementation, and that have placed people with mental health and intellectual disability within the public spotlight.

Policy context and development

In 1971 and 1975 the *Better services* White papers were published by the Department of Health and Social Security for people with mental handicap and for those with mental illness. Since then there has been a gradual progression towards community care, which was at its peak during the 1980s, and which culminated in the introduction of the NHS Community Care Act 1990. Significant changes in policy over this period have also affected the way we communicate inter-professionally.

The review of the Mental Health Act, the introduction of the Mental Capacity Act, now the Equality Act 2010, coupled with the Deprivation of Liberty Safeguards, have compelled professionals to acquire and develop a sound value base, and have required nurses to be more self-aware and emotionally intelligent both in how they perceive themselves and their practice, and also when mediating and collaborating with other professionals and services that directly affect service users.

Recent health policies have emphasised social inclusion. In the UK in 2011, 22.7% of the population was considered to be at risk of poverty or social exclusion, equivalent to 14 million people (Office for National Statistics, 2013). People with mental health and intellectual disability are excluded from mainstream generic health, social, work, leisure and educational services. Professionals across these sectors are required to promote social inclusion for these groups of people.

We are in a policy age of citizenship and personalisation. The recovery approach has been developed for people with mental health needs by listening to service users about what they need to be able to manage their mental illness, to enable them to continue to live a meaningful life as purported by Repper and Perkins (2009). In intellectual disability, person-centred planning effectively means we are required to work with the individuals to maximise their opportunities and move towards the realisation of their aspirations and "dreams". Both the recovery approach and person-centred planning bring challenges not only to people with mental health and intellectual disability, but also to the professionals involved in their care. Contemporary policy that directly affects mental health practice includes the *Ten Essential Shared Capabilities* (Hope, 2004), and when compared with the values base for intellectual disability nursing, we can see that there are similarities in shared philosophy and practice (see *Table 1.1*).

Table 1.1. Ten Essential Shared Capabilities compared with the values base for intellectual disability nursing	
Ten essential shared capabilities for guiding mental health practice (Hope, 2004)	*The values base for intellectual disability nursing (Scottish Government, 2012)*
1. *Working in partnership* with each other and with service users, carers and other agencies in order to develop an effective care plan. 2. *Respecting diversity* by addressing the different needs of individual people and their carers including differences in culture, age, sex, religion and race. It is not ignorant to discuss diversity with people but it can be harmful if we do not.	• *Human rights:* Place the individual at the centre, valuing choice, inclusion, citizenship and social justice. Incorporate equality, individuality, person-centred and strength-based approaches, empowerment, self-determination, dignity and anti-oppression. • *Personalisation:* Supporting the individual's control and choice over their own life and services through empowering people with intellectual disabilities, their families and carers and relinquishing "control".

3. *Practising ethically:* Ensuring that every individual has a chance to express his or her needs and not assuming that we always know best what other people's needs might be. 4. *Challenging inequality:* While it may be difficult at times we must always make sure that there is someone to advocate on behalf of people if they are unable to do so for themselves. 5. *Promoting recovery* by encouraging people to make decisions that maintain their hope and optimism in their individual needs being met. 6. *Identifying people's needs and strengths:* To encourage people along a recovery journey. 7. *Providing service user-centred care:* Working in collaboration at all times to identify and address needs. 8. *Making a difference* in helping people to identify and make choices without assuming that they know what is available to them. 9. *Promoting safety and positive risk taking* by identifying risks and working together to address them. 10. *Ensuring personal development and learning* by taking responsibility for our own learning and providing evidence that our practice is up to date.	• *Equality and inclusion:* Recognising diversity and challenging inequality and inequity by supporting people with intellectual disabilities to use the same services and have the same opportunities and entitlements as anyone else. • *Person-centred:* Meaningful engagement with people to identify goals significant to the person. • *Strengths-based:* Focusing on existing strengths, skills, talents and resources and increasing personal competence. • *Respect:* Valuing the whole person and the diversity of people who support and sustain him or her. Appreciating the contribution of families and carers and, where possible, enhancing the contribution of others. • *Partnerships:* Recognising that health and social outcomes are interdependent. • *Health-focused:* Focusing on the individual's health and well-being to enable inclusive lifestyles.

Intellectual disability nursing

Intellectual disability nursing has consistently been under threat and has at times been almost extinct since the NHS Act 1948 was enacted. Care for people with intellectual disabilities was previously in colonies or hospital and the development of intellectual disability nursing has fractured as nurses moved out with their patients from the institutions.

The introduction of the NHS and Community Care Act 1990 divided services into health and social care. For intellectual disability nurses this brought about a dysfunctional split into what previously had been effective multi-professional team working in the form of community learning disability teams set up by the National Development Group for the Mentally Handicapped in 1976.

The implications of the Community Care Act resulted in social workers being absorbed into social care and intellectual disability nurses into health teams. For the latter this brought about an emphasis on health work and so these nurses were required to forge a specific health agenda and identity.

Health equality had been strived for from the mid-1980s (Howells, 1986) and disparities between the health of the general population and people with intellectual disabilities began to be well reported and subsequently highlighted in government reform on this issue (Department of Health, 1999, 2001).

More recently, a public health role for intellectual disability nurses has been pursued in England (Department of Health, 2007a), specifically relating to developing planning policy and leading service delivery for people with intellectual disabilities (Mufaba, 2009).

The first fracture occurred before the publication of the Jay report in 1979. In this report, Jay's concern was about the recommendations for further development and delivery of more effective services for people with intellectual disabilities. One recommendation proposed joining together intellectual disability nurses and social workers. In essence, this would expand the workforce across services. However, the report was not well received by nurses who saw it as a move towards the dissolution of intellectual disability nursing, to be replaced with a social care/worker model.

The *Nursing Mirror* (1978) reacted vehemently prior to the report recommendations being published, and the unions took to lobbying against it. As a consequence the Labour Government took a long time to release a response. Mitchell (2004) questions what would have happened to the Jay Report if a Conservative Government had not been put in power in 1979? What would services look like today, and what type of professional would exist in such services?

An alternative nursing syllabus was developed by the English National Board for Nursing, Health Visiting and Midwifery. This syllabus, which arrived in 1982, was orientated towards a social, educational ethos, with the nursing process and normalisation being a coherent thread throughout. It must be borne in mind, however, that intellectual disability nursing and services at this time were predominantly still located in hospitals, and that the move to community care and the "ordinary living" model was yet to be fully realised. The mid-1980s could be seen as the point of transition for many services towards providing alternative residential options.

The Consensus conference 10 years later was the second fracture to impact on the future direction of intellectual disability nursing. This was where Brown (1994) coined the phrase "the consensus legacy", reflecting on the fact that the consensus was arrived at without proper consultation. One of the most radical suggestions was that intellectual disability nursing should become a post-registration option.

The profession reacted vociferously to the options proposed, and later there was a retraction of what could have been the death knell for intellectual disability nursing.

The report, *Continuing the commitment* (Kay et al, 1995) confirmed the government's commitment to intellectual disability nursing and began the journey of healing through celebrating and articulating the value and contribution of the specialty across health and social care. Within this report, examples of good practice captured some evidence that intellectual disability nurses provided a unique contribution to people with learning disabilities and their families.

What one can observe from these initial fracturing processes is the ability and presence that senior nurses, positioned within or having alliances with the Department of Health, have to mobilise themselves in times of threat and throw the weight of the profession behind them.

A third fracturing occurred after the announcement in 2005 that nursing would become an all-graduate profession, and that the four fields in nursing would remain. However, although this was positive news for intellectual disability nursing, and strengthened recognition of this field by the Nursing and Midwifery Council (2011), it occurred at a time when student admissions to intellectual disability nursing were declining. Universities offering courses in this field were also in decline and senior staff were openly dissuading students from pursuing the specialty (Parish, 2012).

Gates (2011) submitted a task-group report to the Professional and Advisory Board for Nursing and Midwifery giving an analysis of the results detailing the extent of decline in learning disability nursing courses and in student admissions. According to the Nursing and Midwifery Council (2011) there are just over 21 000 learning disability nurse registrants which represents just over 3% of the total workforce across intellectual disability services. This statistic indicates that the best value from these nurses occurs where direct effect is maximised, and that is within specialist NHS services for people with intellectual disabilities.

Abuse and poor care standards

Amid the periods of fracturing of intellectual disability nursing, and progressively since 1995, we have witnessed, through exposure in the media, blatant abuse of people with intellectual disabilities. In 1995 the BBC programme, *Panorama*, exposed the Longcare scandal in Buckinghamshire, and in 1999, on Channel 4, *MacIntyre undercover* exposed further abuse in residential social care through secret filming.

The Department of Health's (2001) publication, *Valuing people*, was timely. It had been 30 years since a government White paper had strategically addressed the way ahead in promoting a strategy for people with intellectual disabilities, their families and carers. However, although holistic in nature, *Valuing people* has been criticised for not being a National Service Framework which would afford, as with the Frameworks in mental health, a higher profile with more substantive investment (Styring and Grant, 2003).

In 2003, further abuse was exposed in social care on Channel 5, where *MacIntyre undercover* reported on the abuse of vulnerable people with intellectual disabilities with personal care needs who were inappropriately placed into supported living accommodation.

In 2006 the Healthcare Commission and Social Care Inspection had responded to complaints with regard to Cornwall Partnership NHS Trust's services for people with learning disabilities and found widespread poor standards of care in its assessment and treatment centres and in its residential care facilities – and this time involving learning disability nurses. In 2007 the Healthcare Commission inspected Sutton and Merton Primary Care Trust's services for people with a learning disability and once more found poor standards of care. Health inequalities and high rates of "unmet need", which may contribute to early death, were highlighted by the Disability Rights Commission (2006). This in turn brought into the political and societal consciousness what appeared to represent neglect in the NHS, and was followed by the damning report, *Death by indifference* (Mencap, 2007), which cited six unnecessary deaths of individuals with an intellectual disability in hospital. This has been further reported in the latest Mencap report (Mencap, 2012).

In May 2011, further shocking incidences of abuse were reported in the BBC *Panorama* programme on Winterbourne View. Acts of violence and systematic abuse to patients with intellectual disabilities were recorded within a private hospital, and intellectual disability nurses were culpable in this abuse.

In 2012 the Care Quality Commission inspection report identified that 50% of 150 services inspected were below standard.

Briefly reviewing this timeline of critical incidents specific to intellectual disability services presents a somewhat bleak picture in terms of what is going wrong. Given that we have a compendium of reforms that promote person-centred practice, which offers choices and works towards social inclusion, the evidence is undeniably that services and professionals are failing people and that what is required is clear leadership and change management skills at the sharp end of practice.

The Winterbourne View Serious Case Review Inquiry (Flynn and Citarella, 2012) has stated that there was a lack of leadership and supervision at the hospital, and that although it was nurse-led, there was a culture of support workers running shifts. There was little exposure to appropriate intellectual disability education and values-based training, and control and restraint techniques were dominant. It is clear that staff teams had been allowed to develop a subculture of deviance which contributed towards a decay in care services. Staff had become dysfunctional, directionless and caused harm to individuals who were vulnerable.

It is clear that intellectual disability nurses are in the minority within services across the NHS, and independent and third sectors (Gates, 2011), and, since the NHS and Community Care Act (1990), have not been the key influential professionals in the care, development and support of people and families with an intellectual disability. Additionally, they cannot be called to account for the majority of service failures that have been identified, rather it is the way in which services have been configured through multiple providers across sectors that is to blame.

What is clear from the inquiries and controversies is that frontline workers should have more robust training in learning disability – but what exactly does this mean? Both the Winterbourne View Serious Case Review Inquiry and the Francis Report (Mid-Staffordshire NHS Foundation Trust Inquiry, 2010) give clear messages about the necessity for values training, and both inquiries identified professionals' disregard for patients' humanity, and a lack of respect and compassion among staff. In fact it has been reported that management of Stafford Hospital exemplified a total distancing of managers and staff from what patients were experiencing (Moore, 2013). Is, then, what is required in our failing general hospitals today, what was required when long-stay institutions were closing, and staff and patients were transferring into the community – values training and education? What was thought a unique phenomenon to the asylum has now become a reality in the general acute provision of care – the dehumanisation of patients.

We should not disregard our past in terms of what intellectual disability workers have previously been exposed to in promoting a values-based relationship with people and their families. In the 1980s, staff teams were exposed to what values represented. The 10 core themes of social role valorisation were not only articulated, but transplanted into services and individuals' practice. This included recognising how distancing can manifest itself into a person's unconciousness, thereby not allowing him or her to see the poverty that can exist within a relationship when people are not included within any form of decision making or choice. This is doing things *to* people instead of *with* people and not allowing them to have a voice.

Following on from Gates's (2011) *Strengthening the commitment*, the UK Modernising Learning Disabilities Nursing Review report was published (Scottish Government, 2012). In this report the four Chief Nursing Officers of the UK invested support for intellectual disability nursing. Currently, the response from each respective country to the report's 17 recommendations is awaited. Recommendations include action at a UK level, commissioning, and education at a service and individual practitioner level. The report has identified what intellectual disability nurses do that represents good practice, what other health professionals need to do better, and what learning disability nurses can do to extend their role (see *Box 1.1*).

The whole emphasis of *Strengthening the commitment* is a call for the strategic harnessing of intellectual disability nursing, and the recognition that as a field it should be maintained and developed. However, and paradoxically, a previous recommendation from the Department of Health (2007a) advocated regionalising centres of excellence. At a meeting of the recently formed Intellectual Disability Academic Nursing Network at the University of Nottingham, several speakers favoured regionalisation. This was in the absence of any evidence that this proposal is valid, where no discussion papers have been offered, and where there has been a lack of consultation among the profession, or indeed people with learning disabilities, their families and carers. For intellectual disability nursing, this option could potentially result in a fourth, and possibly final fracture and the demise of the profession, as a result of further fragmenting and marginalisation.

Recent developments since the publication of *Strengthening the commitment* include, in England, a multi-professional working party with key stakeholders and partners, and mapping against the six action areas from *Compassion in practice* (Department of Health, 2012).

Learning disability nurse consultants have developed an outcome framework based on the five determinants of health inequalities with the outcome of measuring effectiveness in tackling health inequalities for people with intellectual disabilities (Department of Health, 2013). The five broad determinants of health inequalities are:

Box 1.1. Existing and future competencies for practice

What learning disability nurses do well
- Encourage empowerment and participation.
- Promote communication skills, including accessible communication.
- Carry out health checks, support access to hospital and primary care, help with behaviour and teaching people about health.
- Help people to keep healthy and live in the community.
- Support access to general healthcare (liaison roles are highly valued).
- Raise awareness around learning disabilities through education and training for all professionals.

What learning disability nurses need to do better
- Some people with learning disabilities do not have good experiences in specialist assessment and treatment services. Learning disability nurses need to involve people more in their assessment and treatment in these settings and avoid restrictive practices.
- Learning disability nurses could support services to manage better children with very complex needs who are being excluded from education.
- Provide consistency: people prefer to have the same nurse/named nurse.
- Non-registered workers should have a more robust training in learning disabilities.

Where learning disability nurses want to be
- Supporting transition from children's to adult services: carers would value more involvement from learning disability nurses.
- Developing their role around discharge planning.
- Taking time to get to know people, building trust and recognising that the person is the expert.
- Allowing people with learning disabilities, their families and carers to be more involved in the selection of learning disability nurses, students and the non-registered workforce.
- Involving people with learning disabilities, their families and carers in nurse education for all fields of nursing. Other nurses still need more knowledge and skills in working with people with learning disabilities.
- Expanding their role into other areas, such as mental health and prisons.

Scottish Government (2012: 16–17)

- Social determinants of poorer health, such as poverty, poor housing, unemployment and social disconnectedness.
- Physical and mental health problems associated with specific genetic and biological conditions in learning disabilities.
- Communication difficulties and reduced health literacy.
- Personal health behaviour and lifestyle risks, such as diet, sexual health and exercise.
- Deficiencies in access to and the quality of healthcare and other service provision.

The need for effective practice leadership is required across all populations and sectors, where all workers involved have access to localised education and training in all geographical areas of provision, for all have a responsibility in providing effective support and delivery, and where provision is locally determined amidst a diverse demography.

Leadership

Given the political and social context above, and where intellectual disability nurses are located, there is no doubt that they have a clear impact, identity and influence as trailblazers and champions. This occurs particularly within the healthcare arena, where they promote and support health equality in access to generic mainstream services and acute liaison teams. It is at this interface of services where they are required to demonstrate their values, impacting on service users and services, and working towards a vision that empowers and motivates a workforce across sectors.

If intellectual disability nurses are directly supported through policy by the Department of Health, their presence will be of influence and have credibility with other providers. Commissioning bodies should also be required to acknowledge and have a clear commitment and vision towards the value of intellectual disability nurses' specialist roles in the development of innovations. Such examples are promoting person-centred thinking and planning, and assisting in facilitating accessibility beyond primary healthcare and acute services. Further leadership capacity would also extend into specialist secondary and tertiary services, such as specialist assessment and treatment centres. Further focus for leadership is in mental health (dual-diagnosis) acute services, where collaboration with mental health nurses will promote interprofessional working. Forensic services are an additional specialist area, where to implement a person-centred ethos creates additional challenges for nurses in terms of patients detained under the Mental Health Act 1983.

The General Medical Council, Nursing and Midwifery Council and the Royal College of Nursing have been openly criticised (Winnett, 2013) for not responding to the poor standards of care detailed in the Francis Report (Mid-Staffordshire NHS Foundation Trust Inquiry, 2010).

The Royal College of Nursing was perceived as neither functional as a union nor as a professional body representing standards of good practice. Professional bodies such as the Royal College of Nursing regularly produce guidance documents and role descriptors for nursing, but are not seen as actively representing and supporting good practice initiatives.

As is the case in mental health nursing, intellectual disability nursing has no central representation at government level, minimal representation at the Nursing and Midwifery Council and is left to circumvent its cause and agenda within localised and national networks.

The UK Consultant Nurse Network in 2006 produced a vision for learning disability nursing which recommended that learning disability nurses should develop their leadership capability (Northway et al, 2006). More recently, *Strengthening the commitment* (Scottish Government, 2012) also recommended that it is essential for intellectual disability nurses to be supported through clear career pathways, and to be involved in succession planning to enable such leadership capability to develop and be sustained. Practice leadership education and training is about intellectual disability nurses developing capacity, resilience and having such opportunities available to further hone their skills as an integral part of undergraduate preparation for practice within safe educational environments. Preparing intellectual disability nurses psychologically in subjects such as self-awareness, personality development, emotional intelligence, conflict resolution with additional training and education in the adoption of interpersonal frameworks for effective intervention, are critical for competency-based practice. These concepts and skills are essential requirements within what, at times, is a harsh practice world, where professionals across sectors can be difficult to manage and can demonstrate inappropriate attitudes and values.

Intellectual disability networks are effective and important for communicating good practice and in supporting practice locally. However, such networks are in danger of acting like virtual academies of expertise, promoting interest groups among the converted, and this questions the impact in real terms across wider communities and sectors. For leadership, evidence suggests that intellectual disability nurses are required to break out of their professional boundaries, be more transparent across other sectors and professions, extol their capability in collaborative working and avoid becoming parochial.

Mental health nursing

It is an interesting and challenging time to be considering practice leadership in mental health nursing. In Britain we are experiencing yet another episode of legislative change, following on from the many identified earlier in this chapter. This change comes in the shape of the Health and Social Care Bill 2012 which is likely to have ramifications for mental health nursing well into the 21st century. This section reviews mental health nursing leadership, considers the strengths and weaknesses of the profession, discusses lessons to be learned in parallel with our colleagues in intellectual disability nursing and reflects on the opportunities for mental health nursing practice leadership in the future.

The traditions of mental health nursing have been well documented (see Nolan, 1993). The origins were set in the asylums of Victorian Britain and, as a group, mental health nurses were more typically working class (many were agricultural workers looking for "warmer/inside" winter work). Large numbers were men, although they were still overwhelming female, and during the 20th and early part of the 21st century they came from marginal immigrant population groups notably Irish, Mauritian, and Afro-Caribbean (Royal College of Nursing, 2007). Their work was predominantly to carry out doctors' instructions to keep the patients safe. Over time, mental health nursing began to develop its own theories and ideas of practice (Norman and Ryrie, 2009).

The Department of Health (2006a) focused on nursing moving towards becoming a "research-based profession". Training moved into higher education and, following the Butterworth Report (Department of Health, 1994), "psychiatric" nursing was rejected as an occupational title, being seen to be too illness-focused, and there was a new emphasis on and name for the profession – "mental health" nursing. This was supposed to refocus the profession onto recovery and evidence-based mental health nursing practice. While Barker and Buchanan Barker (2005) acknowledge the potential for positive changes, they illustrate how there have been no significant changes in mental health nursing itself. The practice of mental health nurses and the status of mental health nursing have not changed; there is no public representation of mental health nursing, and no mental health nurses are consulted by the media, politicians or even the Department of Health. In the National Institute for Health and Care Excellence (NICE) guidance to the NHS, rarely, if ever, do they refer to, let alone include, mental health nurses in their work on improving mental health services. For the first time, in 2012, a mental health nurse has been involved in developing guidelines with NICE (Cawthorne and Barron, 2012). Interestingly this individual is a Scottish mental health nurse, perhaps reflecting that Scottish mental health legislation and policy are increasingly independent from the rest of the UK with the more central inclusion of mental health nurses and mental health service users. Peer support work has progressed more widely in Scotland. This has led to some de-professionalisation of mental health services, and while there is a clear potential for good, and alliance with principles of effective recovery for mental health service users, it does leave unanswered questions for the future of mental health nurses.

There have been significant differences in the progression of mental health nurses across the UK. Scotland did not roll out the *Improving access to psychological therapies* programme (Department of Health, 2007b), as their mental health focus tended to be on wider issues around poverty, social exclusion and addiction. In England, Wales and Northern Ireland, although mental health nursing staff will talk readily about excellent clinical leaders at a local level; this is much more nebular at a national level. Clinical mental health nursing staff appear to tie leadership at a national level to academic work. There is recognition of the excellent contribution made by Phil Barker, Kevin Gournay, Peter Nolan, Len Bowers and Liam Clarke to name a few, but these are colleagues recognised for their contribution to academic leadership in mental health nursing and, while their work has and continues to influence clinical practice, clinical mental health nurse leaders are difficult to identify with any real confidence.

Mental health nurses need to heed the lessons of their colleagues in learning disability. We are seeing the implementation of the "big society", the rolling back of health and social care. Mental health nurses are replaceable. In response to opportunities for them to embrace additional and/or expanded roles as nurse consultants, non-medical prescribers, therapists, or allied mental health professionals, or to take on the role of responsible clinician, they seem to have shied away or slowly seen the opportunity eroded through trust policy and practice (Department of Health, 2006b). In some areas these roles have been taken up by mental health nurses and often extremely well, but they are quickly lost in less affluent times. One trust in the West Midlands engaged well with the idea of nurse consultants in mental health, appointing five senior nurses to these posts. Sadly, in 2013, there is only one nurse consultant remaining following several reconfigurations, and that post is likely to be lost to retirement before the end of the year.

There are still opportunities for mental health nurses to lead but they need to adapt and be effective role models; to be positive, assertive and empowering towards mental health service users; to develop others; to promote autonomy; and to encourage independent and critical thinking not only for themselves but

13

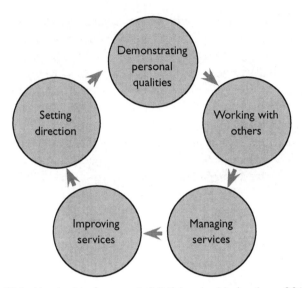

Figure 1.1. Clinical leadership framework (NHS Leadership Academy, 2011).

also in the next generations of mental health nurses; if these opportunities are to continue. In order to be a clinical leader it is necessary for mental health nurses to have a vision of what they are hoping to achieve, what they are trying to do and to understand why. They need to be visionary, not blindly following, and this means developing their own theories and evidence to support their clinical practice as mental health nurses.

The NHS has developed a clinical leadership framework (NHS Leadership Academy, 2011) (see *Figure 1.1*). The framework acknowledges that the necessary personal qualities of a clinical leader include self-awareness, managing yourself, continuing personal development, and acting with integrity. In order to work effectively with others, a clinical leader needs to develop networks, build and maintain relationships, encourage contribution, and work with teams. In managing services, an effective clinical leader must plan and manage resources, including people and their performance. If a clinical leader is working to improve services then he or she must ensure patient safety, evaluate critically, encourage improvement and innovation, and facilitate transformation. The framework also states that in setting direction it is important to identify the contexts for change, apply knowledge and evidence, make decisions, and evaluate the impact on services.

Concerns over the apparent lack of autonomy and initiative among the next generation of mental health nurses is apparent when colleagues report hearing nurses say, "Tell me what you want me to do", rather than, "This is my vision and is what I'm going to do". Mental health nurses are struggling to deal with increasingly complex needs within the mental health service user population alongside their own feelings of compassion fatigue and stress (Clarke, 2008; Taylor, 2011). Mental health nurse leaders need to engage with colleagues in a way that helps to build resilience and robustness and that provides effective clinical supervision with appropriate protective measures (White and Whitstanley, 2010).

Clinical leaders will need to help provide a space for mental health nurses to engage in reflexive practice and process supervision (Carthy et al, 2012). Part of this provision by leaders must be to enable nurses to care about and with service users. In order to capture the essence of how and why leadership seems inadequate to this task and why mental health nurses persistently fail to care, it is necessary to consider the perceived overwhelming need for care and attachment that people with mental health problems demonstrate. Faced with such neediness mental health nurses appear to retreat hastily into traditional and established patterns of behaviour such as excessive documentation, reliance on medication and physical treatments rather than carrying out interpersonal work with their service users (Clarke and Flanagan, 2003). The use of professional language, such as "boundaries", is much manipulated and has come to mean emotional distance and a lack of availability rather than working with service users in a way that is genuine, honest, person-centred and patient-focused. Claims of "confidentiality" also provide mental health nurses with the opportunity to avoid dealing with the emotional needs of families and carers of service users. Mental health service users respond well to small gestures of care and attention on one hand yet mental health nurses appear entrenched in a position of avoidance and distancing from this "burden" of excessive neediness. Is it due to fear of failing the service user, so we never even try? Is it that we fear we will be the only person fully committed to this so we pre-emptively resent others' lack of support and that we are doing more than them, and blame them for our inability to meet the demands of service users? Mental health nurses are used to expectations that they will carry the burden of emotional labour, that they will be with mental health service users more and will deal those with the greatest complexity of need more than any other health professional. Have they become so damaged, traumatised and fatigued that they have stopped caring? Do they feel so badly done to that they are now doing badly to others?

Mental health nursing leaders need to show the way in caring through role modelling good practice. Service users need time, but not every moment of the working day; leaders need to demonstrate how to give time effectively. One of the key ways to do this is through group processes that can help to meet service users' needs in a way that promotes independence, social interaction and networking, which are all transferrable skills for successful inclusion in society (Perese and Wolf, 2005).

Clinical leaders in mental health nursing also need to remember the importance of the nurse–patient relationship (Peplau, 1988); washing a person and making sure they eat and drink enough. There needs to be an emphasis on the therapeutic use of self; being with the person in distress physically, emotionally and psychologically is essential if these specialist nurses are going to be part of mental health services in the 21st century and reflect the importance of care and caring (Royal College of Nursing, 2012).

Barker's (2009) Tidal Model is a useful metaphor for the current situation in mental health nursing. The sea around mental health nurses is not gently swaying, it is not static or frozen, rather there are huge swells (the challenge to mental health professionals from peer support workers, inter-professionalism, the Department of Health's [2011] *Payment by results*), whirlpools (the Mid-Staffordshire NHS Foundation Trust inquiries, 2010; stigma; rising demand for a high quality service with less and less resources), storms (the Health and Social Care Act 2012) and tidal waves (the global economic crisis) to contend with. How we weather these conditions will be largely dictated by how effective our clinical leaders can be. Now, more than ever, is the time to be with mental health service users, their families and friends and to offer real care. Hopefully mental health nursing will be swimming not drowning in the 21st century.

Acknowledgements

Mark would like to acknowledge the first 2010/11 student intake for the BSc(Hons) Learning Disability Nursing degree and Vicky would like to acknowledge Mayuri Senpati (Consultant Clinical Psychologist) and Rachel Clarke (RN:MH, and Senior Lecturer) for their invaluable contribution to this chapter.

References

Barker P (Ed) (2009) *Psychiatric and mental health nursing: The craft of caring.* (2nd edn). Hodder Arnold, London

Barker P, Buchanan-Barker P (2005) Still invisible after all these years: Mental health nursing on the margins. *Journal of Psychiatric and Mental Health Nursing* **12**: 255–6

Brown J (1994) *Analysis of responses to the Consensus Statement on the Future of the Specialist Nurse Practitioner in Learning Disabilities.* Department of Social Policy and Social Work, University of York

Carthy J, Noak J, Wadey E (2012) Clinical supervision in a high secure hospital. *British Journal of Mental Health Nursing* **1**(1): 24–32

Cawthorne P, Barron DT (2012) Developing the new SIGN schizophrenia guidelines. *British Journal of Mental Health Nursing* **1**(1): 45–51

Clarke L, Flanagan T (2003) *Institutional breakdown: Exploring mental health nursing practice in acute in-patient settings.* APS Publishing, Wiltshire

Clarke V (2008) Working with survivors of trauma. *Mental Health Practice* **11**(7): 14–8

Department of Health (1994) *The Butterworth Report. Working in Partnership.* HMSO, London

Department of Health (1999) *Facing the facts.* Department of Health, London

Department of Health (2001) V*aluing people. A strategy for people with learning disabilities in the 21st Century.* Department of Health, London

Department of Health (2006a) *From values to action: The Chief Nursing Officer's review of mental health nursing.* Department of Health, London

Department of Health (2006b) *Modernising nursing careers. Setting the direction.* Department of Health, London

Department of Health (2007a) *Good practice guidelines for learning disability nursing.* Department of Health, London

Department of Health (2007b) *Improving access to psychological therapies.* Department of Health, London

Department of Health (2011) *Payment by results in mental health services.* Department of Health, London

Department of Health (2012) *Compassion in practice. Nursing, midwifery and care staff. Our vision and strategy.* Department of Health, London

Department of Health (2013) *The CNO Bulletin.* Issue 113, February 2013, Gateway No. 18809

Department of Health and Social Security (1971) *Better services for the mentally handicapped.* Department of Health and Social Security, London

Department of Health and Social Security (1975) *Better services for the mentally ill.* Department of Health and Social Security, London

Disability Rights Commission (2006) *Equal treatment: Closing the gap.* Disability Rights Commission, London

Flynn M, Citarella V (2012) *Winterbourne View Hospital. A serious case review.* South Gloucester Council, Gloucester

Gates B (2011) *Learning disability nursing: Task and Finish Group Report for the Professional and Advisory Board for Nursing and Midwifery.* University of Hertfordshire, Hatfield

Hope R (2004) *The ten essential shared capabilities: A Framework for the whole mental health workforce.* HMSO, London

Howells G (1986) Are the health needs of mentally handicapped adults being met? *Journal of the Royal College of General Practitioners* **36**: 449–53

Kay B, Rose S, Turnbull J (1995) *Continuing the commitment. Report of the Learning Disability Nursing Project.* Department of Health, London

Mencap (2007) *Death by indifference! Follow up of the Treat Me Right report.* Mencap, London

Mencap (2012) *Death by indifference! 74 deaths and counting.* Mencap, London

Mid-Staffordshire NHS Foundation Trust Inquiry (2010) *The Francis Report. Independent Inquiry into care provided by Mid-Staffordshire NHS Foundation Trust. January 2005–March 2009.* Stationery Office, London

Mitchell D (2004) The Jay Report: 25 years on. *Learning Disability Practice* 7(6): 20–3

Moore C (2013) Let's face the truth about our uncaring, selfish and cruel NHS. *Daily Telegraph* **Feb 9**: 26

Mufaba K (2009) The public health role of learning disability nurses. A review of the literature. *Learning Disability Practice* **12**(4): 33–7

NHS Leadership Academy (2011) *Leadership framework.* Available from: http:/www.leadershipacademy.nhs.uk/develop-your-leadership-skills/leadership-framework/supporting-tools-and-documents/documents-to-download

Nolan P (1993) *A history of mental health nursing.* Chapman & Hall, London

Norman I, Ryrie I (Eds) (2009) *The art and science of mental health nursing: A textbook of principles and practice* (2nd edn). Open University Press/McGraw Hill, Maidenhead

Northway R, Hutchinson C, Kingdon, A (eds) (2006) *Shaping the future: A vision for learning disability nursing.* UK Learning Disability Consultant Nurse Network, London

Nursing and Midwifery Council (2011) *Standards for competency.* Available from: http://standards.nmc-uk.org/PreRegNursing/statutory/competencies/Pages/Competencies.aspx

Nursing Mirror (1978) No way, Mrs. Jay. **June 29**: 1

Office for National Statistics (2013) *Poverty and social exclusion in the UK and EU, 2005-2011.* Office for National Statistics, London

Parish C (2012) Learning disability students "discouraged" by senior staff. *Learning Disability Practice* **15**(1): 5

Peplau H (1988) *Interpersonal relations in nursing: A conceptual frame of reference for psychodynamic nursing.* Macmillan, London

Perese EF, Wolf M (2005) Combating loneliness among persons with severe mental illness: Social network interventions' characteristics, effectiveness and applicability. *Issues in Mental Health Nursing* **26**: 591–609

Repper J, Perkins R (2009) Recovery and social inclusion. In C.Brooker, J Repper (eds) *Mental health: From policy to practice* (pp 1–13). Elsevier, Oxford

Report of the Committee of Enquiry into Mental Handicap Nursing and Care (1979) *The Jay Report*. Department of Health and Social Security, London

Royal College of Nursing (2007) *Black and minority ethnic and internationally recruited nurses: Results from the RCN Employment/Working Well Surveys 2005 and 2002.* Royal College of Nursing, London

Royal College of Nursing (2012) *The Willis Report. Quality with compassion: The future of nursing education. Report of the Willis Commission on Nursing Education.* Royal College of Nursing, London

Scottish Government (2012) *Strengthening the commitment. Report of the UK modernising learning disabilities nursing review* (pp 16-17). Scottish Government, Edinburgh

Styring L, Grant G (2005) Maintaining a commitment to qualities In Grant et al (Eds) *Learning disability: A life cycle approach to valuing people.* Open University Press, Berkshire

Taylor R (2011) The interface between forensic psychiatry and general adult psychiatry. In Rubitel A, Reiss D (Eds) *Containment in the community: Supportive frameworks for thinking about antisocial behaviour and mental health.* Karnac Books, London

White E, Whitstanley J (2010) A randomised control trial of clinical supervision. Selected findings from a novel Australian attempt to establish the evidence base for causal relationships with quality of care and patient outcomes, as an informed contribution to mental health nursing practice development. *Journal of Research Nursing* **15**(2): 151–67

Winnett R (2013) Minister calls for police enquiry into NHS. *Daily Telegraph* **Feb 9**: 1

Chapter 2

Self-awareness and personality

Helen Goulding and Emma Lyall

Nurse leaders and managers who lose sight of their values are the ones who we least admire.

(Bach and Ellis, 2011: 13)

This chapter seeks to explore the concept of self-awareness, its practical acquisition and how this relates to the fields of intellectual disability and mental health nursing.

To practise the art of nursing within mental health and intellectual disability, nurses are required to embrace the fundamental values of dignity, respect and compassion which are considered to represent the core values that are intrinsic to the role. It is these values that lend themselves to the effective delivery of practice leadership, through an increased level of self-awareness coupled with desired individual personality traits in those who have selected to work within such specialist areas of practice.

However, it would be blind to assume that personal characteristics alone can lead to successful leadership practice and the role of knowledge, experience and reflection when seeking to effect change within the clinical environment are explored. A person's character may even be shaped by these processes themselves, and this relationship between self-awareness and personality and the joint and separate parts they play in developing positive and effectual change within nursing are examined.

As well as providing a model for achieving self-awareness and demonstrating the practical application of this in practice, the distinctive challenges faced within the intellectual disability and mental health nursing professions are also explored. These can include working with acutely psychotic patients, those displaying difficult and challenging behaviour, individuals with extremely complex health needs, and working within in-patient forensic environments.

In addition to working within these environments, other challenges are encountered within these two fields of nursing. Examples of these would include a commitment to person-centred care, working towards empowerment of vulnerable individuals and advocating the rights of those who are unable to do so for themselves. To undertake such challenges as an intellectual disability or a mental health nurse demands a discerning level of personal self-awareness.

Defining self-awareness

Self-awareness is often portrayed as a complex set of concepts that are at times defined as separate components. Rungapadiachy (2008), for example, refers to cognitive, affective and behavioural components. These three elements are not mutually exclusive but directly affect each other in the development of self-awareness.

For the purposes of this chapter, the terms and concepts of self-awareness and reflective practice can be seen as mutually inclusive and interchangeable. Reflection is key within a nursing environment and critical in actualising a development of self-awareness. This is not a new concept. In 1952 Peplau (cited in Vandemark, 2006: 606) highlighted that every nurse, in order to be effective, must first learn to "tackle her own problem" before she is able to move on to tackling the problems of others. This not only need apply to the nurse–patient relationship, which is key to Peplau's theory, but also to the nurse–colleague relationship. In order to understand the way others function within a particular setting, we surely need to know how our own behaviours and values impact upon them. To do this we are required to achieve a certain level of insight. This is aided by either a structured or unstructured process of reflection (see *Chapter 4*).

Nurses can at times be almost overwhelmed by the amount of reflection they are required to do as part of their role. It is a skill they are required to learn and to practise as undergraduates, and one they are then required to perfect throughout their working lives. A number of reflective models can be used to aid the clinician, but ultimately, the goal remains what Margaret Newman termed as achieving "consciousness". Like Peplau, Newman discusses her concepts relating to "consciousness" of self-awareness as being a skill that can be learned and that very much depends upon reflecting upon one's interactions with others and the impact of the environment in which a person carries out that interaction (Newman, 1994). This implies that self-awareness is a learned process and not something that a nurse may instinctively possess.

So how do we become self-aware?

Self-awareness is ultimately knowing and understanding oneself, and reflection is key to this process. When we reflect on our strengths, areas of development, our personalities and values we begin to understand ourselves better. However, to develop self-awareness we need to identify our strengths and look at ways to cope with our weaknesses or develop them. It can be difficult to accept areas of weakness and these need to be viewed positively and accepted. This will identify and offer opportunities for professional development and personal growth.

There are a number of models that can be utilised to develop reflection. Kolb's Experiential Learning Theory (Kolb, 1984) is a cycle that focuses on feeling, watching, thinking and doing, a cycle that develops perception and processing. This aids the development of self through experience and will lead to increased self-awareness. While Kolb's theory is often adopted within a learning and teaching context, as a pure reflective process, it can also be applied to other areas, including practice leadership.

Other tools may be used alongside reflective cycles and most of these assist with the thinking part of the cycle. Such tools focus on skills, personality traits and styles adopted by the practitioner. SWOT analysis (Ansoff, 1987, cited in Barr and Dowding, 2012), for example, explores a practitioner's strengths, weaknesses, opportunities and threats. The Myers-Briggs Type Indicator is described by Barr and Dowding (2012) as a tool for gathering and evaluating information from individuals to ascertain their problem solving and decision-making skills. Personality tests are also available, e.g. Wiggins (1996). This information helps practitioners to reflect on themselves and explain how the findings influence their practice.

While feedback from others is imperative, practice leaders also need to have an understanding of how others view them as well, since this may be different to their own self-perceptions. The Royal College of Nursing's 360 degree feedback is widely used and gives practitioners a full indication of themselves as individuals. The way individuals are viewed can also vary considerably within different settings or groups. Within a work environment, as a practitioner you may be expected to have specific leadership skills and qualities and these may be observed within the workplace. Sometimes, more authoritarian traits may be seen when you have a lead within a group, however, where the hierarchy changes, less authoritarian traits may not be evident.

Through the development of self-awareness, the awareness of others will evolve. If leaders begin to understand how their own characteristics impact upon their work and on other people, then their understanding of others can also evolve. Argyris and Schön (1978) describe double loop learning where reflection may then lead to an alteration of how the individual practices, thus any reflection needs to be critical and develop both the practitioner and his or her practice.

Nurses are raised on reflective models. As they become more experienced and more self-aware they may choose to abandon models they have previously relied upon in favour of their own style. However, within the context of this chapter, reflection must ultimately support the development of self-awareness and subsequent leadership skills. To this extent, the cycle shown in *Figure 2.1* is proposed. This cycle allows practitioners, or practice leaders, to develop their own self-awareness, and resonates with Kolb's reflective cycle (1984). One aspect of Kolb's cycle that is replicated in *Figure 2.1* is the ability to access any part of the cycle at any time, and not necessarily in any particular order. The cycle acknowledges the importance of reflection within the process, as well as the underpinning of knowledge and experience. However, these do not necessarily need to express a continuum, but rather a cycle where each element contributes equally. For example, through self-awareness, perhaps through training or reflection upon practice, the practitioner may more readily effect change. However, change could equally occur due to external factors or events (experience) beyond the control of the clinician, which then initiates the process of reflection and subsequent awareness of self.

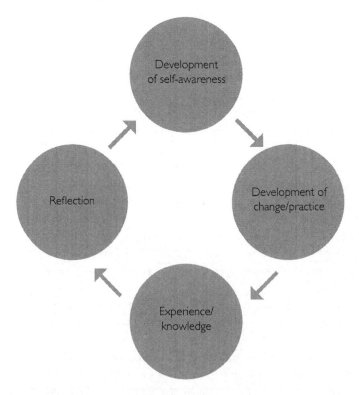

Figure 2.1. The self-awareness model.

How is leadership linked to personality?

The effect of personality on effective leadership has been explored by a number of researchers. In order to attempt to link personality type to the experiences people have and the situations they find themselves in, a number of writers have chosen to use empirically established psychological models. The most popular of these is the Five Factor Model or "The Big Five".

The Five Factor Model (Digman, 1990; Wiggins and Trapnell, 1996) has been adapted by psychologists over the decades, but first came into being in the 1960s. It incorporated openness to experience, conscientiousness, extraversion, agreeableness and neuroticism. These issues began to be explored further within a psychological and theoretical context. More recently, the Five Factor Model has been applied directly to clinical environments and practice leadership. King (2011) examines how the Model's traits may translate into leadership. For example, King (2011) states that "traits and behaviours that make clinicians good at the technical aspects of patient care may serve them less well in the arena of clinical leadership". King therefore highlights a difference between leadership and the clinician. One example of this could be someone who is extrovert and very confident when interacting with patients and carrying out technical work, but whose behaviour may spill over into an over-confidence and become intimidating to others at times in a leadership role. Judge et al (2002) also uses the Five Factor Model in order to establish links between personality traits and leadership styles.

Work by those such as King would indicate that a degree of self-awareness is key to effective channelling of personality traits. However, others, such as Hogan and Kaiser (2005), state that "personality predicts leadership" and it is in fact who we are that defines us as a leader. It is not the intention of this chapter to analyse in depth the part that personality does or does not potentially play in leadership styles, however, what is interesting is the part that personality may play within the areas of mental health and intellectual disability nursing. At this point it is helpful to refer back to the opening statement of this chapter, which highlighted the importance of our own values upon our clinical work.

It could be said that different personality types tend to orientate towards different therapeutic styles when meeting the needs of particular client groups. Chessum (2006) explores this further, in the investigation of "moral habitability" within a nursing role. It is here that we can divide the orientation of the nurse into one of three broad therapeutic styles, namely therapist, carer and rehabilitator in their interaction and focus with clients (see *Table 2.1*).

Table 2.1. Framework of care-giving relationships: Therapeutic orientation	
Therapist	Agent of change. Assuming role of expert in a particular therapy. Disciplined application of models used by a generic therapist with skills in many approaches. Someone who views their interventions as broadly "therapeutic" in whatever they undertake with the client.
Carer	Someone who sees him or herself as "looking after" another or doing things for people unable to do them for themselves, either permanently or temporarily. Giving care in a timely and appropriate manner, reflecting the expressed needs and wishes of the client and not disempowering. Undertaking a role that has fluidity, i.e. it can decrease and increase, nurturing but not static, so that care can be developmental and progressive too. The perspective can be impeded by conceptualisation of a mother–child relationship from psychoanalytic metapsychology: mother = nurse, client = child. Therapeutic care is not necessarily custodial care or control that can be restricting of personal growth and development.
Rehabilitator	A restorative or even developmental process for some clients, suggesting dynamic change over time, which is progressive but determined by the pace and needs of the client. It is of a varied focus depending upon the needs of the client. Essentially empowering for clients who move from less to more independence and autonomy, experiencing personal growth and development in the process. It assumes expectations of change because of the capacity inherent in the client, through support, assistance and encouragement, for example.
	Source Chessum (2006: 50)

It is therefore important to consider how, as a practice leader, individual practice may fall into such a conceptualisation, and equally so across staff teams, and how individual members prefer to exercise certain relational characteristics. In mental health and intellectual disability nursing such relational characteristics are more likely to be found where the quality and extent of relationships are over significant periods of time, as opposed to adult or children's nurses where time for developing relationships and knowing the person is limited. The ethos in intellectual disability and mental health nursing is towards the recovery model and person-centred planning and care, where mental health and intellectual disability nurses are focused on health within a social model across a variety of sectors and environments, and concentrate on the growth and development of clients where the aim is to ensure their maximum potential, whatever their limitations.

Within the field of intellectual disability nursing, besides the Nursing and Midwifery Council Code of Professional Conduct (2008), nurses also adhere to the four guiding principles of *Valuing people* (Department of Health, 2001, 2009). These are rights, inclusion, independent living and control. Mental health nursing echoes these principles within its own National Service Framework (Department of Health, 2007). The Framework has 10 guiding values and principles, which also include those of choice, independence and empowerment. Readers will already know and uphold these values, yet it is suggested that there is a link between these guiding values and the personality of the clinician.

Much of the discussion up to this point has been quite general and has used a number of generic sources in order to take a look at self-awareness, personality and practice leadership. However, in order to aim the discussion specifically at intellectual disability and mental health nurses, it is useful to use a more focused and specialist example. One such example is that of forensic nursing, which is almost exclusive to the fields of mental health and intellectual disabilities. McCourt (1999) introduced five concepts for forensic nursing, one of which included the use of self. McCourt acknowledged the need for nurses working in secure environments to be extremely self-aware, since self-awareness is key in "shaping a positive culture and preventing a negative culture". While the idea of a positive and negative culture may resonate with forensic nurses, both within mental health and intellectual disability environments, it is by no means exclusive to this field.

As stated previously, self-awareness increases awareness of others. In some respects this may be easier for mental health and intellectual disability nurses, as an important part of their role is to develop an awareness of patients. Nurses need to work with people and make conclusions regarding a person's well-being from behaviour they observe or through, possibly limited, communication. A large part of these nurses' time is spent interpreting what a person is communicating through their behaviour or body language. This in turn leads to a greater propensity and awareness of their own communication skills as well as those of others. There is no reason why these highly developed skills are exclusive to the nurse–patient relationship; they can also be used within a leadership role with other staff.

Mental health and intellectual disability nurses also work with people who have conditions that are taboo, and as a result of their personal experience in practice often have a highly developed sense of equality and diversity. The people these nurses care for are not always readily accepted into society, they may be perceived as different and experience social exclusion and oppression. As part of intellectual disability and mental health nurse education, ensuring individuals are treated equally is paramount and training should include such concepts as advocacy and empowerment. Having a developed sense of equality and diversity can thus have an effect on how practice leaders treat the diverse needs of the staff they lead, who in turn can model that behaviour to offer the best possible care to those already marginalised within society.

The current climate of intellectual disability and mental health nursing presents many challenges for nurses working in these fields of practice. The abusive practices at Winterbourne View (Department of Health, 2012) have shocked not only the profession but also society generally. This catalogue of inhumane infliction of abuse cries out for skilled, trained, knowledgeable and effective practitioners who can exercise leadership within intellectual disability services and nursing. The recent announcement to close all hospitals for the learning disabled needs a rigorous implementation plan and not just rhetoric. Mental health nurses also have to care for those who are often ostracised and abandoned by wider society. The death of Sean Rigg in police custody in 2008 (Independent Police Complaints Commission, 2012) is just one example that highlights the need for leaders capable of effecting change, so that these incidents do not occur in the future.

Conclusion

As stated at the beginning of this chapter, values which epitomise an ethical approach in providing dignity, respect and compassion are of pivotal importance, and vital to embrace within mental health and intellectual disability nursing. This chapter has attempted to link these values to the personality traits of those that uphold them. However, it is also clear that personality alone cannot always effect positive change and that clinicians must engage in reflective practice and training and channel their personal qualities in order to increase their self-awareness. To echo Peplau (1952) (cited in Vandemark, 2006), it is not possible to bring about the changes so desperately needed in mental health and intellectual disability nursing and make a significant impact without first understanding yourself.

It could be argued that to be an effective clinical leader, a person does not necessarily have to possess a wealth of knowledge. However, as stated previously, knowledge and practice certainly play their part in the development of self-awareness. This is echoed by Callaly and Minas (2005) who refer to natural charisma and "inherent personal qualities" as playing a part but that these alone cannot ensure good leadership without a "commitment to action".

Self-awareness and developed knowledge build self-esteem and a more confident practitioner. As a leader, credibility is important as it can directly affect the way in which others react to leadership efforts. Leadership is not simply defined in terms of a managerial role. Therefore, all practice nurse leaders, regardless of their band or job title, should be able to support their decisions with a sound evidence base.

References

Argyris C, Schön D (1978) *Organization learning: A theory of action perspective.* Addison Wesley, Reading, MA

Bach S, Ellis P (2011) *Leadership, management and team working in nursing.* Learning Matters Ltd, Exeter

Barr J, Dowding L (2012) *Leadership in health care* (2nd edn). Sage, London

Callaly T, Minas H (2005) Reflections on clinical leadership and management in mental health. *Australasian Psychiatry* **13**(1): 27–32

Chessum C (2006) Interpersonal therapeutic relationships. In Jukes M, Aldridge J (Eds) *Person-centred practices – A therapeutic approach* (pp 44–59). Quay Books, London

Department of Health (2001) *Valuing people: A new strategy for learning disability for the 21st century.* Department of Health, London

Department of Health (2007) *National Service Framework for Mental Health: Modern standards and service models.* Department of Health, London

Department of Health (2009) *Valuing people now.* Department of Health, London

Department of Health (2012) *Department of health review: Winterbourne View Interim Report.* Department of Health, London

Digman JM (1990) Personality structure: Emergence of the five-factor model. *Annual Review of Psychology* **41**: 417–40

Hogan R, Kaiser RB (2005) What we know about leadership. *Review of General Psychology* **9**(2): 169–80

Independent Police Complaints Commission (2012) *Independent investigation into the death of Sean Rigg whilst in the custody of Brixton police.* IPCC, Sale

Judge TA, Bono JE, Ilies R, Gerhardt MW (2002) Personality and leadership: A qualitative and quantitative review. *Journal of Applied Psychology* **87**(4): 765–80

King J (2011) Understanding yourself as leader.. In Swanwick T, McKimm J (Eds) *ABC of clinical leadership* (pp 50–3). Wiley-Blackwell, BMJ Books, London

Kolb DA (1984) *Experiential learning: Experience as the source of learning and development*. Prentice-Hall, Upper Saddle River, NJ

McCourt M (1999) Five concepts for the expanded role of the forensic mental health nurse. In Tarbuck P, et al (Eds.) *Forensic mental health nursing: Strategy and implementation*. Whurr, London

Newman M (1994). *Health as expanding consciousness* (2nd edn). National League for Nursing Press, New York

Nursing and Midwifery Council (2008) *The code: Standards of conduct, performance and ethics for nurses and midwives.* Nursing and Midwifery Council, London

Rungapadiachy DM (2008) *Self awareness in health care*. Palgrave Macmillan, Basingstoke

Vandemark LM (2006) Awareness of self and expanding consciousness: Using nursing theories to prepare nurse-therapists. *Issues in Mental Health Nursing* **27**: 605–15

Wiggins JS, Trapnell PD (1996) A dyadic-interactional perspective on the five-factor model. In Wiggins JS (Ed) *The five-factor model of personality: Theoretical perspectives* (pp 88–162). Guilford, New York, NY

Chapter 3

Practice leadership and emotional intelligence

Fred Ruddick

This chapter considers the relationship between emotional intelligence (Goleman, 1996) and effective practice leadership within mental health and intellectual disability nursing. It suggests that such leadership is fundamentally an interpersonal event that is strengthened by a leader's enhanced self-awareness, ability to form person-centred relationships and possession of certain qualities that motivate and inspire others. We all know of leaders who use power in an authoritative or coercive manner in order to drive through change, with the misguided belief that the "followers" will eventually come around to their way of thinking. This approach rarely results in true engagement or ownership from those being led and is largely at odds with ideas expressed within contemporary leadership programmes (Sparrow and Knight, 2006; Marshall, 2010).

The mental health and intellectual disability fields of nursing have both changed dramatically in the past 30 years or so from predominantly institutional systems that robbed clients of their personhood and human rights towards a more humane and person-centred ethos. Practice leadership, if it existed as such, previously took the form of maintaining control and obedience to regimented regimes, with the consequence that custodial environments were created where both clients and staff were expected to conform (Goffman, 1961). The current climate in these constantly evolving nursing disciplines now demands something very different from those leading practice, including a more transformational style that shares much with the notion of emotional intelligence (Burns, 1978; Bass and Riggio, 2005). It has become a greater priority that clinical leaders excel in an ability to influence and motivate others towards future-orientated goals that turn healthcare policy into reality. They need to possess a high degree of self-understanding that serves to strengthen their ability to form influential relationships with those around them. Effective communication is the medium through which these leaders create an expectation of positive change which is then transfused to others, including individual nurses, nursing teams, clients and their families.

Emotional intelligence and personal qualities

Goleman (1996) identified the components of emotional or social intelligence which involves knowing and managing your own emotions and those of others. He suggests that such abilities are characteristics of effective human interactions and, by association, leadership, where it is important to understand people in terms of what they value or what inspires them. A primary focus of practice leadership is to be a visionary and to inspire positive change in others. This can only be accomplished through engagement and meaningful relationship development that amplifies interpersonal influence. Goleman, in his book, *Emotional intelligence: Why it can matter more than IQ*, highlights five key domains of emotional intelligence:

- Knowing your own emotions.
- Managing your own emotions.
- Motivating yourself.
- Recognising and understanding the emotions of others.
- Managing relationships.

People with these qualities are adept at dealing with social or emotional conflicts which are a part of everyday working life for clinical leaders in mental health and learning disability settings trying to achieve constructive change through debate, persuasion and negotiation and by adopting a facilitative/enabling role (Edmonstone, 2009).

Research

There is evidence to support the importance of emotional intelligence as a deeply influential set of personal leadership qualities. Ruderman et al (2001) from the Centre for Creative Leadership, in a study of 302 participants attending a leadership development programme, concluded that:

> *Key leadership skills and perspectives are related to aspects of emotional intelligence and the absence of emotional intelligence is related to career derailment.*

Parker and Sorenson's (2008) study of 43 managers working in a mental health setting showed a strong relationship between high levels of emotional intelligence and transformational leadership styles. A meta-analysis by O'Boyle et al (2010), claiming to be "the most comprehensive, and focused emotional intelligence meta-analysis to date", concluded that, "the overall relation between emotional intelligence and job performance is positive and significant". In terms of leadership, Goleman (1996) supports the position that all effective leaders (not managers) are alike in one crucial way in that they all have a high degree of emotional intelligence.

Self-awareness

Self-awareness is a pivotal quality of emotional intelligence and is a continuous journey of personal reflection and exploration. Two American psychologists, Luft and Ingham (1955), considered ways of enhancing our self-understanding to increase our interpersonal effectiveness. They suggested that we learn about ourselves in three main ways. Firstly, through a process of introspection whereby we take time to reflect upon and evaluate the beliefs, values and attitudes that significantly influence the perception we hold of ourselves, others, and the daily challenges we face. Secondly, they indicate that we must be willing to share some of our "hidden self" where our fears and anxieties reside, contaminating our ability to be confident and open in our relationships. Thirdly, we need actively to seek and respond to feedback received from external sources rather than sitting in a fortress of self-protection. A willingness to engage with these processes can heighten awareness of our strengths and areas for personal development, engender greater sensitivity to our feelings and those of others, and improve our ability to engage and communicate effectively. The core of mental health and learning disability nursing practice is rooted in the "interpersonal", and the emotionally intelligent practitioner is what clients and families want. Therefore, leaders in such services must lead by example, creating an environment in which emotional intelligence is seen to be as important as cognitive intelligence or strategic managerial prowess (Department of Health, 2009).

Actively seeking feedback regarding our interpersonal effectiveness helps identify strengths and things we may need to change. How we are perceived by others within the clinical setting is an important source of information. Human nature and a fear of negative feedback may, however, instil a reluctance to enter such sensitive territory, thereby denying the practitioner access to personal growth-based opportunities. The Royal College of Nursing (2010) leadership programme recognises the importance of external feedback in expanding self-awareness and includes a 360 degree feedback tool incorporating evaluations from a range of other people including managers, co-workers and people who report direct to the clinical leader. In a multiple case study evaluation (Royal College of Nursing, 2005), findings revealed that the clinical leaders involved in the programme "show a greater sense of appreciation of the contributions of individuals within teams, with an increased intent to share knowledge and facilitate the development of other members of the team".

Person-centred relationships

It therefore appears that clinical leaders who are prepared to engage with initiatives that increase their self-awareness are not only enriched at a personal level but also come to "value" those around them more, with a consequence of maximising their own effectiveness and that of others. It could be argued that enhanced self-awareness helps develop a more transformational and emotionally intelligent style of leadership so crucial within nursing services that purport to be person-centred in relation to the clients they serve (Ruddick, 2010). It could also be suggested that without person-centred practice leadership the likelihood of mental health and learning disability teams delivering authentic person-centred care is significantly reduced. Burns (1978) suggests that true leadership should not only be concerned with stimulating organisational change and achieving goals, but it is also concerned with changing the people involved as well. Much of what has already been written within this chapter on emotional intelligence and practice leadership resonates closely with the work of Carl Rogers (Mearns and Thorne, 1999), his humanistic approach to understanding human nature and the ingredients of growth-promoting relationships. He focused upon therapeutic relationships and personal qualities that, when present, create a positive psychological environment in which personal growth can be cultivated. His renowned "core conditions" of acceptance, genuineness and empathy are also qualities characteristic of the emotionally intelligent leader.

Acceptance refers to valuing a person as someone of worth, without preconceived judgement (verbal or non-verbal). The fear of negative judgement can stifle development and helps create a culture of risk avoidance. Staff and clients alike sense from a person's communication style whether it is safe to share their thoughts and feelings, and they predict how this will be received and what the potential consequences of this might be. If a message of acceptance is communicated from the first encounter with a person then this impression tends to last over time, however, the opposite is also true (Demarais and White, 2005). You only get one chance to make a first impression and emotionally intelligent leaders appreciate the lasting impact of their initial contact with those they lead. Being accepting demands an ability to listen actively to others, their hopes, dreams and concerns. A person-centred approach also rests upon a relationship built upon genuineness in which the practice leader avoids using professional status as a barrier or abusing power to dominate or control staff. Nursing practitioners seem to appreciate being kept informed in a transparent and genuine manner, thus generating an atmosphere of mutual loyalty. Congruence between what leaders do and what they say is important in building reciprocal trust-based relationships. Empathic understanding of another's situation is perhaps the most empowering quality of all and often helps dissolve potential conflict situations. Rogers (2003), while acknowledging that you cannot actually experience the world of another human being, considered the act of considering their perspective "as if" you were that person could help develop a deeper understanding of their situation and emotions. Having the skills and awareness to communicate such an understanding can help leaders deal with their staff in a more sensitive manner, building rapport rather than erecting relationship-long barriers.

Solution-focused communication

Through person-centred relationships, Rogers (see Thorne, 2003) would assert a climate for growth can be created in which it is assumed that any individual has inner resources and strengths that can be nurtured to maximise their potential. Practice leaders therefore need to develop a means of communication that amplifies and exposes such qualities in others. It is also acknowledged that by creating a sense of hope, optimism and expectation that change will occur, there is a greater probability that it will actually take place (Ruddick, 2008). Solution-focused approaches to communication, originating from the field of family therapy, may be helpful in equipping leaders in the practice setting with a range of simple techniques that increase the probability of success with both individuals and teams (de Shazer, 1985; Sharry et al, 2003; O'Connell, 2005; Macdonald, 2007). In agreement with person-centred values, the solution-focused way of working is more interested in what people can do rather than being preoccupied with what they cannot do. When a leader becomes focused on problems rather than solutions this tends towards a more critical communication style that diminishes people and reduces their motivation, commitment and confidence. Goleman (1996: 151) suggests that destructive criticism, "displays an ignorance of the feelings it will trigger in those who receive it", reinforcing the benefits of emotional intelligence for those who wish to inspire, and the need to have compassion and sensitivity for the human condition.

Leaders can develop the skills of communication, including those of active listening that tune into and amplify a person's strengths and resources, with the intention of enhancing their confidence and self-esteem. Many leaders and practitioners use problem-based thinking and communication rather than solution-based questions that help others see future possibilities and goals. The principles and skills that underpin solution-focused forms of communication can be translated into everyday working lives but they also demand a shift from problem-orientated thinking habits to more constructive and optimistic ones. According to Sharry et al (2003) we need to learn how to question others in a way that communicates a belief in them, and they suggest that we need to develop a psychological disposition whereby the words and actions of others are "passed through a strengths-based filter which frames understanding in ways that open up possibilities and choices" (Sharry et al, 2003: 16). When the motivation and inspiration of others forms a central pillar of emotionally intelligent leadership this type of optimism would seem to be another desirable personal characteristic. Seligman (2006), a leading motivational expert, through his lifelong research in exploring this phenomenon considers it a virtue in jobs where there is a requirement for resilience in the face of high stress situations, and where public relations are a focal point of the role. In his book, *Learned optimism*, he reports that, "over 50 companies now use optimistic questionnaires in their selection procedures" (Seligman, 2006: 256). He also claims that as well as being able to screen for the optimistic tendency in jobs, where it is seen as a desirable trait, it is possible to provide training to enhance such an explanatory style (see Sparrow and Knight, 2006).

Implications for practice

Modern practice leaders are the driving force behind patient-orientated change within a dynamic NHS. They are at the behest of managers who ask them to turn policy into reality, often within short timeframes and with limited resources. These leaders also have to engage with the individuals and clinical teams that will need to implement and own visions of a future that maximises the quality of service delivered to patients and their families. Clients want a humane service in which they are treated with acceptance, genuineness and empathy above all else. Emotional intelligence and the so-called "soft management skills" should be seen as complementary to cognitive intelligence and a prerequisite for strong and effective practice leadership. It is no good having brilliant ideas or future visions if the leader in question cannot then engage with those whose cooperation is paramount for them to be put into practice. (See Appendix 1 at the end of the chapter.)

There exists some persuasive evidence distilled by renowned experts to suggest a greater emphasis ought to be placed upon emotional or social intelligence when selecting those considered suitable for practice leadership positions (Goleman, 1996; Rogers, 2003; Seligman, 2006). Emotional intelligence would seem to fit well within a nursing context where the relationship is the pivotal instrument of change. There may be significant barriers in persuading managers with more traditional values that emotional intelligence should be given equal billing to the acquisition of knowledge (cognitive intelligence) when developing the workforce, and in particular that such characteristics are desirable in practice leaders. Traditional training schemes and in-service coaching (clinical supervision) may also need a radical overhaul to accommodate a more experiential learning ethos that focuses a "constructive" magnifying glass upon the individual's self-awareness and interactional style.

Table 3.1 highlights the key characteristics of emotional intelligence and some developmental actions that will encourage personal growth. It is acknowledged that intellectual understanding of emotional intelligence is important, however it must also be understood that we cannot hope to develop our abilities unless we engage in meaningful "experiential learning" that truly stimulates emotional reflection and self-awareness.

Table 3.1. Emotional intelligence	
Key characteristics	*Developmental actions*
Recognise and manage one's emotions and their effects on self and others	Share fears and anxieties with a trusted person. Personal "reflection time". Person-centred clinical supervision or coaching. Stress management strategies.
Know one's own strengths and limitations	Structured self-reflection (e.g. Johari window). 360 degree feedback initiatives. Goal-orientated action planning.
Develop self-confidence	Acknowledge strengths/successes. Assertiveness training. Clinical supervision or personal coaching.
Effectively manage change in self and others	Develop understanding of the stages and process of change. Develop coaching skills. Change management skills.
Adopt an optimistic style	Challenge pessimism (cognitive techniques). Enhance solution-focused thinking and communication.
	Table 3.1/cont

Social awareness and relationship development	Become a skilled communicator. Develop verbal and non-verbal attending skills. Read and respond to others' non-verbal communication. Develop person-centred relationships based upon acceptance, genuineness and empathy. Develop conflict-resolution skills. Create positive first impressions.
Inspire and motivate others	Be solution-focused. Understand and implement motivational theory. Recognise the achievement of others. Contribute to a positive working atmosphere.

Conclusion

In summary there are a number of potential strategies to enhance emotional intelligence in practice leadership. We must develop organisational cultures where the presence of person-centred qualities is genuinely encouraged and valued, and reflection upon interpersonal relationships is incorporated into coaching/clinical supervision (Ruddick, 2010). Enhancing self-awareness through actively seeking 360 degree feedback from significant others either informally or through more structured programmes has to be seen as an essential ingredient of practice leadership development (Royal College of Nursing, 2010). Practice leaders can also be encouraged to engage in self-development through accessing more person-centred, experiential training programmes that enhance self-awareness, self-regard and regard for others. They can also commit to developing a more solution-focused and optimistic communication/explanatory style that targets the strengths and resources present in their followers in order to maximise both individual and team potential (Sharry et al, 2003; Seligman, 2006; Ruddick, 2011). Finally, but most importantly, practice leaders can develop their active listening skills that are fundamental in all productive relationships and which communicate a sense of value to the other person, helping him or her to feel understood (Freshwater, 2003).

Effective leadership in a mental health or learning disability nursing context is different from simply managing others. The "visibility" of clinical leaders and their personal characteristics are as influential as intellectual ability in affecting those they lead. Recognition of how emotional intelligence, relationship-building skills and communication style impact on individuals, teams and organisations has resulted in identification of what are seen as important and desirable attributes of practice leadership (Sparrow and Knight, 2006). Adair (2010: 4) suggests that, in terms of attributes, as a leader, "you should possess, exemplify and perhaps even personify the qualities expected or required in your working group". Leaders who can understand themselves and others at an emotional level can inspire others, develop better relationships, and positively motivate staff. In a modern health service the consequence of choosing practice leaders only for their academic qualifications will hopefully become a historical tradition because the benefits for practice generated from leaders who hold and develop person-centred relationships with their "followers" should positively influence the person-centred services organisations aspire to provide for clients and their families.

Appendix I

The underperforming team: An emotionally intelligent approach

Picture a scenario where a nursing team is in the midst of what seems unrelenting organisational change. Uncertainty prevails and morale is low. Team members feel let down, their motivation has been sapped and as a result they are not reaching the expected organisational targets.

The practice leader has to turn things around and realises that much work needs to be done at both individual and team level. He understands the team's fears and anxieties because he is experiencing some of this himself (self-awareness – recognises and manages own feelings and stress responses). He notices that team members are constantly engaging in "problem talk" and he observes that this is depleting morale even further (recognises the emotional impact on others). How can the situation be managed?

The leader wants to let team members know that their concerns are important and spends time listening to the individuals involved (relationship development). Employing solution-focused communication techniques, he asks questions about how things will be different when the current situation is resolved (optimism and motivation). The feedback received may provide him with some immediate short-term future-orientated goals, and encourages team members to consider solutions rather than problems. He understands that helping people visualise a future when the problems are resolved can instil a greater sense of hopefulness and direction.

The leader is mindful that the team will respond to genuine and transparent communication regarding the organisational changes, and that this is more likely to lead to a trusting and respectful relationship. Individual worries are genuinely acknowledged (empathic communication) and the leader engages in a supportive coaching role (developing others and creating a culture of support) which in turn communicates a sense of personal value to those in the team (enhancing self-worth).

Team meetings follow a similar solution-orientated style with the aim of developing a shared vision (co-operation and relationship development) and direction. Leaders understand that as a role model their sense of optimism and confidence are paramount in creating a positive and supportive environment in which the necessary changes can be managed and organisational objectives met. The approach, based upon the practice leader's person-centred values, affirms that the people at the heart of the team need to be nurtured and valued in order to provide high quality caring services for clients and their families.

It would be helpful for the reader to now reflect upon the following questions to explore their reactions to the "underperforming team" scenario.

- How would you respond to such a leader?
- How does your leadership style compare?
- What benefits do you see for the individual?
- What benefits do you see for the team?
- What benefits do you see for the organisation?

References

Adair J (2010) *Develop your leadership skills.* Kogan Page, London

Bass BM, Riggio RE (2005) *Transformational leadership* (2nd edn). Lawrence Erlbaum Associates, London

Burns JM (1978) *Leadership.* Harper Row, New York

Demarais A, White V (2005) *First impressions: What you don't know about how others see you.* Bantam Books, New York

Department of Health (2009) *Valuing people now: A new three year strategy for people with learning disabilities.* Department of Health, London

de Shazer S (1885) *Keys to solutions in brief therapy.* Paulist Press, New York

Edmondstone J (2009) Clinical leadership: The elephant in the room. *International Journal of Health Planning Management* **24**: 290–305

Freshwater D (2003) *Counselling skills for nurses, midwives and health visitors.* Open University Press, Maidenhead

Goffman E (1961) *Asylums: Essays on the social situation of mental health patients and other inmates.* Anchor Books, New York

Goleman D (1996) *Emotional intelligence.* Bloomsbury, London

Luft J, Ingham H (1955) *The Johari window, a graphic model of interpersonal awareness.*

Proceedings of the Western Training laboratory in Group Development, Los Angeles, UCLA

Macdonald A (2007) *Solution focused therapy: Theory, research and practice*. Sage, London

Marshall E (2010) *Transformational leadership in nursing: From expert clinician to influential leader.* Springer, New York

Mearns D, Thorne B (1999) *Person-centred counselling in action*. Sage, London

O'Boyle EH, Humphrey RH, Pollack JM, Hawver TH, Story PA (2010) The relation between emotional intelligence and job performance: A meta-analysis. *Journal of Organisational Behavior*. DOI 10.1002/job.714

O'Connell B (2005) *Solution focused brief therapy*. Sage, London

Parker PA, Sorenson J (2008) Emotional intelligence and leadership skills among NHS managers: An empirical investigation. *International Journal of Clinical Leadership* **16**(3): 137–42

Rao PR (2006) Emotional intelligence: The sine qua non for a clinical leadership toolbox. *Journal of Communication Disorders* **39**: 310–19

Rogers C (2003) *Client-centered therapy*. Constable, London

Royal College of Nursing (2005) *A multiple-case study evaluation of the RCN clinical leadership programme in England*. RCN, London

Royal College of Nursing (2010) *RCN clinical leadership programme*. Available from: www.rcn.org.uk/development/practice/leadership

Ruddick F (2008) Hope, optimism and expectation. *Mental Health Practice* **12**(1): 33–5

Ruddick F (2010) Person centred mental health care: Myth or reality? *Mental Health Practice* **13**(9): 24–8

Ruddick F (2011) Coping with problems by focusing on solutions. *Mental Health Practice* **14**(8): 28–30

Ruderman MN, Hannum K, Leslie JB, Steed JL (2001) *Leadership skills and emotional intelligence: Research synopsis number 1*. Centre for Creative Leadership, Greensboro, NC

Seligman M (2006) *Learned optimism: How to change your mind and your life*. Vintage Books, New York

Sharry J, Madden B, Darmody M (2003) *Becoming a solution detective*. Routledge, London

Sparrow T, Knight A (2006) *Applied emotional intelligence: The importance of attitudes in developing emotional intelligence*. John Wiley & Sons, London

Thorne B (2003) *Carl Rogers*. Sage, London

Chapter 4

Reflective practice and its relationship to practice leadership

Nicola Clarke

Follow effective action with quiet reflection. From the quiet reflection will come even more effective action.

Peter F Drucker – renowned management guru

In nursing, reflective practice has become a key issue for all those involved in curriculum development and has become a requirement within many nurse education programmes (Mantzoukas and Jasper, 2004; Nicholl and Higgins, 2004). Not only are healthcare professionals required to utilise reflective practice within their initial training and during continuing professional development, it is also seen as a higher education transferable skill, evidence of which is required by the Quality Assurance Agency (Mantzoukas and Jasper, 2004; Tate and Sills, 2004).

The inclusion of critical reflection into the curriculum is also promoted by professional and statutory bodies (Driscoll, 2007). The Nursing and Midwifery Council stipulates that reflection is a competence that needs to be demonstrated in order to gain entry onto the register as a mental health and intellectual disability nurse (Nursing and Midwifery Council, 2010).

The use of reflection and reflective practice in nursing has been reinforced further by the Clinical Leadership Competency Framework (Department of Health, 2011). This Framework came out of the *Next stage review* (Darzi, 2008) and demonstrates a commitment to ensuring that the "undergraduate curricula for all medical and nursing students reflect the requirement for leadership skills in the NHS", and the need to develop leadership capability among all clinicians within the NHS. The Framework has five leadership domains within which clinicians are required to demonstrate competency. Domain 1 "Demonstrating personal qualities" where "clinicians demonstrating effective leadership are required to draw upon core values which are commensurate with delivering person-centred care" is of relevance to reflective practice.

This chapter is concerned with acknowledging the reasons underpinning the importance of being an effective reflective practitioner and how, in embodying this notion, the clinician will be enabled to acquire and maintain competence in relation to Domain 1 and to develop personal qualities.

Twenty first century nursing demands a person-centred/patient-led focus, requiring commitment, with a strong practice and evidence-based ethos from which to face daily challenges. Taylor (2006) suggests that systematic approaches to reflection and action are needed so as to strengthen personal resolve and to be effective and happy in our work. Bolton (2010) concurs with this observation and suggests that reflection and reflexivity are essential for responsible and ethical practice. Reflective practice/writing, or as Bolton (2010) terms it, "through the mirror writing", allows discovery of who and what we are in practice, and why we act as we do. It can help practitioners towards perceiving and taking full responsibility for themselves and their behaviour, thus supporting the demonstration of competence in the domain of developing personal qualities, in particular, self-awareness. The Clinical Leadership Competency Framework requires clinicians to demonstrate leadership through the development of self-awareness and, in essence, reflexivity. In the words of Beckett (1969: 169) "to be capable of helping others to become all they are capable of becoming we must first fulfil that commitment to ourselves". Boyd and Fales (1983) support this view stating that reflection is the core difference between whether an individual repeats the same experience several times and becomes highly proficient at certain behaviour, or learns from experience in such a way that he or she is cognitively or affectively changed.

On further examination of the importance of reflection, Tate and Sills (2004) refer to the work of Schön (1983) who categorised knowledge into two types: technical rationality and professional artistry. Technical rationality was Schön's idiom for scientific knowledge that has been generated by research, referred to as "knowing that". In contrast, professional artistry is intuitive knowledge derived from individual experiences and is referred to as "knowing how". Tate and Sills (2004) suggest that both types of knowledge are needed by practitioners, and it is at the interface of these two types of knowledge that the professional artistry that is required by practitioners to offer holistic patient-centred care exists. Tate goes on to suggest that professional artistry is developed through critical reflection, and Benner (1984) identified this as a characteristic skill of expert nurses by which they will be able to describe and demonstrate their skills, thereby gaining credit and recognition. The Competency Framework alludes to the management of oneself in relation to demonstrating personal qualities. Managing oneself further develops the concept of reflexivity, recognising the impact we have on others in relation to the "self", and in more practical matters of workload and commitments. Professional artistry, developed through critical reflection, may enable clinicians to engage in personal and professional development that demonstrates managing themselves in accordance with the Competency Framework.

The Framework further supports the importance of "learning" under personal qualities, by formalising the need to demonstrate personal development and integrity. Kolb (1984) saw reflection as an integral part of the way in which we learn. The purpose of reflection on experience is to stimulate further inquiry and so generate new cycles of meaningful activity (further experiences), in turn aimed at constructing new knowledge. The development of cognitive, intellectual and practical skills is a product of activity (Kolb, 1984). Therefore, learning by means of reflection can best be conceived as a process that is grounded in and emergent from experience or experiences. (See *Figure 4.1.*)

Thus Kolb considered reflection as a mental activity that has a role in learning from experience. Dewey also viewed reflective practice as a tool for learning, enabling us "to know what we are about when we act". It "converts action that is merely appetitive, blind, and impulsive into intelligent action" (Dewey, 1964: 211), and if we relate this information to Domain 1 of the Competency Framework "demonstrating personal qualities", the process of effective reflection and engaging in the reflective process enables the clinician to demonstrate a development of personal qualities, and learning from the experience, which in turn demonstrates personal development and integrity.

However, if practitioners/clinicians are going to engage in reflective practice they first need to ensure they understand what is meant by this term. In my experience it is not uncommon for even seasoned clinicians to not own a fully

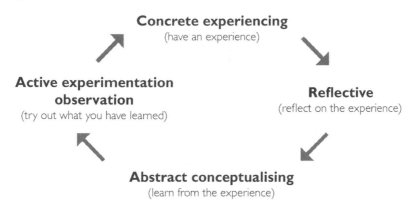

Figure 4.1. Kolb's Learning Cycle (Kolb, 1984).

comprehensive understanding of reflection and its complex nature. An extended definition of reflection, derived from my own studies and research into this concept, indicates that reflection is an essential, engaging process that allows the reflector to frame and reframe his or her reality that is being experienced moment by moment. It requires us to use communication skills, to become our own person-centred therapists, understanding ourselves in relation to experiences we are about to have, are having or have had, empathically and with accuracy, then step beyond the self and use this knowledge gained to understand how we may then have impacted on those around us.

For this process to be fruitful we must leave arrogance and complacency at the door; be actively engaged in mindfulness; consciously aware of the self in the moment; open to learning and sourcing new knowledge if the knowledge is not already known to us; using the new knowledge gained to develop ourselves personally and professionally; and be critically analytical. When fully engaged in the reflective process the experience can be humbling as we realise we are perhaps not what we assumed ourselves to be, yet also rewarding as we confirm that our best may have at that time been good enough.

Horan (2005) describes reflection as a complex activity of psychologically and emotionally processing the issues that trouble nurses/midwives in everyday clinical practice. He suggests that the term does not accurately portray the complexity of this process and instead refers to Schön who he describes as coining the term "framing". This term, Horan believes, has more value and would be better suited to describe the process that occurs when reflecting. He believes that this is because an experience can be pre-framed before it happens, framed as it happens, and reframed both as it happens and after it has happened. He believes that by terming this complex process of reflecting as framing:

...we become the nursing artists of our own experience...through framing, our thinking can be as creative as we wish.

(Horan, 2005)

Johns (2000) affirms this and describes reflection as:

...a window through which the practitioner can view and focus self within the context of her lived experience in ways that enable her to confront, understand and work towards resolving the contradictions within her practice between what is desirable and actual practice.

(Johns 2000: 34)

There appears to be a consensus of opinion within the literature that reflecting on action develops individuals' skills as reflective practitioners and provides a way for them to frame and reframe the situations they have experienced. It opens up individuals to criticise the tacit knowledge they hold about given situations and to make new sense or reframe these experiences as they see fit (Schön, 1983). Gaining this level of self-awareness, or getting to know what frames individuals give to situations or experiences and reflecting on them, allows them to create new frames that are stored and utilised in future events. This also opens the person up to viewing situations from many different angles; in essence, reflection supports the development and enhancement of personal qualities.

Perusing the brief amount of information alluded to on what reflective practice is, the importance of it and what it means for the individual engaging in it, it would seem that there is a clear link between reflective practice and the clinician's ability not only to demonstrate personal qualities but also to develop them in accordance with the Clinical Leadership Competency Framework requirements.

It has been acknowledged in the literature that spontaneous reflection in action is not only a product of the development of reflecting on action skills but also of the development of the internal supervisor (Casement, 1985; Bond and Holland, 1998; Todd, 2005). The term "internal supervisor" has been coined to describe the internal Socratic dialogue that occurs in the consciousness of the reflector within the moment of the experience (Todd, 2005) or the conversation that takes place with the self about the event as the event or experience occurs. The internal supervisor questions personal bias and subjectivity towards finding an objective perspective (Todd, 2002). The internal supervisor is a way of questioning the self at the time of engaging in any given situation; it allows individuals to be fully aware of their own engagement and be mindful of the outcome. The critical friend, whether this part is taken on by your own internal supervisor or an external party, will listen more than talk but will use reflective questioning and be mindful of the salient points as the reflector speaks (Taylor, 2006). In essence, development of Socratic dialogue and the internal supervisor would, it seems, enhance self-awareness and thus have an indirect impact on acting with integrity as required by the Competency Framework. The Framework requires that clinicians are able to recognise and articulate their own values and principles, understanding how these may differ from others; be able to identify their own strengths and limitations, and how these may impact upon others; understand their own emotions and prejudices, and how this can affect behaviour; communicate effectively with individuals, taking into account diversity and equality, and act promptly if ethics and values are compromised. On review of the literature, all these qualities can be enhanced and gained through reflective practice.

To support this notion, Atkins and Murphy (1993) made reference to academic abilities when they outlined the five main skills helpful for reflection. Four out of the five skills sit within the category of higher order cognitive skills, these are:

- *Description*: the ability to recognise, recollect and describe situations as well as feelings and emotions.
- *Critical analysis*: the challenging of assumptions, exploring alternatives and asking the relevance of knowledge in specific situations.
- *Synthesis*: the amalgamation of new and previous knowledge in the move towards a new perspective.
- *Evaluation*: the making of value judgements involving the use of criteria and standards.

Taylor (2006) refers to the amalgamation of these four skills as critical thinking. She suggests that critical thinking processes and the possession of critical thinking skills are important if practitioners require careful, fully analytical reasoning to assure them of the conclusions they have drawn in relation to some objective issues in their practice.

However, it is the skill of self-awareness that has been noted as the foundation upon which reflective practice is built. It underpins the entire notion of reflection as it enables individuals to see themselves in a particular situation and honestly observe how they have affected that situation and how the situation has affected them. It also allows individuals to analyse their feelings regarding that particular event (Atkins, 2004). It is suggested by Atkins that self-awareness enables a person to analyse his/her own feelings, beliefs, and values as an essential part of the reflective process. So by engaging in the reflective process the clinician will be demonstrating the requirement of self-awareness under Domain 1 of the Clinical Leadership Competency Framework.

Johns (2000) went so far as to integrate the aspects of attitude required for reflection into a mode of being. He purported that in order to engage effectively in the critically reflective process the individual needs to engage with the 10 "C"s of reflection (see *Box 4.1*).

Here we can see that engaging the 10 "C"s of reflection is about reflectors' attitude to learning; their openness to learn about themselves, to be able to

Box 4.1. The 10 "C"s of reflection
(Johns, 2000: 36, adapted)

Commitment
Believe that self and practice matter; accepting responsibility for self; the openness, curiosity and willingness to challenge normative ways of responding to situations. In leadership this would be openness to change and an attitude of responsiveness to situations rather than a one size fits all approach.

Contradiction
Exposing and understanding the contradiction between what is desirable and actual practice. In leadership this would mean supporting staff in attaining desirable practice by gentle confrontation and exposure of what is poor practice.

Conflict
Harnessing the energy of conflict within contradiction to become empowered to take appropriate action. In leadership, being confident in applying conflict-resolution strategies.

Challenge and support
Confronting the practitioner's normative attitudes, beliefs and actions in ways that do not threaten the practitioner. In leadership this would mean having the ability to act as the critical companion (Titchen, 2003) to staff in a manner that is conducive to change rather than judgemental of attitudes and beliefs or coercive.

Catharsis
Working through negative feelings. In leadership not only would this mean seeking supervision for themselves, but ensuring provision for staff whereby staff members can work through any issues without being judged, within a supportive safe environment. Being a leader that enhances staff members' ability to express themselves appropriately rather than seeing expression of feeling requiring suppression.

Creation
Moving beyond self to see and understand new ways of viewing and responding to practice. In leadership this would mean the clinician being reflexive, taking on board the views and comments of staff, recognition of individual expertise within the team. Recognition that as a leader they are not all knowing.

Box 4.1/cont

Connection

Connecting new insights within the real world of practice; appreciating the temporality of experience over time. In leadership this means sensing, feeling the palpable world of practice, and being able to create, adapt or adopt new perspectives.

Caring

Realising desirable practice as everyday reality. In leadership terms this would mean leading by example, acknowledging that best practice is the norm not the exception.

Congruence

Reflection as a mirror for caring. In leadership this would mean openness and transparency on behalf of the leader. Not acting the role of the leader but as a person individuals can make a psychological connection with.

Constructing personal knowledge in practice

Weaving personal knowing with relevant extant theory in constructing knowledge. In leadership this would mean the clinicians would ensure they were evidence based in their practice, but humble enough to acknowledge when personal knowing needs enhancement with the creation of new knowledge from training, etc.

---

acknowledge what their attitudes and perceptions are, to be open to challenging those current ideologies, to have the ability to be empathic, to view the world as others may see it, and to be able to combine evidence-based theory with personal knowing in the construction of new knowledge.

In conclusion, reflection requires individuals to hold a level of knowledge on the experience upon which they are reflecting so that they, through the process of reflecting, can determine if that knowledge was correct, and construct new knowledge if needed. It requires people to be open, congruent, confident, honest and self-aware, to be able to critique and analyse a situation they have experienced in a manner that goes beyond a description of the event and allows people not only to understand themselves in relation to the experience but also to understand empathically how others were affected by their experience. At the end of the process it requires the person to be able to synthesise new knowledge and amalgamate it with current knowledge in the development of self, thus as a result demonstrating competence in Domain 1 (Demonstrating Personal Qualities) of the Clinical Leadership Competency Framework.

References

Atkins S (2004) Developing underlying skills in the move towards reflective practice. In Bulman C, Schutz S (Eds.) *Reflective practice in nursing* (3rd edn). Blackwell Publishing, Oxford

Atkins S, Murphy C (1993). Reflection: A review of the literature. *Journal of Advanced Nursing* **18**: 1188–92

Beckett T (1969). A candidate's reflections on the supervisory process. *Contemporary Psychoanalysis* **5**: 169–79

Benner P (1984). *From novice to expert*. Addison-Wesley, Menlo Park, CA

Bolton G (2010). *Reflective practice, writing and professional development* (3rd edn). SAGE Publications, London

Bond M, Holland S (1998) *Skills of clinical supervision for nurses*. Open University Press, Buckingham

Boyd E, Fales A (1983) Reflective learning: The key to learning from experience. *Journal of Humanistic Psychology* **23**(2): 99–117

Casement P (1985) *On learning from the patient*. Guilford Press, New York

Darzi A (2008) *High quality care for all: NHS next stage review. Final report.* Department of Health, London

Department of Health (2011) *Clinical Leadership Competency Framework*. NHS Institute for Innovation and Improvement, Coventry

Dewey J (1964) *John Dewey selected writings*. Heath and Co, New York

Driscoll J (2007) *Practising clinical supervision. A reflective approach for healthcare professionals* (2nd edn). Elsevier, Edinburgh

Horan P (2005) Framing the new reflection. *Nurse Education in Practice* **5**(5): 255–7

Johns C (2000) *Becoming a reflective practitioner*. Blackwell Science, Oxford

Kolb DA (1984) *Experiential learning*. Prentice-Hall, New Jersey

Mantzoukas S, Jasper MA (2004) Issues in clinical nursing. Reflective practice and daily ward reality: A covert power game. *Journal of Clinical Nursing* **13**: 925–33

Nicholl H, Higgins A (2004) Issues and innovations in nurse education; Reflection in pre-registration nursing curricula. *Journal of Advanced Nursing* **46**(6): 578–85

Nursing and Midwifery Council (2010) *Standards for pre-registration nurse education.* NMC, London

Schön DA (1983) *The reflective practitioner: How practitioners think in action*. Basic Books, New York

Tate S, Sills M (2004). *The development of critical reflection in healthcare professionals. Occasional Paper No.4.* Health Sciences and Practice, London

Taylor BJ (2006) *Reflective practice. A guide for nurses and midwives* (2nd edn). Open University Press, Berkshire

Titchen A (2003) Critical companionship: Part 1. *Nursing Standard* **18**(9): 33–40

Todd G (2002) The role of the internal supervisor in developing therapeutic nursing. In D Freshwater (ed) *Therapeutic nursing*. Sage, London

Todd G (2005) Reflective practice and Socratic dialogue. In C Johns, D Freshwater (eds) *Transforming nursing through reflective practice*. Blackwell Publishing, Oxford

Chapter 5

Maximising capacity and creativity through coaching

Stephen Conlon and Dean-David Holyoake

To understand something is to stand under it, so that you may foster its development.
Heinz Von Foerster Observing Systems (1984)

Introduction

This chapter aims to explore the relationship between leadership and coaching. It brings to the fore ideas about how employees, colleagues and managers find themselves interwoven in relationships, behavioural patterns and organisational routines that are not as easily identified as traditional coaching models might suggest. The solution-focused coaching ideas introduced here ally themselves to the most recent leadership framework within health and social care organisations (NHS Institute for Innovation and Improvement and Academy of Medical Royal Colleges, 2010). In this model, leadership skills are arranged in three clusters containing 15 key skill domains (see *Figure 5.1*).

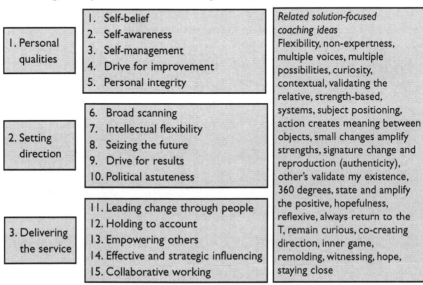

1. Personal qualities	1. Self-belief 2. Self-awareness 3. Self-management 4. Drive for improvement 5. Personal integrity	*Related solution-focused coaching ideas* Flexibility, non-expertness, multiple voices, multiple possibilities, curiosity, contextual, validating the relative, strength-based, systems, subject positioning, action creates meaning between objects, small changes amplify strengths, signature change and reproduction (authenticity), other's validate my existence, 360 degrees, state and amplify the positive, hopefulness, reflexive, always return to the T, remain curious, co-creating direction, inner game, remolding, witnessing, hope, staying close
2. Setting direction	6. Broad scanning 7. Intellectual flexibility 8. Seizing the future 9. Drive for results 10. Political astuteness	
3. Delivering the service	11. Leading change through people 12. Holding to account 13. Empowering others 14. Effective and strategic influencing 15. Collaborative working	

Figure 5.1: The Medical Leadership Competency Framework.

Today, healthcare is confronting an uncertain future and attempting to meet challenging service expectations in relation to the leaders it develops. The aims of the Medical Leadership Competency Framework are founded on a concept of shared leadership and shared responsibility. This chapter reveals how adopting a strength-based solution-focused approach to coaching maximises both individual and organisational capacity to share creatively.

Defining coaching

Whitmore (2002) broadly defines coaching as the process of "unlocking a person's potential to maximise their performance". Jarvis et al (2006) offer a more specific work-oriented definition and suggest that coaching is a process that aims to develop a "person's skills and knowledge so that their job performance improves, leading to the achievement of organisational objectives". Coaching, therefore, in both the solution-focused and Clinical Leadership Competency Framework sense, has the intention of recognising and acting upon at least two practical ideals. These are cultural meaning and local context which are both systemically driven concepts. The notion of "meaning" relates to how people think about and actively plug into their cultural surroundings and how "they know what it is they know" about any given thing such as "the way things work around here". The second notion of context relates to the way meaning is always relative and dynamically connected to the individual experiencing it. In this sense leadership should be considered contextually and always in situ as opposed to the traditional individualistically trait-driven models so often promoted in management textbooks. In the words of Somers (2002, 2006) situated coaching recognises that people are not empty vessels into which knowledge and skills must be poured, but rather "seedlings who require careful nurturing and support".

Top tip: Coaching always attempts to be transparent and promote an exploration of both meaning and context of the process. Remember you are not the expert in others' lived or memorised experience.

Personal qualities: Multiverse as opposed to universe

Coaching can build capacity and skills, enable the achievement of personal goals and improve system insight in organisations. A complete pallet of important psychotherapeutic approaches, including client-centred, cognitive, systemic, psychodynamic and psychoanalytic models, inform most coaching practice. The solution-focused model, similar to the Clinical Leadership Competency Framework model, draws on curiosity, systemic and Socratic thinking, and modelling related to range and flexibility as originally outlined by Ashby (1956). Solution-focused coaching, as with the ideals of the Clinical Leadership Competency Framework, emphasises a sense of positioning which is contextual, and culturally and socially relative. So instead of focusing purely on the good and bad points of "the individual" there is a shift towards examining the contextual forces of culture which are seen to inform actions and reverberate back to inform culture (Cronen et al, 1982) and provide what Hawkins and Smith (2006) term the context for positive coaching experience.

The solution-focused approach is strength-based (de Shazer, 1988; Hubble et al, 1999) and offers both the theoretical and practical tools to get the most out of the Clinical Leadership Competency Framework. The emphasis is on the examination of the "multiple" personal and institutional dynamics that constitute a working culture rather than a critique of an individual's skills or ability per se to relate to the organisational standards and other team members. For example, solution-focused coaching asks questions about the nature of multiple intra-personal relationships that people have with themselves (confidence, beliefs, awareness, flexibility), the multiple inter-personal relationships they have with their colleagues (attitude, values, perception and integrity) and the multiple organisation connections at different strategic levels (motivation. clarity of role, function and purpose). In short, similar to coaching inspired by the Competency Framework, the solution-focused approach recognises there is no longer a one size fits all approach to achieving the desired definition of organisational leadership coaching. As such, O'Hanlon's (1999) more inclusive style invites coaches to explore people's multiple strengths or skill set rather than perceive them as having a single strength or skill set, not just a batter or bowler but an all-rounder, and that the real strength of the leader is to draw out existing or develop new knowledge and skills by increasing possibilities and perspectives and shifting from a limited singular strength-based view (universe) to a broader multi-strength view (multiverse) (Maturana and Varela, 1986).

Top tip:The notion of "multiverse" reminds us that everything is possible. It is not simply the coach and the "personal qualities" being coached in the relationship, but everyone and thing they have ever known.

Amplifying personal qualities and subject positioning

For the solution-focused coach the emphasis on the individual is always via the shared social experience, that is, the way an individual relates to and is constituted by the organisational social world around him or her. In healthcare organisations the type of systems that position you are determined by the relationships you have with others, such as managers, subordinates, colleagues, clients and so on. The idea of "subjecthood" or "subject positioning" also emphasises that to be solution-focused is wary of 20th century coaching ideas promoting "individuality", "autonomy" and "freewill", that is the dominant idea that people within organisations can simply improve themselves independently of context and have an impact on organisational functioning.

This has an impact on the outcomes of coaching in relation to the personal qualities of professionals even if they are in the same profession and organisation, such as the newly qualified medic who is expected to "learn the ropes" when compared to the consultant who has been qualified for over 20 years and rules with a subtle iron rod. As such, there is a recognition that leadership and coaching is sited (situated) as fragments of personal qualities which, according to Watzlawick et al (1974), are rooted in an interactional approach. This invites us to consider how repetitive interactions maintain attitudes, behaviours and cultural cycles. These dynamics are created in the action between people and emphasise that the real challenge of coaching is to introduce change (do something different) and offer novel interruption into patterns that are working (amplify strengths). Personal qualities therefore are important to the solution-focused coach, but not a distraction from the broad social influences acting on the individual.

Top tip: Never negotiate, instead collaborate and blend the theory you trust to achieve a desired goal.

New signatures, 360 degree change style and focusing on the positive

Like many coaching approaches the solution-focused coach aims to facilitate an identification of the strengths and resources supervisees already have in order to substantiate change. The solution-focused approach, as does the Clinical Leadership Competency Framework, takes on board the idea that "authenticity" and fixed characteristics of identity are fluid possibilities open for change. This is a strange concept which can be likened to the way, as children, we practised our signature until we settled on the one we thought made us look more adult or flamboyant or whatever. The point is that when coaching, the solution-focused coach identifies that the individuals are more than able to come up with a new signature given the right conditions within which to construct a new organisationally managed image of themselves.

To do this, the solution-focused supervisor will employ a number of skills to elicit, not necessarily new modes of thinking, but rather changed behaviour (see *Box 5.1* for an overall solution-focused ethos). One key aim of the solution-focused coach is to get the client to commit to new ways of "doing", the outcome being that their colleagues can actually "see a difference". In this sense, the development of personal qualities is less about the personal and more about the public validation of change. For example, the coach might ask: "What would your manager see you doing when the change has happened?" or "What will you do differently if I secretly watched you in a week's time go about your daily chores on the ward?" This idea of the personal becoming public is the key to understanding the theoretical difference between solution-focused coaching and other approaches. And the way to emphasise this personal/public dichotomy is through the age-old pastime of "watching the doing". It reminds us that we should not judge a man by what he says, but rather through the action he takes.

For the solution-focused coach, another primary concern is social review and feedback, "What would your colleagues tell me you were good at?" Such a question asks, "What would they see you doing consistently?" The qualities of the personal is truly public and as such more pragmatic than we would want to admit. The work of Collins (2000) highlights the value of 360 degree feedback which uses a person's immediate eco system to capture both qualitative and quantitative data, highlighting strengths and potential for development in areas that include performance, role and function. As previously noted, the gossip and secret views of colleagues, as part of the grapevine, is a "systemically" derived example of organisational personal quality feedback. As cruel as the process can be, the authors note that from their own practice they invite participants to "state the positive", commenting on what they see a person do well and what they would like to see a person do differently or do more of, rather than stating the negative, identifying what they do not like or do not want. Taking this approach can build a culture of acceptance, if not celebration, of difference. "When I focus on people's bad qualities, they multiply; when I focus on people's good qualities, they seem to grow and grow" (Alcoholics Anonymous, 2001).

Top tip: Regarding personal qualities, expect more and hope for the best.

Box 5.1. Best future(s) scenario for coaching delivery

- A community-endorsed set of standards
- A peer-led programme
- A balanced equal approach to access
- A needs-led framework approach
- A realistic fit for practice
- Debriefing
- Shadowing
- A flattening of hierarchy
- Development of a new lexicon
- Emphasis on the dynamic between actions
- Emphasis on the impact of systemic action
- An accepting and welcoming of vulnerability
- A promotion of new modes of performance
- Recognition of the multiples (selves, meanings, actions)
- A wariness of humanist essentialism
- Replacement of a way of knowing with a plan of action
- Alienation
- Deconstruction
- An expectancy of hope
- A decentring of the individual
- Systemic principles of ward communication (in handover – debriefing)
- Milieu
- Recognition of the confirming dynamics of language
- Big fat feedback loops
- Increased feedback
- A notion of small change
- Blurring of boundaries and authorship
- Partnership
- Co-collaboration
- Cultural ownership of a colleague's improvement

Clinical Leadership Competency Framework setting direction

Coaching plays a key part in raising awareness of the systemic nature of organisations as large families of individuals interacting; heightening awareness of the reflexive relationships people have with themselves and others to create productive cultures that can shape organisational success and direction. Campbell et al (1991) recognise that patterns of interaction influence thinking and behaving within and between individuals, creating the attitudes and cultures that mould, "set direction", and shape the organisational fabric and function.

Direction, range, curiosity, not knowing and histories

Solution-focused coaches recognise that people are a composite collection of social influences. So when exploring organisational issues it is possible to invite supervisees to consider who they have metaphorically brought into the room and how that might be informing the reflexive interaction. Specifically, the relationship with the uptake or not of new or challenging information is a technique that emphasises what Cronen et al (1982) term multiple levels of context. Similarly, the notion of someone "bringing in their history (his-story)" offers a method to explore with curiosity the notion of signature themes and a reflexive evaluation of how the coach might use elements of the relationship. O'Hanlon and Weiner-Davis (1989) draw attention to the iatrogenic influence that we as coaches can have on clients, how a solution or strength-based style contrasts with a deficit or problem-focused style and how this can influence both our own and our clients' perceptions and experience of their situation in both positive and negative directions. So, when considering the importance of "setting direction", the coaching experience becomes one of co-creating realities where meanings, interpretations and constructs are exchanged in what Cronen et al (1982) identify as an evolving reflexive discourse that moves individuals' thinking and behaviour from one point to another.

A coach subscribing to this approach adopts what Anderson and Goolishian (1992) describe as a curious or "not knowing" style, where questions are asked, not necessarily to get answers but as an intervention into the client's thinking. This prompts the generation of new or different meanings or perspectives, which increase a person's range and agency. Increasing a client's range so much that he or she is able to exert a greater degree of control over a system, team or organisation is supported in Ashby's early work (1956), which recognised that the part of the system with the most range or flexibility controls the system. Lewis and Pucelik (1982) recognise that for interventions or change strategies to work these core skills must be evident and employed.

> *Top tip: Identifying people's range allows them to determine and evaluate their direction of travel.*

The cast and systems around the performer (culture)

The language of "setting direction" is an attempt at simplifying that which has been hijacked and absorbed into everyday management speak. The importance of how language operates rather than the actual content is the concern for the solution-focused coach. This involves ideas about contextuality, intertextuality and the multivoice of meaning previously discussed. Coaching plays a key role in helping organisations and individuals create a dynamic, supportive and inspiring culture where change is embraced and people feel valued and supported. O'Neill (2000) acknowledges the systemic opportunities that coaching offers for individuals to map patterns of their own thoughts and behaviours and reference them against performance indicators and organisational outcomes, identifying what they are doing that works and doing more of it, and, where something is not working, introducing change or difference. A coaching culture encourages a focus on valuing all members of the team, inviting workers to reflect and review how what they do helps or hinders their own, their team's and their organisation's functioning.

Experience shows that coaching invites the emergence of ideas and feedback (even 360 degree) and creates a feeling within teams of acknowledgement and validation. The benefits for the organisation include a reduction in sickness and absence and a high staff retention in those teams where there is a coaching culture in comparison to those teams where there is not. Evered and Selman (1989) recognised that some people believe they know all they need to know and are reluctant to engage in coaching type discussions. Most teams can identify with managers, colleagues and fellow workers of this type. Experience here is that some are skeptical because they have seen others undergo coaching and there has been no noticeable change in their thinking or behaviour. Remembering the ethos that solution-focused coaching is mostly about recognising systems, the setting of leadership direction for the solution-focused coach is promoted and built on the following ideals:

- What will your colleagues notice that is different about you that will tell them the coaching is having a positive effect?
- Who will be most/least surprised by the changes you make?
- What small part of your work will change as a result of coaching?
- Who will notice when you implement your next change?
- What else will be different?
- What else will people say to you?
- How will you notice that things are changing for other team members?
- How convinced are you that you will succeed?
- When you finish this coaching session what will you do that shows it has been successful?
- What will you want to see your colleagues doing?

Top tip: Feedback loops enable an answer to the organisational intertextual "will" questions.

Setting "inner" direction

Gallwey (1986) argues that organisations wanting to develop their workforce should focus attention on the "inner game", developing values, attitudes, beliefs, confidence, esteem and culture as opposed to focusing excessively on the "outer game" of outcomes and the achievement of performance targets. Marshall and McLean (1985) extend Gallwey's position and argue that the individual's belief systems or meaning systems influence both the way in which people view reality and how they subsequently choose to act. They go on to connect individual belief systems (e.g. of success and failure) with organisational belief systems (e.g. of loyalty, achievement, right and wrong) that they believe have a direct influence and therefore relate to the setting of direction on the way people behave in roles. Leithwood et al (2006) challenge this position as difficult to quantify or measure, instead preferring a shift towards the more tangible quantitative measures of organisational success, namely that targets or outcomes have been reached. One might argue that there is merit in both, systemically encouraging a focus on the relationship between the way people think about their world, their role and the part they play, will have a direct bearing on their actions and ultimately the organisation's performance.

A survey conducted by Gallup over 25 years and involving over one million people (Buckingham and Coffman, 2005) revealed some of the key abilities and

---

Box 5.2. Key abilities and performance characteristics of effective leaders (Buckingham and Coffman, 2005)

- Recognise that each person is motivated differently, with their own way of thinking and own style of relating to others.
- Know there is only so much remoulding they can do to someone.
- Work with people's strengths and put them into positions that draw on their strengths. Rather than "waste time trying to put in what was left out, they draw out what was left in".
- Reach inside each employee and release his or her unique talents into performance.
- Act as catalysts by speeding up the reaction between the employee's talents and the company's goals and between the employee's talents and the customer's needs.
- Perform four key activities:
  - (i) Select the person
  - (ii) Set expectations (hope)
  - (iii) Motivate the person
  - (iv) Develop the person.
- Meet regularly (minimum quarterly) with employees, focus on the future, learn from the past and encourage employees to take responsibility for their own performance and learning.

---

performance characteristics of effective leaders (see *Box 5.2*). The "delivery of service" is something that happens "between actors" in terms of action which is always relative and ongoing. The skeptical employee will be one who has been subjected to doses of coaching and probably not a supportive ongoing arrangement intrinsic to his or her work role, in that adage that supervision is not socially dangerous until you say the wrong thing. So one of the guiding principles in solution-focused practice is the idea of hope. The idea that the supervisor attempts to instil a feeling of hope relates to a number of factors including witnessing, non-expertness, and the expectation that people have the persona, resources and expertise to sort their own lives. In the supervision sense this shows itself in the air of expectation. It allows for the exploration of future possibilities and at least reduces a reliance on problem focusing. Hence the solution-focused (not forced) foundation of skills introduced in this chapter (see *Box 5.3* and *Figure 5.2*).

Box 5.3. Traditional coaching models versus solution-focused approach

Traditional (Modernist)	*Solution-focused* (Post-modern)
Nurture	Nature
Outcome	Process
Motivation (will)	Impingement of position
Individual	Object/subject
Organisation	Culture
Personality traits	Technologies of the self
Development	Validation
Authorship	Reproduction and representation
Language as expression	Language as entrapment
Deductive	Inductive
Responsive	Receptive
Individual	Systemic
Certainty principle	Slippery signifiers
Holism	Fragmentation
Deep	Shallow
Rational	Relative
Simple	Complex
Reflective	Reflexive
Production	Consumption
Linear	Cluster
Diachronic	Synchronic
Atomist	Organicist
Knowledge	Intuition
Intellect	Emotion
Universal	Multiversal
Fixed	Fluid
Authorship	Collaborative

Summary

Primarily one could argue that the most important requirement for delivering effective leadership coaching can be found in the opening definitions given at the beginning of this chapter, principally how to maximise another person's capacity

Figure 5.2. Delivering new ideas.

in whatever context. Bentley (1996) argues that coaches are people who model desired behaviours and are trusted with knowledge and experience to help people less experienced but with skills and talent to develop. Whitmore (2002) argues that coaches do not need to have any experience; their role is that of "awareness raiser" with faith in the individual's ability. Personal experience has shown that as a coach there is no need to have any prior knowledge or experience of the client's business, one is always measured by, among other things, how productive the client found the coaching interaction. Listening skills that enable the coach to acknowledge, validate and create what O'Hanlon (1999) describes as a joining, where clients feel heard, that the coach is empathising and able to make sense of their experience. Covey (2004) argues that the coach needs to listen and "seek to understand" the client first before moving to a position where they seek to be understood. He goes on to say that problem solving follows listening. Experience indicates that listening and solution building are linked in the very early stages of the interaction with the identification of outcomes for the session opening with, for example, "What needs to happen in this session for you to feel that it has been productive and time well spent?" A key characteristic of an effective coach is the ability to "stay close to the client". De Jong and Kim Berg (2002) emphasise the importance of staying close, adopting a one-down curious posture stimulating the client's thinking and resisting the temptation for instructive interaction and the "telling expert" position.

References

Alcoholics Anonymous (2001) *Big book* (4th edn). AA World Services, USA

Anderson H, Goolishian H (1992) The client is the expert: A not-knowing approach to therapy. In S McNamee, K Bergen (eds) *Therapy as social construction.* Sage, Newbury Park, CA

Ashby R (1956) *Introduction to cybernetics.* Chapman & Hall, London

Bentley T (1996) *Bridging the performance gap.* Gower, Farnham

Buckingham M, Coffman C (2005) *First break all the rules: What the World's greatest managers do differently.* Pocket Books, London

Campbell D, Draper R, Huffington C (1991) *A systemic approach to systemic consultation.* Karnac Books, London

Collins LeDuff M (2000) *360^0 feedback: A manager's guide.* Thin Book Publishing Company, Plano, TX

Covey S (2004) *The seven habits of highly effective people.* Simon and Schuster, London

Cronen VE, Johnson KM, Lannamann JW (1982) Paradoxes, double binds and reflexive loops. *Family Process* **21**: 91–112

De Jong P, Kim Berg I (2002) *Interviewing for solutions.* Brooks Cole, San Francisco, CA

De Shazer S (1988) *Clues: Investigating solutions in brief therapy.* Norton, New York

Evered R, Selman J (1989) Coaching and the art of management. *Organisational Dynamics* **18**: 165–75

Gallwey WT (1986) *The inner game of tennis.* Pan Books, London

Hawkins P, Smith N (2006) *Coaching, mentoring and organisational consultancy – supervision and development.* Open University Press, Buckingham

Hubble M, Duncan B, Miller S (1999) *The heart and soul of change*. APA Press, Washington DC

Jarvis J, Lane D, Fillery-Travis A (2006) *The case for coaching: Making evidence-based decisions*. CIPD Publishing, London

Leithwood K, Day C, Sammons P, Harris A, Hopkins D (2006) *Successful school leadership. What it is and how it influences pupil learning*. University of Nottingham, Nottingham

Lewis B, Pucelik F (1982) *Magic demystified: A pragmatic guide to communication and change*. Metamorphous Press, Oregon

Maturana H, Varela F (1986) *The tree of knowledge: Biological roots of human understanding*. Shambhala Publishers, London

NHS Institute for Innovation and Improvement and Academy of Medical Royal Colleges (2010) *Medical Leadership Competency Framework*. NHS Institute for Innovation and Improvement, Coventry

O'Hanlon W, Weiner-Davis M (1989) *In search of solutions*. W.W. Norton, New York

O'Hanlon W (1999) *Do one thing different*. William Morrow Publishing, New York

O'Neill M (2000) *Executive coaching with backbone and heart*. Jossey Bass, San Francisco, CA

Somers M (2002) *Coaching in a week*. Hodder and Stoughton, Oxford

Somers M (2006) *Coaching at work*. Wiley and Sons, London

Von Foerster H (1984) *Observing systems*. Intersystems Publications, San Francisco, CA

Watzlawick P, Weakland J, Fisch R (1974). *Change: Principles of problem formation and problem resolution*. Norton, London

Whitmore J (2002) *Coaching for performance*. Nicholas Brearley, London

Further reading

Bateson G (1972) *Steps to an ecology of mind*. University Press, Chicago, IL

Berne E (1964) *Games people play*. Penguin Books, London

Fisch R, Weakland J, Segal L (1982) *The tactics of change: Doing therapy briefly*. Jossey Bass, San Francisco, CA

Goleman D (1994). *Emotional intelligence*. Bantam Books, New York

Goleman D, Boyatzis R, McKee A (2002) *Primal leadership*. Harvard Business School Press, Boston, MA

Marshall J, McLean A (1985) Exploring organisation culture as a route to organisational change. In Hammond V (ed) *Current research in management* (pp 2–20). Francis Pinter, London

Maslow AH (1943) A theory of human motivation. *Psychological Review* **50**(4): 370–96

Neighbour R (2006) *The inner consultation: How to develop an effective and intuitive consulting style*. Radcliffe Publishing, Oxford

O'Hanlon W, Beadle S (1996) *A field guide to possibility land*. BT Press, London

Paul R, Elder L (2006) *The art of Socratic questioning*. Foundation for Critical Thinking, Dillon Beach, CA

White M, Epston D (1990) *Narrative means to therapeutic ends*. Norton, New York

Chapter 6

Practice development: Mental health and learning disability

Cheryl Chessum

Practice development focuses on enhancing the experience and outcomes of the service user receiving care by improving the processes and systems in delivery of care. McSherry and Warr (2006) describe how practice development as a concept and process was primarily introduced into the UK by the nursing profession in the late 1970s and early 1980s. Nursing at the time was attempting a shift from nursing based on tasks towards a patient-centred approach based on quality, standards, education and evaluation (McCormack et al, 1999). Nursing, aiming for increased professional identity and autonomy, used practice development as a vehicle for a professionalism based on providing individualised patient-centred care, and independent, accountable and autonomous decision making and practice (Glover, 2002). From the outset a strong focus on individual practice, teamwork and the culture of the workplace has distinguished practice development approaches from other improvement and innovation methodologies. It has retained, probably to the detriment of the generic benefits, an over-identification with the nursing profession.

This proposed a cultural shift in nursing skills from "technical orientation" to facilitating person-centred initiatives, thus creating a culture of innovation. Practice development should be ethical, and central to this are the fundamentals of embedding the principles of choice, involvement and empowerment and ensuring timeliness for patients. This happens from learning; by asking the right questions and being willing to learn from mistakes. A key tenet is engaging in a process of shared learning with many stakeholders and using this to facilitate change. A spectrum of personal change can then happen in the domains of skills, attributes and knowledge; enabling "putting the person at the heart of everything we do" and offering the practical delivery of "no decisions about me without me" (Department of Health, 2012a). Since the early days of practice development much has changed, and resources to support and enable staff have evolved which incorporate the fundamental principles and ideas described below (See Resources section at end of the chapter).

The concerns and expectations raised in the document *Valuing people* (Department of Health, 2001a, 2009a) set out the aspirations and agenda for people with a learning disability. It placed significant emphasis on delivering person-centred care and planning, linking this to the principles of personalisation and healthcare facilitation, adding to the "Putting People First" agenda (Robertson et al, 2005; Department of Health, 2007). However, ongoing revelations of abuse, neglect on all levels, serious social exclusion and stigmatisation resulting in a scandalous number of deaths demonstrates that policy alone does not lead to better practices or service user experience (Department of Health, 2012b; Mencap, 2012). For other vulnerable groups, such as the elderly, dignity in care and providing acceptable standards of basic nursing care in the face of recurring criticisms of neglect and abuse has been highly publicised and profiled (Department of Health, 2008; Mid Staffordshire NHS Foundation Trust, 2010). Appalling failures continue to disappoint many, professionals and public alike, who called for innovations and improvements in quality of care. So while the concept of "putting people first" and "person-centred planning" is mainstream and supported by much policy, guidance and tools, the translation into practice remains inadequate.

Since the Bristol Royal Infirmary Inquiry (Department of Health, 2001b), the concept that the patient should be central to the healthcare experience has been a key factor for the whole modernisation agenda. It is clear, despite a range of quality improvement initiatives over time, that there are still major failings in the culture within healthcare that perpetuates these scandals. The bridge from rhetoric to reality in practice has proved an immense challenge to services trying to improve the care given, to patient outcomes and the patient's experience of the journey through services.

The practice development community argues that the complex intervention that is "practice development" offers an approach leading to transformational, sustainable change in workplace cultures. This can assist in addressing recurrent serious failings and, with reform based on commissioning, and marketing placing an emphasis on outcomes and quality, there is a powerful argument for mainstream practice development initiatives.

Traditional definitions of practice development

The process and principles of practice development remain pertinent and are clearly aligned with innovation and improvement. Early exposure to these ideas and approaches, allowing identification and involvement by nurses at the earliest stages of their careers and as part of their ongoing personal development, is much needed.

Ideas about what defines practice development have evolved over time. It is seen differently by different proponents but, as is often the case, there are many consistent, recurring elements. Here practice development is defined as:

...a continuous process of developing person-centred cultures. It is enabled by facilitators who "authentically" engage with individuals and teams to blend personal qualities and creative imagination with practice skills and practice wisdom. The learning that occurs brings about transformations of individuals and team practices. This is sustained by embedding both processes and outcomes in corporate strategy.

Manley et al (2008)

It was defined earlier as:

Practice development is a continuous process of improvement towards increased effectiveness in patient-centred care, through the enabling of nurses and healthcare teams to transform the culture and context of care. It is enabled and supported by facilitators committed to a systematic rigorous continuous process of emancipatory change.

McCormack (1999)

Some subtle changes take place and the notion of "facilitation" is not shared by all. Wenger's work (Wenger, 1998; Wenger et al, 2002) relates not only to health or social care. He writes of "communities of practice" and summarises his ideas as:

Communities of practice are groups of people who share a concern or passion for something they do and learn how to do it better as they interact regularly.

Wenger (2006)

Communities of practice have three characteristics in common:

1. *Domain of interest*: They value collective experience and learn from each other.
2. *The community*: They engage in joint activity and discussion. They share information and interact in a variety of activities, building relationships.
3. *The practice*: Practitioners have a repertoire of resources which they share to inform practice and learn from each other with learning linked to performance.

71

Practice development and its relevance to context and policy over recent decades

In the 1990s a series of policy initiatives set out the intentions to reform, improve and invest in the NHS, with mental health services identified as one of three key priority areas in 1999 (Department of Health, 1999). It consolidated the move into community-based services. The aim was to balance care and support against control and public safety, plus improve the health outcomes of the nation, and to modernise and improve health services with an emphasis on the quality of care delivered within the NHS. The policy document, *A first class service* (Department of Health, 1997) introduced us to the principles and "pillars" of clinical governance (a framework of NHS accountability and service improvement) and demanded effectiveness, efficiency and improved outcomes and experiences.

The National Service Framework for Mental Health (now superseded by *No health without mental health*, HM Government, 2011) was described as "evidence-based", utilising epidemiology and grades of evidence. There was significant expansion of services and new service models (Department of Health, 2000). Nursing personnel were seen as key professionals in delivery (Department of Health, 2002). Drivers for the modernisation programme (Department of Health, 1998) were variable, standards were inconsistent between clinicians, departments and organisations, and there was all-round inflexibility. In the context of this, nursing as a profession had been trying to promote changes in attitude and practice with a move to person-centred care being part of the professional identity.

The challenge to deliver well on key elements (safety, outcomes and experience) is still exercising the minds of people providing clinical services to a wide range of people. The present situation in the NHS is rapidly changing with many concerned about the impact the demand for massive savings (£20 billion by 2015) will have on the level and provision of services in general. A research study by the NHS Service Delivery and Organisation (Department of Health, 2006a) identified massive numbers of changes at the same time, all being externally imposed with target pressures resulting in failures in delivery across the NHS. However, quality of care remains "a major priority" and highly profiled as a central tenet of the contentious NHS and Social Care Act 2012. The NHS Constitution (Department of Health, 2013) enshrines seven key principles (see *Box 6.1*), as well as a range of rights and pledges.

These principles are underpinned by values from a breadth of stakeholders. The Constitution captures, as a "right", some of the essence of choice,

---

Box 6.1. Values underpinning the NHS constitution

- Respect
- Dignity
- Commitment to quality of care
- Compassion
- Improving lives
- Working together for patients
- Everyone counts

---

empowerment, control and person-centeredness that practice development has concerned itself with for many years.

With a continual high volume of demand for healthcare services, delivering on quality of experience is a significant challenge for outcome-focused services. This is a dominant challenge to the nursing profession. Alongside this there is a real need to find ways to address the demographic challenges of our population – changing health needs, advanced age, long-term conditions, complex co-morbidities, hard-to-reach groups, or conditions for early diagnosis. This is as well as the expectations of the service users who are encouraged to be active partners in their care and treatment.

It is in this complex arena that supporters of practice development approaches suggest that innovation, creativity and sustainable change can be harvested to meet the challenge. For more than two decades a number of academic nurses from different countries have sought to collaborate and develop theories and frameworks to promote practice development (McCormack et al, 2006). The assertion now is:

Practice development is an internationally recognised and sustainable approach that achieves multiple aims in healthcare workplaces and organisations to improve patient or service user experiences of care.

England Centre for Practice Development (2013)

If practice development is, as some exponents describe, about teamwork, visioning and taking people with you, then omitting these elements in any change process would disable potential practice developers or initiatives, and this needs to be addressed. Practice development approaches offer a way forward to assist in meeting these challenges. Established or "traditional methods" continue to include clinical supervision and reflection (where adopted), case management supervision, learning beyond registration and experience plus statutory and mandatory training requirements. Service development can be a driver or opportunity for practice development with the potential to benefit enormously the delivery of services from the improved processes and outcomes achieved. Working in this way, practice can be localised, having a fingerprint unique to that particular team or organisation but ensuring best evidence and research informs practice and is woven into care delivery. Manley et al (2011) propose the main challenge of the moment is to develop and demonstrate an effective evaluation framework to link outcomes to the current health and social care policy agenda and commissioning brief.

There is constant change and revision of the knowledge and skills needed by nurses in rapidly changing healthcare, and this influences both pre- and post-registration training for nurses, as evidenced in *The capable practitioner* (Sainsbury Centre for Mental Health, 2001) and by the Chief Nursing Officer's review of mental health nursing (Department of Health, 2006b). However, critics argue that despite this revision, the education system for nursing has failed to deliver on the quality and care agenda, although this assertion is contested by a recent report on nurse education (Willis Commission, 2012). More reasonable claims are that the university system of education fails successfully to integrate learning from practice into cycles of improvement or to develop research and leadership skills in its students. As a part of the reform process there will be changes in the commissioning and provision of workforce education and development, with Local Education and Training Boards formed to oversee this challenge. Incorporating more robustly the principles and approaches of practice development into these programmes is an opportunity to prepare and equip nurses from the earliest stage of their socialisation into nursing.

Practice development, quality and change

The science of quality improvement within health services can appear to be forbidding territory... However, there are fundamental principles applicable throughout a systematic, team-based, problem-solving process to continually move up the level of care provided – to implement and test the effects of ideas.

Department of Health (2009b)

The Rapid Assessment Interface Discharge service in Birmingham (Parsonage and Fossey, 2011) has proved to be award winning. It is the commissioning of a new type of mental health service, where multi-disciplinary teams work proactively within large general hospitals, often based in accident and emergency departments to rapidly assess, advise and signpost on mental health problems. By using existing skills in a different setting, patients receive a timely service with earlier intervention. It is also leading to a greater liaison with professionals in acute medicine and to an expansion in the concept of who is a "colleague", with mental health awareness being widely disseminated over time. An analysis of the approach has shown it leads to significant financial savings and fewer bed days for patients needing an alternative service provision (Parsonage et al, 2012). The King's Fund (2012) supported the findings from the report on this service and highlighted the need for care staff to be educated and for screening for mental health problems. A recommendation is integrating both mental health and physical interventions into packages of care.

Another example of developing practice based on person-centred approaches is the promotion of a personalisation agenda. Personalisation is considered to be an opportunity to further reduce stigma for people with mental health problems and learning disabilities. It emphasises use of personal budgets and personal plans to increase self-determination, independence, choice and control. There are specific challenges of implementation within mental health. These include the need to manage particular types of risk, fluctuations in mental capacity, and the challenge of effective social care delivery within integrated NHS provider organisations. This is in its infancy but as practice development concerns itself with reform of care to an improved person-centred individualised approach, clearly it has scope to bring some of the aspiration to reality (McCormack, 2007; Manley et al, 2009).

Manley et al (2009) put the case for practice development and what it can deliver. It can keep the service user at the centre of the care process:

- By always involving the service user in decision-making about care.
- By using systems and cultures developed to deliver quality services that enable evidence-based practice.
- By investing in staff to take responsibility for change and new ways of working, where change is systematic, owned and evaluated.

According to Manley et al (2011) development work should:

- Work with people using collaborative, inclusive and participative principles.
- Agree values and beliefs about what is to be achieved, developing a shared framework facilitating self-direction and agreement.
- Benefit from multiple perspectives through joint and shared responsibility and engagement in improvement processes.

- Provide care that is both person-centred and effective, the principles reflected in the relationships between all stakeholders in the care process, combining all five elements of evidence-based practice.
- Use systematic evaluation and learning to promote cycles of positive change and innovation, with emphasis on learning from practice.
- Achieve sustainable change through embedding the above patterns of behaviour in workplace culture.

Additionally, Manley (2011) recognises barriers to the wider adoption of practice development into healthcare and which are summarised in *Box 6.3*.

Box 6.2. Practice skills (Woodbridge and Fulford, 2004)

1. *Awareness*: being aware of the values in a given situation.
2. *Reasoning*: thinking about values when making decisions.
3. *Knowledge*: knowing about values and facts that are relevant to a situation.
4. *Communication*: using communication to resolve conflicts or complexity.

Models of service delivery
5. *User-centred*: considering the service user's values as the first priority.
6. *Multidisciplinary*: using a balance of perspectives to resolve conflicts.

Values-based practice and evidence-based practice
7. *The "two feet" principle*: all decisions are based on facts and values.

Evidence-based practice and values-based practice therefore work together
8. *The "squeaky wheel" principle*: we only notice values if there is a problem.
9. *Science and values*: increasing scientific knowledge creates choices in healthcare, which introduces wide differences in values.

Partnership
10. *Partnership*: In values-based practice, decisions are taken by service users working in partnership with providers of care.

The practice development process

Conflicts in values can lead to clashes in teams and affect care delivery, working relationships, and team morale and effectiveness. It can lead to what Crisp and Wilson (2011) describe as the disengagement of staff from their work. Skilled facilitation is considered a key role in eliciting the dominant values by some (McCormack et al, 2004), but disputed by others (Unsworth, 2002).

Woodbridge and Fulford (2004) advocate using the 10 pointers outlined in *Box 6.2* as a guide to developing "good" process. They assert that these pointers can offer guidance on systematically dealing with "difference" in teams that can give rise to a clash of or dominant cultures. These have the potential to undermine the quality of care delivered and adversely affect the service user experience. Skills are needed in dealing with the emotional milieu of the workplace. This will include understanding and responding to staff who face constant change and challenge, the demands of which frequently cause stress and anxiety in care workers. Identifying and examining these factors and their impact on care is a critical starting point.

The concept of "facilitation", rather than telling, instructing or teaching, is central to change. In the context of practice development, where facilitation is central (Shaw et al, 2008), reflective, self-reflective or critical questioning is a core component of the role undertaken by a "facilitator", and consistently requires intellectual, emotional and practical energy. The practice development community agrees there are many dimensions to facilitators and they must evolve a set of complex skills to be effective in the role (see below).

- Planning (the work programme, for example).
- Meaning (creating understanding).
- Confronting (challenging rigid behaviours).
- Feeling (working with emotional processes in teams).
- Structuring (how learning happens, to include action learning approaches).
- Valuing (how group members are helped to feel valued).

Facilitators will need to be able to sustain this spectrum of activity over time, through a diverse range of experiences and potential setbacks. Therefore, it is suggested that the facilitator will also need support from a mentor through the process. A broad skill set is required: questioning, being curious, enabling and encouraging reflection, active listening, and clarification, especially in supporting the development of clear endpoints or markers in change. This approach has been used to create "visions" and guide improvements in clinical care, with staff coming together in clinical groups to deliver on the NHS next stage review (Department of Health, 2009b). Additional leadership skills are required for group activities on a number of levels: staying focused and purposeful and being able to deliver personally when working on the "high support, high challenge spectrum"

(Daloz, 1986). In addition, there are phases of identifying and refining what needs to be improved and changed.

There are different perspectives on the role of facilitator, with different opinions on the extent to which facilitators need to embrace the range of responsibilities. Facilitators can be within or outside service and may be a hybrid (someone with links both to practice and academia or research). Overall, the process of facilitation would need organisational support as healthcare settings are complex, varied and have many stakeholders.

Crisp and Wilson (2011) offer the framework of critical creativity, a three-stage process, to map and support practitioners in the development of facilitation and leadership skills. The skills are based on humanist principles of "helping" (Egan, 2010) and will be developmental for the facilitator and clinical practitioner, enabling them to become "effective".

Box 6.3. Possible barriers to the wider adoption of practice development into healthcare

- Practice development has evolved within a nursing context so it can seem irrelevant to other disciplines, despite the fact that multi-disciplinary teams are the norm in healthcare, especially where needs are complex, enduring and occur across the life span.
- The language around the concept and process of practice development does not always emphasise its potentially positive impact and benefits for a whole systems approach.
- As a "complex intervention" it demands a range of evaluation processes to demonstrate outcomes, impact and benefits and these must be accessible and understandable to stakeholders and commissioners.

Summarised from Manley et al (2011)

Conclusion

Support for practice development has come from a wide range of disciplines and links into NHS improvement and innovation. Internationally and locally there has been adoption of and support for the approach and links between the practice development community, academics and clinicians has been recognised by stakeholders and commissioners. However, practice development is intensive and very demanding in terms of time and effort.

Recognition of change, and supporting changes in practice, have been synthesised in the "Change Model" (www.changemodel.nhs.uk) which embodies principles of support for staff with parallels in practice development. Ten working principles have been agreed to ensure that staff are valued and developed and a training programme supporting business priorities has been funded.

Resources

Resources to support practice development are more widely available from:

- NHS Evidence (www.evidence.nhs.uk). Among other things, supports access to a library of national quality standards of care, which is continually being grown by the National Institute of Health and Care Excellence (NICE) in collaboration with other standard setters.
- The resources providing methodologies for innovation and improvement, previously hosted at the Improvement Centre (www.institute.nhs.uk) are now available at NHS Improving Quality (Part of NHS England). Archived material is available at: http://webarchive.nationalarchives.gov.uk/*/http://institute.nhs.uk. The site hosts the PDSA (Plan, Do, Study, Act) cycle which is a resource offering guidance on testing ideas for innovation, improvement and change before full implementation.
- The NHS Change Model (www.changemodel.nhs.uk) is a framework with eight key components that promote improvements in patient experience, quality of care and outcomes.
- The Foundation of Nursing Studies is a registered charity which operates UK wide and whose aim is to support practice development across all healthcare settings. See http://www.fons.org/about-us/about-us.aspx. It hosts the *International Practice Development Journal*, available free to registrants at http://www.fons.org/library/journal.aspx.
- Support for innovation and improvement (www.improvement.nhs.uk): Improvement programmes link up clinical networks and communities of practice development, offering help and links in developing networks and mentoring.
- The NHS information centre (www.ic.nhs.uk) allows access to data and reports on a wide range of services.
- A range of resources and publications to aid person-centred planning, supporting change and practice development initiatives to deliver on personalisation and supporting people is available from: www.inclusion.com.

- The England Centre for Practice Development was set up to support practice development and is a UK centre for nursing innovation. It promotes a patient-centred culture of care. The centre is hosted by Canterbury Christ Church University and is part of an international network of practice developers who are members of the International Practice Development Collaborative. More information can be found at: http://www.canterbury.ac.uk/health/EnglandCentreforPracticeDevelopment/

References

Crisp JM, Wilson VJ (2011) How do facilitators of practice development gain the expertise required to support vital transformation of practice and workplace cultures? *Nurse Education in Practice* 11(3): 173–8

Daloz L (1986) *Effective teaching and mentoring: Realising the transformational power of adult learning experiences* (pp 209–35). Jossey Bass, San Francisco

Department of Health (1998) *Modernising mental health services: Safe, sound and supportive*. HMSO, London. Available from: http://webarchive.nationalarchives.gov.uk/+/www.dh.gov.uk/en/publicationsandstatistics/publications/publicationspolicyandguidance/browsable/DH_4096400

Department of Health (1999) *The National Service Framework for mental health – Modern standards and service models*. Department of Health, London

Department of Health (2000) *The NHS Plan: A plan for investment, a plan for reform*. Department of Health, London

Department of Health (2001a) *Valuing People: A new strategy for learning disability for the 21st century*. Department of Health, London. Available from: http://www.dh.gov.uk/en/Publicationsandstatistics/Publications/PublicationsPolicyAndGuidance/DH_4009153. Accessed 25/5/2012.

Department of Health (2001b) *Learning the lessons: The Department of Health's response to the Bristol Royal Infirmary Inquiry Report (Kennedy report)* Command Paper: CM 5207. Available from: http://www.bristol-inquiry.org.uk/

Department of Health (2002) *Liberating the talents*. Department of Health, London

Department of Health (2006a) *Making change happen in the NHS: clinical and management tasks*. Briefing paper. Available from: http://www.netscc.ac.uk/hsdr/files/project/SDO_BP_08-1201-021_V01.pdf

Department of Health (2006b) *From values to action: The Chief Nursing Officer's review of mental health nursing*. Available from: http://www.dh.gov.uk/en/Publicationsandstatistics/Publications/PublicationsPolicyAndGuidance/DH_4133839

Department of Health (2007) *Putting people first: A shared vision and commitment to the transformation of adult social care*. Department of Health, London

Department of Health (2008) *High quality care for all – NHS next stage final review*.

Department of Health, London

Department of Health (2009a) *Valuing people now: A new three-year strategy for people with learning disabilities.* Department of Health, London. Available from: http://www.dh.gov.uk/en/Publicationsandstatistics/Publications/ PublicationsPolicyAndGuidance/DH_093377

Department of Health (2009b) *High quality care for all. Our journey so far.* Department of Health, London

Department of Health (2010) *Personalisation through person-centred planning.* Department of Health, London

Department of Health (2012a) *Liberating the NHS: No decision about me, without me.* Department of Health, London

Department of Health (2012b) *Transforming care: A national response to Winterbourne View Hospital Department of Health Review: Final Report.* Department of Health, London

Department of Health (2013) *NHS Constitution: The NHS belongs to us all.* HMSO, London. Available from: https://www.gov.uk/government/publications/the-nhs-constitution-for-england

Egan G (2010) *The skilled helper: A problem management approach and opportunity development approach to helping* (9th edn.) Brooks/Cole Cengage Learning, Belmont, California

England Centre for Practice Development (2013) *What is practice development?* Available from: http://www.canterbury.ac.uk/ healthEnglandCentreforPracticeDevelopment/Whatispracticedevelopment/ Whatispracticedevelopment.aspx

Glover D (2002) What is practice development? In McSherry R, Bassett C (eds) *Practice development in the clinical setting: A guide to implementation.* Nelson Thornes, Cheltenham

HM Government (2011) *No health without mental health: A cross-government mental health outcomes strategy for people of all ages.* HMSO, London

King's Fund and Centre for Mental Health (2012) *Long-term conditions and mental health: The cost of comorbidities.* Available from: www.centreformentalhealth.org. uk/pdfs/cost_of_comorbidities.pdf

Manley K, Crisp J, Moss C (2011) Advancing the practice development outcomes agenda. *International Practice Development Journal* **1**(4): 1–16

Manley K, Titchen A, Hardy S (2009) Workplace learning in the context of contemporary health care education and practice; a concept analysis. *Practice Development in Health Care* **8**(2): 87–127

Manley K, McCormack B, Wilson V (eds) (2008) *International practice development in nursing and healthcare.* Blackwell Publishing, Oxford

McCormack B, Dewar B, Wright J, Garbett R, Harvey G, Ballantine K (2006) *A realist synthesis of evidence relating to practice development.* NHS for Scotland and NHS

Quality Improvement Scotland. Available from: http://www.nes.scot.nhs.uk/

McCormack B, Manley K, Garbett R (eds) (2004) *Practice development in nursing.* Blackwell, Oxford

McCormack B, Manley K, Kitson A, Harvey G (1999) Towards practice development – a vision in reality or reality without vision. *Journal of Nursing Management* **7**(5): 255–64

McCormack B, Wright J, Dewar B, Harvey G, Ballantine K (2007) A realist synthesis of evidence relating to practice development: Recommendations. *Practice Development in Healthcare* **6**(1): 76–80

McSherry R, Warr J (2006) Practice development: Confirming the existence of a knowledge and evidence base. *Practice Development in Health Care* **5**: 55–79

Mencap (2012) *Out of sight: Stopping the neglect and abuse of people with learning disabilities.* Available from: www.mencap.org.uk/outofsight

Mid Staffordshire NHS Foundation Trust (2010) Robert Francis Enquiry Report into Mid Staffordshire NHS Foundation Trust. Available from: http://www.dh.gov.uk/ publicationsandstatistics/publications/PublicationsPolicyAndGuidance/DH_113018

Parsonage M, Fossey M (2011) *Economic evaluation of a liaison psychiatry service. Report produced for the Centre for Mental Health.* Available from: http://www. centreformentalhealth.org.uk/pdfs/economic_evaluation.pdf

Parsonage M, Fossey M, Tutty C (2012) *Liaison psychiatry in the modern NHS. Centre for Mental Health.* Available from: www.centreformentalhealth.org.uk/publications

Robertson J, Emerson E, Hatton C, Elliott J, McIntosh B, et al (2005) *The impact of person centred planning for people with intellectual disabilities in England: A summary of findings.* Institute for Health Research, Lancaster University

Sainsbury Centre for Mental Health (2001) *The capable practitioner: A framework and list of the practitioner capabilities required to implement the National Service Framework for Mental Health.* Sainsbury Centre for Mental Health, London

Shaw T, Dewing J, Young R, Devlin M, Boomer C, Legius M (2008) Enabling practice development: Delving into the concept of facilitation from a practitioner perspective. In Manley K, McCormack B, Wilson V (eds) *International practice development in nursing* (pp 147–69). Blackwell Publishing, Oxford

Unsworth J (2002) Practice development: A concept analysis. *Journal of Nursing Management* **8**(6): 317–26

Wenger E (1998) *Communities of practice: Learning, meaning, and identity.* Cambridge University Press, Cambridge

Wenger, E (2006) *Communities of practice – A brief introduction.* Available from: www. ewenger.com/theory/

Wenger E, McDermott R, Snyder WM (2002) *Cultivating communities of practice.* Harvard Business Press, Boston, MA

Willis Commission (2012) *Quality with Compassion: The future of nursing education. Report of the Willis Commission on Nurse Education.* Royal College of Nursing,

London. Available from: http://www.williscommission.org.uk/__data/assets/pdf_file/0007/495115/Willis_commission_report_Jan_2013.pdf

Woodbridge K, Fulford KWM (2004) *Whose values? A workbook for values based practice in mental health care.* Sainsbury Centre for Mental Health, London

Chapter 7

Learning disability nursing in the UK: Issues and challenges

Michael Brown and Karen Nankervis

Introduction

Historically, some people with learning disabilities were cared for in congregated institutional settings with limited influence and choice, while others lived at home with their families. There have been significant changes in recent decades regarding the understanding of the needs of children, adults and older people with learning disabilities, with moves to community-based care and services. As a population children, adults and older people with learning disabilities experience significant health inequalities that impact on their health and wellbeing, their social inclusion and their quality of life. A range of practitioners in health, social care and non-government organisations all have important contributions to make in relation to supporting ordinary and inclusive lives. Central to the changing and evolving models of care is the need for leadership that contributes to reducing health inequalities and enables person-centred care, thereby facilitating social inclusion and citizenship.

People with learning disabilities

A range of terminologies has been used over the decades to describe learning disability, including mental retardation, mental handicap, cognitive impairment, intellectual disability and developmental disability. Within the UK, for example, the term adopted within government policy is learning disability; internationally, in the research literature, the term intellectual disability is used (Scottish Executive, 2000; Department of Health, 2001; Welsh Assembly Government, 2001; Department of Health, Social Services and Public Safety, 2005).

A learning disability is not a single condition; rather it is developmental in nature as a result of a range of issues such as genetic, biological, social and other factors and is an irreversible, lifelong condition that starts at or around the time of birth. A diagnosis of intellectual disability requires each of the following to be present:

- A significant global intellectual impairment with a functional IQ of less than 70.
- Significant limitations of adaptive behaviour.
- Onset during childhood, before the age of 18.

> (American Association on Intellectual and Developmental Disabilities, 2010; Department of Health, 2001; Scottish Executive, 2000)

Globally, prevalence rates vary from between 1 and 3% of the population (Harris, 2006, cited in Maulik et al, 2011). However, estimates of prevalence can vary with higher rates seen in countries with low and middle incomes (Maulik et al, 2011). From the perspective of the UK, 1.5 million people have a learning disability, with some 300 000 children and adults presenting with a severe disability (Scottish Executive, 2000; Department of Health, 2001).

The changing population of people with learning disabilities

The population of people with learning disabilities is increasing and living longer and, as a consequence, all government and non-government services will need to provide more education, support and interventions in the future (Patja et al, 2000; Maaskant et al, 2002; Parrott et al, 2008; Emerson and Baines, 2010). Population growth has occurred because of a number of factors, including improvements in general socio-economic standards, improvements in health and social care service delivery, developments in neonatal intensive care and the delivery of technological interventions within the home (Glendinning et al, 2001; Oullette-Kuntz, 2005; Emerson and Hatton, 2007; McKay et al, 2010). As a result, there is an increase in the number of people with learning disabilities at both ends of the age continuum, many presenting with co-morbid health needs and experiencing deprivation (Emerson et al, 2006; Kwok and Cheung, 2007; Tyrer et al, 2007; Cooper et al, 2011). It is important to recognise that while life expectancy in this group is increasing, it remains significantly shorter than the general population, with mortality three times higher in adults with learning disabilities, notably in relation to young adults and women with learning disabilities and people with Down syndrome (Tyrer et al, 2007; Tyrer and McGrother, 2009; Cooper et al, 2011).

Health needs of people with learning disabilities

There has been an increasing focus internationally on the health needs of people with learning disabilities. The population has a different health profile when compared to the general population, presenting with significant health inequalities that impact on life expectancy, quality of life and health and wellbeing (Cooper et al, 2004; Krahn et al, 2006; Tyrer and McGrother, 2009; Emerson and Baines, 2010; Emerson, 2011). With this attention it is apparent that too often health needs go unrecognised and untreated, with significant consequences for the individual, the family and carers, and more broadly on government and non-government services that are required to respond (Morgan et al, 2000; NHS Health Scotland, 2004; Ouellette-Kunz et al, 2005; Cooper et al, 2006; Disability Rights Commission, 2006; Emerson, 2011). All children, adults and older people with learning disabilities have what can be termed everyday health needs. They include the need to access universal health services available to the whole population, such as GPs, practice nurses, universal programmes such as cervical screening, primary care and emergency services (Lennox et al, 1997; Morgan et al, 2000; Brown, 2005; Ouellette-Kunz et al, 2005; Cooper et al, 2007; Robertson et al, 2011). Many people with learning disabilities have co-morbid health needs, referred to as complex health needs. All require equal access to universal health services and some also need access to more specialist services. These services have an important role to play in facilitating equal access and health outcomes when attending universal health services, and in providing assessment, treatment and interventions for specific issues (Smiley et al, 2002; Brown and Marshall, 2006; Cooper et al, 2006, 2007; Whitaker and Read, 2006; Mason, 2007; Slevin et al, 2007; Backer et al, 2009; Brown et al, 2011).

There is an increase in the diagnosis of children with learning disabilities resulting from foetal alcohol spectrum disorder, attention deficit hyperactive disorder and autism spectrum disorder. The new generation of children with learning disabilities brings a pattern of disability that presents new challenges in relation to education, care delivery and treatment (Carpenter, 2005; Baron-Cohen et al, 2009; Blackburn et al, 2010; Lange et al, 2010). Research has demonstrated that the prevalence of psychiatric disorders is significantly higher in children with learning disabilities than those without (Emerson and Hatton, 2007). Further, it has been found that, because children with an intellectual disability are at significantly greater risk of exposure to social disadvantage, they are at increased risk of psychiatric disorders (Emerson and Hatton, 2007). These conditions, if not assessed and treated, are likely to persist into adulthood and may co-exist with challenging behaviours (Allen, 2008) and result in high and complex support needs.

These points are important since evidence highlights that 40% of the learning disabled population develops mental health problems at some point. The mental health issues include anxiety disorders, depression, eating disorders, compulsive disorders and psychosis. There is a need for effective treatment and intervention options, beyond those available pharmacologically (Hatton, 2002; Sturmey,

2004; Whitaker and Read, 2006; Cooper et al, 2007; Bouras, 2008; Emerson and Baines, 2010). Despite the increasing need, the treatment options available may be inadequate, not evidence based, inconsistently implemented, or unable to be implemented by inadequately trained staff. There is a need for practitioners to develop their knowledge and skills to deliver interventions and for researchers to grow the evidence base regarding what works (Hatton et al, 1999; Hollins and Sinason, 2000; Hatton, 2002; Whitehouse et al, 2006).

The education context

All health practitioners require preparation to ensure people with learning disabilities experience safe and effective care and have their health needs addressed (Scottish Executive, 2002; Royal College of Nursing, 2011; Scottish Government, 2012). Adequate preparation is necessary to meet the increasingly complex needs and changing demographics of the learning disability population. There will be more demand in the future, not less. With this comes the need for a workforce with appropriate knowledge, skills and attitudes to meet the challenges of the future, across health, social care and non-government sectors (Scottish Government, 2012).

In the UK, learning disabilities is a specific area of nursing that has had a separate part on the Nursing and Midwifery Council professional register for over a century (United Kingdom Central Council for Nursing, Midwifery and Health Visiting, 1998; Nursing and Midwifery Council, 2010). Yet, there have been numerous ongoing debates over the years regarding the need for this field of practice. Today there is recognition and acceptance of the need to grow the learning disability nursing workforce to respond to the changing requirements of the population and ensure there is access to skilled nursing (Mitchell, 1998; Mitchell, 2003; Griffiths et al, 2007; Scottish Government, 2012). This is not the case in the majority of countries across the world where nurse preparation is generic in nature. To this end, the Nursing and Midwifery Council in the UK published Standards of Proficiency for pre-registration nursing education (Nursing and Midwifery Council, 2010). The Council have strengthened the position of learning disability nursing and this has resulted in a positive focus on reducing health inequalities, promoting positive health, and providing nursing assessment, treatment and interventions, thereby contributing to enabling social inclusion and wider citizenship (Scottish Government, 2010; Royal College of Nursing, 2011).

It must be noted that while in the UK there has been an expansion and strengthening of the role of the learning disability nurse, other countries have eliminated such roles and moved to a generalist registered nurse, such as in Australia and New Zealand. Part of the apparent rationale arose from a move away from an institutional medical model of care, while in other countries the profession never existed in the first place (Barr and Sines, 1996; Barr, 2004; Robinson and Griffiths, 2007). Such decisions, however, failed to take account of the significant health inequalities and the requirement for a specialist health worker with the knowledge and skills to respond to the population; now even more imperative given the demographic changes and increasing complexity of need. Even so, in specialist learning disability services there is an imperative to provide quality supports to people with learning disabilities who have complex needs; the service must include specialist learning disability practitioners. These can be learning disability nurses, behaviour support specialists or other professions with relevant expertise.

The role of the specialist learning disability practitioner is not only to implement evidence-based and effective supports to people with complex needs, but also to support and educate others involved who are integral to the success of care, such as family and support workers. Thus, specialist learning disability practitioners are leaders, educators and knowledgeable practitioners. They will ideally work within a clinical and practice governance framework that encompasses: (1) learning and development; (2) research and innovation through evidence-based practice and practice-based evidence; (3) clinical and practice audit and review; (4) clinical and practice effectiveness; (5) openness and accountability; and (6) safety through risk assessment and management (Starey, 2001; Pridmore and Gammon, 2007).

While clinical governance has most commonly been described in the healthcare sector, its elements have direct relevance to the provision of services to people with learning disabilities as it offers an opportunity to: (1) monitor quality; (2) set quality standards; and (3) improve quality across service delivery, and across diffuse and varied services, systems and practitioner levels and experience (Newman et al, 2003). Where there are no identified specialist learning disability practitioners there will be a significant challenge in ensuring quality and safe service delivery through the components that comprise clinical and practice governance. These components cannot be delivered and supported by staff without such expertise. This is particularly the case in specialist disability services where direct care workers may be inadequately trained to support the needs and complexities of service users with learning disabilities (Mansell, 2010). Often it is the case that direct care practitioners themselves need extensive knowledge and skills to address the complex nature of the needs of the users and carers. In this practice context, leadership is fundamentally important.

Leadership and advancing practice

As a result of service failures and poor standards of care, there have been investigations and inquiries into the care of people with learning disabilities accessing both universal and general services (Mencap, 2007). The findings have significant implications for the education of the workforce and care services. The investigations have resulted in concerns about the quality and standard of care being delivered to the most vulnerable in society and the role and purpose of the caring professions and professional practice (Mencap, 2007; Department of Health, 2008; House of Commons and House of Lords, 2008; NHS Quality Improvement Scotland, 2009; Brown et al, 2010).

Consistently, it has been found that leadership and organisational factors influence staff outcomes, such as well-being, and the quality of care being delivered. In an Australian study, Vassos and Nankervis (2012) found that leadership and organisational factors, such as a lack of supervisor support, job feedback and role clarity, were predictors of staff burnout. This research indicated the need for better staff supervision and support practices.

People with learning disabilities have the right to expect and receive high quality support from skilled and knowledgeable staff (Nankervis and Matthews, 2006). Thus, leadership by both practitioners and managers is critical to ensuring treatment and programme fidelity by support staff and high quality health and other services for people with learning disabilities. Supervision has clear benefits to workers in health-related professions. Nurses who work with people with learning disabilities find supervision useful as it allows them not only to reflect on their own practice, but also provides them with the opportunity to improve their skills and increase their knowledge (Sines and McNally, 2007).

Skilled practitioners are essential to high quality services for people with learning disabilities, particularly those who have complex needs, such as co-morbid health, mental health, or behavioural conditions. Adequately trained and skilled individuals will be those who are provided with professional development based on best practice, and who are supported through leadership and supervision by specialist learning disability practitioners providing modelling, coaching and feedback. They will also require workplaces that support the use of these skills and knowledge consistently in day-to-day practice (Nankervis and Matthews, 2006). Therefore, specialist learning disability practitioners need to be skilled and knowledgeable; they need to have the leadership skills to share their expertise to support less experienced and trained workers in disability services as well as the individuals with learning disability themselves and their family members.

Effective leadership at all levels is essential in delivering the goals of the health and social care services and to ensure high quality, safe and effective care as well as creating a culture of innovation and support in the workplace (McCray, 2003).

Practitioners in leadership must appreciate the role of the five key workforce challenges that exist in public services in the 21st century:

• Tackling health inequalities.
• Shifting the balance of care.
• Ensuring a quality workforce.
• Delivering best value across the workforce.
• Moving towards an integrated workforce.

During periods of austerity and the rising cost of care, strong visible leadership is vital to build shared visions with users, carers and service providers to ensure the effective use of resources and to minimise the duplication of time and effort (Dickenson and Glasby, 2008).

Strong leadership for specialist learning disability practitioners is necessary as there are increasing demands on their knowledge and skills to support future service delivery (Royal College of Nursing, 2011). Networking forums need to share best practice to ensure nurses function effectively and successfully. It is important to ensure there are practice-focused networks, with clear leadership to promote the use and dissemination of best practice across all government and non-government services (Page Brown and Horan, 2009). To help achieve this, leadership needs to support the development of appropriate attitudes and behaviours that are vital to improve and develop standards of practice and care (Michael and Richardson, 2008). Promoting and supporting access to everyday, universal health services is an area where learning disability nurses and other practitioners can provide assessment, treatment, interventions, positive role modelling and local leadership, thereby facilitating compliance with disability legislation (Gibbs et al, 2008; NHS Quality Improvement Scotland, 2009; Brown et al, 2012).

As well as undergraduate education and preparation, there is a need to ensure leadership in the delivery of post-registration education with a learning disability focus, setting out the professional development and advanced practice requirements to ensure the workforce is fit for purpose. With this comes the possibility of developing new international collaborations, thereby ensuring access to quality and contemporary education provision. New approaches to education will require web-based, online solutions, with opportunities for wider shared learning across disciplines and professions. This will have the advantage of ensuring education is sustainable and accessible, thereby developing a workforce that is fit for purpose in the future.

Conclusion

The model for nurse preparation in the UK differs from the majority of other countries, and an initial nurse registration focusing exclusively on people with learning disability is viewed as necessary to ensure health needs are met. Irrespective of the route of preparation, either pre-registration or post-registration, the evidence base in relation to the changing demographics and extent of the care needs of children, adults and older people with learning disabilities is well established, and there is an increasing requirement for skilled, competent and compassionate nursing support. Future research should aim to identify the impact of the nursing contribution to improving the health of people with learning disabilities. Models of care that support community presence and participation are becoming well established. These developments herald further change in the lives of people with learning disabilities. There is therefore a pressing need for nurse leaders, planners and educationalists to ensure that there are education pathways available to prepare nurses to provide care and treatment for people with learning disabilities within new models of integrated teams, and to contribute to the challenges of the future.

References

Allen D (2008) The relationship between challenging behaviour and mental ill-health in people with intellectual disabilities: A review of the current theories and evidence. *Journal of Intellectual Disabilities* **124**: 267–94

American Association on Intellectual and Developmental Disabilities (2010) *Definition of intellectual disability.* Available from: http: //wwwaaiddorg/content_100cfm

Backer C, Chapam M, Mitchell D (2009) Access to secondary healthcare for people with learning disabilities: A review of the literature. *Journal of Applied Research in Intellectual Disabilities* **22**: 514–25

Baron-Cohen S, Scott F, Allison C, Williams J, Bolton P, Mathews F, Brayne C (2009) Prevalence of autism-spectrum conditions: UK school-based population study. *British Journal of Psychiatry* **194**: 500–9

Barr O (2004) Nurses for people with learning disabilities within the United Kingdom: An overview and some challenges for the future. *International Journal of Nursing in Intellectual and Development Disabilities* **12**(3): 231–3

Barr O, Sines D (1996) The development of the generalist nurse within pre-registration nurse education in the UK: Some points for consideration. *Nurse Education Today* **16**: 274–7

Bouras N (2008) Mental health of people with intellectual disabilities. *Current Opinion in Psychiatry* **21**(5): 439–40

Brown M (2005) Emergency care for people with learning disabilities: What every nurse and midwife needs to know. *Journal of Accident and Emergency Nursing* **13**(4): 224–31

Brown M, Duff H, Karatzia T, Horsburgh D (2011) A review of the literature relating to psychological interventions and people with learning disabilities: Issues for research, policy, education and clinical practice. *Journal of Intellectual Disabilities* **15**(1): 31–45

Brown M, MacArthur J, MacKechanie A, Mack S, Hayes M, Fletcher J (2012) Learning disability liaison nursing services in South East Scotland: A mixed methods impact and outcomes study. *Journal of Intellectual Disability Research* **56**(12): 1161–74

Brown M, MacArthur J, McKechanie A, Mack S, Hayes M, Fletcher J (2010) Equality and access to general health care for people with learning disabilities: Reality or rhetoric? *Journal of Research in Nursing* **15**(4): 351–61

Brown M, Marshall K (2006) Cognitive behaviour therapy and people with learning disabilities: Implications for developing nursing practice. *Journal of Psychiatry and Mental Health Nursing* **13**: 234–41

Carpenter B (2005) Early childhood intervention: Possibilities and prospects for professionals, families and children. *British Journal of Special Education* **32**(4): 176–83

Cooper S-A, McConnachie A, Allan L, Melville C, Smiley E Morrison J (2011) Neighbourhood deprivation, health inequalities and service access by adults with intellectual disabilities: A cross-sectional study. *Journal of Intellectual Disability Research* **55**(3): 313–23

Cooper S-A, Melville C, Morrison J (2004) People with intellectual disabilities: Their health needs differ and need to be recognised and met. *British Medical Journal* **239**: 414–15

Cooper S-A, Morrison J, Melville C, Finlayson J, Allan L, Martin G (2006) Improving the health of people with intellectual disabilities: Outcomes of a health screening programme after one year. *Journal of Intellectual Disability Research* **50**: 667–77

Cooper S-A, Smiley E, Morrison J, Williamson A, Allan L (2007) Mental ill-health in adults with intellectual disabilities: Prevalence and associated factors. *British Journal of Psychiatry* **190**: 27–35

Department of Health (2001) *Valuing people: A new strategy for learning disability for the 21st Century.* HMSO, London

Department of Health (2008) *Health care for all: Independent inquiry into access to health care for people with learning disabilities.* HMSO, London

Department of Health, Social Services and Public Safety (2005) *Equal lives: Review of policy for people with learning disabilities.* DHSSP, Belfast

Dickenson H, Glasby J (2008) Not throwing out the partnership agenda with the personalisation bathwater. *Journal of Integrated Care* **16**(4): 3–8

Disability Rights Commission (2006) *Equal treatment: Closing the gap.* Disability Rights Commission, London

Emerson E (2011) Health inequalities and people with learning disabilities in the UK. *Learning Disability Review* **16**(1): 42–8

Emerson E, Baines S (2010) *Health inequalities and people with learning disabilities in the UK: 2010.* Improving Health Lives, Learning Disabilities Observatory, Durham

Emerson E, Graham H, Hatton C (2006) Household income and health status in children and adolescents in Britain. *European Journal of Public Health* **16**: 354–60

Emerson E, Hatton C, (2007) Mental health of children and adolescents with intellectual disabilities in Britain. *British Journal of Psychiatry* **191**: 493–9

Gibbs S, Brown M, Muir W (2008) The experiences of adults with intellectual disabilities and their carers in general hospitals: A focus group study. *Journal of Intellectual Disability Research* **52**(12): 1061–77

Glendinning C, Kirk S, Guiffrida A, Lawton D (2001) Technology-dependent children in the community: Definitions, numbers and costs. *Child Care Health Development* **27**(4): 321–34

Griffiths P, Bennett J, Smith E (2007) *The research base for learning disability nursing: A rapid scoping review.* Kings College, London

Hatton C (2002) Psychosocial interventions for adults with intellectual disabilities and mental health problems: A review. *Journal of Mental Health* **11**(4): 357–73

Hatton C, Hastings R, Vetere A (1999) A case for inclusion? *The Psychologist* **12**(5): 230–3

Hollins S, Sinason V (2000) Psychotherapy, learning disability and trauma: New perspectives. *Journal of the Royal College of Psychiatrists* **176**: 32–6

House of Commons and House of Lords: Joint Committee on Human Rights (2008) *A life like any other? Human Rights of Adults with Learning Disabilities.* HMSO, London

Krahn G, Hammond L, Turner A (2006) A cascade of disparities: Health and health care access for people with intellectual disabilities. *Mental Retardation and Developmental Disabilities Research Reviews* **12**: 70–82

Kwok H, Cheung P (2007) Co-morbidity of psychiatric disorder and medical illness in people with intellectual disabilities. *Current Opinion in Psychiatry* **20**: 443–9

Lange K, Reichl S, Lange K, Tucha L, Tucha O (2010) The history of attention deficit hyperactive disorder. *Attention Deficit Hyperactive Disorder* **2**: 241–55

Lennox N, Diggens J, Ugoni A (1997) The general practice care of people with intellectual disabilities: Barriers and solutions. *Journal of Intellectual Disability Research* **41**(5): 380–90

Maaskant M, Gevers J, Wierda H (2002) Mortality and life expectancy in Dutch Residential Centres for individuals with intellectual disability 1991–1995. *Journal of Applied Research in Intellectual Disabilities* **15**: 200–12

Mansell J (2010) Raising our sights: Services for adults with profound impairments and multiple disabilities. *Tizard Learning Disability Review* **15**(3): 5–12

Mason J (2007) The provision of psychological therapy to people with intellectual disabilities: An investigation into some of the relevant factors. *Journal of Intellectual Disability Research* **51**(3): 244–9

Maulik P, Mascarenhas M, Mathers C, Dua T, Saxena S (2011) Prevalence of intellectual disability: A meta-analysis of population-based studies. *Research in Developmental Disabilities* **32**: 419–36

McCray J (2003) Inter-professional practice and learning disability nursing. *British Journal of Nursing* **12**(22): 1335–44

McKay D, Smith G, Dobbie R, Pell J (2010) Gestational age at delivery and special educational need: Retrospective cohort study of 407,503 schoolchildren. *PLoS Medicine* **36**(6): 1–10

Mencap (2007) *Death by indifference*. Mencap, London

Michael J, Richardson A (2008) Healthcare for all: The independent inquiry into access to healthcare for people with learning disabilities. *Tizard Learning Disability Review* **13**(4): 28–34

Mitchell D (1998) The origins of learning disability nursing. *International History of Nursing Journal* **4**(1): 10–16

Mitchell D (2003) A chapter in the history of nurse education: Learning disability nursing and the Jay Report. *Nurse Education Today* **23**: 350–6

Morgan C, Ahmed Z, Kerr M (2000) Health care provision for people with a learning disability: Record linkage study of epidemiology and factors contributing to hospital care uptake. *British Journal of Psychiatry* **176**: 37–74

Nankervis K, Matthews J (2006) Building staff capacity. In I Dempsey, K Nankervis (Eds) *Community disability services: An evidence-based approach to practice* (pp. 324–51) UNSW Press, Sydney

Newman D, Kellett S, Beail N (2003) From research and development to practice-based evidence: Clinical governance initiatives in a service for adults with mild intellectual disability and mental health needs. *Journal of Intellectual Disability Research* **47**: 68–74

NHS Health Scotland (2004) *People with learning disabilities in Scotland: The health needs assessment report*. NHS Health Scotland, Glasgow

NHS Quality Improvement Scotland (2009) *Tackling indifference: Health care services for people with learning disabilities. National overview report*. NHS Quality Improvement Scotland, Edinburgh

Nursing and Midwifery Council (2010) *Standards for pre-registration nurse education*. Nursing and Midwifery Council, London

Ouellette-Kuntz H (2005) Understanding health disparities and inequities faced by individuals with intellectual disabilities. *Journal of Applied Research in Intellectual Disabilities* **18**: 113–21

Ouellette-Kuntz H, Garcin N, Lewis S (2005) Addressing health disparities through promoting equity for individuals with intellectual disability. *Canadian Journal of Public Health* **96**(2): S8–S22

Page Brown M, Horan P (2009) An international evaluation of networks and networking in learning disability nursing. *Learning Disability Practice* **12**(8): 32–7

Parrott R, Tilley N, Wolstenholme J (2008) Changing demography and demands for services for people with complex needs and profound and multiple learning disabilities. *Learning Disability Review* **13**(3): 26–34

Patja K, Iivanainen H, Oksanen H, Ruoppila I (2000) Life expectancy of people with intellectual disability: A 35-year follow-up study. *Journal of Intellectual Disability Research* **44**: 591–9

Pridmore J, Gammon J (2007) A comparative review of clinical governance arrangements in the UK. *British Journal of Nursing* **16**(12): 720–3

Robertson J, Roberts H, Emerson E, Turner S, Greig R (2011) The impact of health checks for people with intellectual disabilities: A systematic review of evidence. *Journal of Intellectual Disability Research* **55**(11): 1009–19

Robinson S, Griffiths P (2007) *Approaches to specialist training at pre-registration level: An international comparison.* King's College, London

Royal College of Nursing (2011) *Learning from the past – setting out the future: Developing learning disability nursing in the United Kingdom.* Royal College of Nursing, London

Scottish Executive (2000) *The same as you? A review of services for people with learning disabilities.* The Stationery Office, Edinburgh

Scottish Executive (2002) *Promoting health, supporting inclusion: The national review of the contribution of all nurses and midwives to the care and support of people with learning disabilities.* The Stationery Office, Edinburgh

Scottish Government (2012) *Strengthening the commitment: The report of the UK Modernising learning disability nursing review.* The Stationery Office, Edinburgh

Sines D, McNally S (2007) An investigation into the perceptions of clinical supervision experienced by learning disability nurses. *Journal of Intellectual Disabilities* **11**(4): 307–28

Slevin E, McConkey R, Truesdale-Kennedy M, Barr O, Taggert L (2007) Community learning disability teams: Perceived effectiveness, multidisciplinary working and service user satisfaction. *Journal of Intellectual Disability Research* **11**(4): 329–42

Smiley E, Cooper S-A, Miller S, Robertson P, Simpson N (2002) Specialist health services for people with learning disability in Scotland. *Journal of Learning Disability Research* **46**: 585–93

Starey N (2001) *What is clinical governance?* Hayward Medical Communications,

London

Sturmey P (2004) Cognitive therapy with people with intellectual disabilities: A selective review and critique. *Clinical Psychology and Psychotherapy* **11**: 222–32

Tyrer F, McGrother C (2009) Cause-specific mortality and death certificate reporting in adults with moderate to profound intellectual disabilities. *Journal of Intellectual Disability Research* **53**: 898–904

Tyrer F, Smith L, McGrother C (2007) Mortality in adults with moderate to profound intellectual disability: A population-based study. *Journal of Intellectual Disability Research* **51**: 520–7

United Kingdom Central Council for Nursing, Midwifery and Health Visiting (1998) *Project 2000. A new preparation for practice.* UKCC, London

Vassos M, Nankervis K (2012) Investigating the importance of various individual, interpersonal, organisational, and demographic variables when predicting job burnout in disability support workers. *Research in Developmental Disabilities* **33**: 1780–91

Welsh Assembly Government (2001) *Fulfilling the promises: Proposals for a framework for services for people with learning disabilities.* Welsh Assembly Government, Cardiff

Whitaker S, Read S (2006) The prevalence of psychiatric disorders among people with intellectual disabilities: An analysis of the literature. *Journal of Applied Research in Intellectual Disabilities* **19**: 330–45

Whitehouse R, Tudway J, Look R, Stenfert Kroese B (2006) Adapting individual psychotherapy for adults with intellectual disabilities: A comparative review of the cognitive-behavioural and psychodynamic literature. *Journal of Applied Research in Intellectual Disabilities* **19**: 55–65

Chapter 8

Mental health: UK and international perspectives

Mervyn Morris

Mental health nurses have so much to offer as well as learn from developing an international perspective, and potentially much to lose if they do not. Increasingly, evidence is generated from services in other countries, and this has had a significant influence here in the UK. The core service initiatives identified in the National Service Framework (Department of Health, 1999a) were the result of international collaboration and knowledge transfer. Assertive outreach was originally developed in the USA (Stein and Test, 1978, 1980), while Home Treatment and Early Intervention incorporated early experience from Australia (Hoult, 1986; McGorry, 1993). Taking ideas and making them work in other contexts, the challenge of knowledge transfer, requires many leadership qualities, whether within organisations or between countries, and it is often nurses with the day-to-day responsibility of delivering services who understand most the issues involved. This means we have much to gain from international collaboration in developing our leadership capacity, and much to offer others in developing theirs.

With the aim of encouraging widening horizons and raising awareness of our contribution and potential, this chapter provides an international perspective on mental health and nursing. It does not define or specify a role for mental health nurses, but rather provides a better understanding of the context in which professional leadership can evolve.

The global development of mental health

Mental health undoubtedly has significant and growing political currency, even though it is notably absent from the United Nations Millennium Development Goals set in 2000 (see World Health Organisation, 2010a: 165; United Nations, 2012). For example, in terms of global "burden of disease" (disability adjusted life years) major depressive disorder has increased from 15th to 11th rank, a 37% increase since 1990 (Murray et al, 2012). An earlier World Health Organization (WHO) estimate of disease burden placed unipolar depression to be in:

...third place worldwide and eighth place in low-income countries, but at first place in middle- and high-income countries.

WHO (2004)

The burden for low income countries is predicted to increase, with the Institute for Health Metrics and Evaluation (2012) stating:

African nations have not even begun to confront the consequences of exploding cases of mental illness, depression, pain, and the enormous burden of substance abuse that stem from those conditions. The direct link between mental illness and physical well-being is at the core of this unexplored terrain, and can only grow as the years go by.

Much of the emphasis around WHO policy is focused on low income countries where there is least resource directed towards mental health. The Lancet Global Mental Health Group (2007) published *Scaling up services for mental disorders – a call for action* alongside a series of papers providing supporting evidence, and this was followed up by further papers and "a renewed agenda for global mental health" (Patel et al, 2011). The WHO mental health Gap Action Programme (mhGAP; WHO, 2008, 2010b) identified a core range of psychiatric conditions and related interventions to address the shortfall in detection and treatment. It is important to note that the global agenda is predominantly set by psychiatrists, and nursing is virtually absent as a voice, either by individuals who have contributed as authors, or as a professional body.

Mental health nurses, as elaborated below, are certainly recognised as a key human resource, but interventions do not identify the domain of any particular profession. While it might be assumed that the evolution of nursing stems from its traditional presence in psychiatric hospitals, WHO (2008) give evidence that this presence is relatively small in many countries. This is supported by other reports, such as the National Human Rights Commission (1999), which, in separate studies of hospitals in India, identified that trained psychiatric nurses were present in less than 25% of the hospitals, even less present than psychologists and psychiatric social workers. In the absence of established nurse training programmes that have specialisation in mental health, and also services where practical experience can be developed, the promotion of mental health nursing is meaningless because there is no mental health nursing to promote. In the shift to community care, the skill gap can be filled by developing new workforces ("cadres") that are potentially cheaper and quicker to train and employ. To this end there is growing recognition of the value and evidence for the role of community health workers in the field of mental health (WHO, 2010a).

The other strand of international activity is driven by economic globalisation; the commodification of health and commercial interests, in particular, but not exclusively, those of drug companies. BCC Research (2011) estimated the global market in psychiatric medication to be worth $80 billion dollars in 2010, and growing at around 1.9% per annum. Much of the market is in high income countries. For example, Thomas Insel, Director of the US National Institute for Mental Health estimates the cost to be $25 billion alone (Insel, 2012), although alongside this Hyman warns that:

> ...drug discovery is at a near standstill for treating psychiatric disorders... despite high prevalence and unmet medical need, major pharmaceutical companies are de-emphasising or exiting psychiatry.
>
> Hyman (2012)

Unsurprisingly given its predominantly medical authorship, medication forms the core of interventions identified in the WHO mental health Gap Action Programme (mhGAP; WHO, 2008), although increasingly the evidence for psychological intervention is being incorporated into pilot studies for interventions in low resource countries. The focus of service development is primarily on intervention, and the relevance of nursing is related to its ability to contribute to intervention programmes. As will be discussed further below, there is evidence to suggest that the relevance of nursing is driven by contextual factors rather than professional identity and role.

The role of mental health nurses: UK perspective

Identifying the significance and distinct contribution of mental health nursing seems crucial to a secure future. In many ways mental health nursing in the UK has benefited from the broader development of nursing; degree status has been achieved, primary Registered Nurse qualification has been retained; and career pathways in academia, practice and organisations are established (Nurse Consultants – Department of Health, 1999b; Modern Matrons – Department of Health, 2001) as is the requirement for a Registered Nurse to be an executive director of each NHS trust. However, the role of mental health nurses in practice and operational management appears much more fluid. Community care has created significant role overlap in case and team management, and has also led to "extending" the role to incorporate statutory roles in compulsory admission (previously a social work domain) and (albeit limited) prescribing of medication. These "developments" can be argued as solutions to problems rather than professional advancement, and many nurses see such responsibilities as compromising the nurse–patient relationship. Nursing in the NHS seems to be a daily experience of being led by organisational demands, contracts, targets, procedures and even the minutiae of hourly ward-rounds. Services are deliberately managed to ensure thinking inside the box through constant recording and reporting on compliance. This not only takes time, but also impacts on the way nurses practise through the requirements to ask particular questions, use particular interventions and measure particular outcomes. While these new roles and responsibilities have become incorporated into what might be called nursing knowledge and practice, it raises the question of whether there is a sense of mental health nursing beyond what is defined by the particular healthcare system we work in.

With the future development of mental health care towards de-institutionalisation, there is a particular case for promoting the value and contribution of nurses who were integral to the development of community mental health services, a long tradition in the UK that included the creation of a national Community Psychiatric Nurses' programme and recorded qualification in the early 1980s. Much has developed since, and the National Service Framework for Mental Health (Department of Health, 1999a) paved the way for a wholesale transformation of services, and meant a dramatic shift in the locus of the profession and the role of nurses. The move to care at home has fundamentally changed the way nurses meet their responsibility for 24-hour care, and has placed far greater emphasis in working not just with the patient but with family and friends to ensure needs were being met. Community working has now become part of the core training of nurses rather than a specialist post-qualifying programme, and of course hospitals have continued to be a core part of services, although markedly changed in their role as a result of community care. Mental health nurses now have vast experience in developing a comprehensive range of accessible community-based services, and working in and managing multi-disciplinary teams. The move to community-based care has also evolved alongside a strengthening of the service user voice, emphasising recovery that focuses on personal goals rather than professional outcomes. In terms of promoting the international agenda for mental health nursing, UK nursing has a credible history and enormous potential for offering leadership.

International development of mental health nursing

The registration of mental health nurses is not found globally and falls under the broader statutory requirements for registered nurses. In Europe there is no statutory equivalence for training mental health nurses, again the European Union legislates for recognition of a single registered nurse qualification among member states. The UK Registered Nurse, Mental Health, is recognised in some countries across the Commonwealth, but usually requires transcripts of training to provide evidence of meeting local requirements. Globally, mental health nursing is largely a post-registration specialisation and, for example in Europe, this is not regulated (see European Commission, 2013 for various details on individual EU countries). However, it is important that in the European Union and other high income countries such as the USA, Canada, Australia and New Zealand, mental health nurses benefit from their status as registered nurses, professionalised in terms of statutory regulation and, by being established within higher education, benefit from academic as well as practice career paths.

It is important that WHO not only recognises but also promotes the development of mental health nursing as a significant contributor to resources available to deliver mental health services. While much of WHO policy develops the broader focus of the nursing and midwifery agenda (WHO, 2010c), the mental health department has produced data about mental health nursing. Published as the *Atlas: nurses in mental health* (WHO, 2007), it brought into stark contrast the enormous differences in nursing numbers, reporting a 100-fold difference between countries reporting the lowest and highest number of mental health nurses per head of population. These data must be approached with caution in interpreting what is meant by "mental health nurse", as there is little elaboration on the role of nurses. However, there is consistent reference to nurses undertaking the roles of doctors and, in particular, nurses are more likely to be involved in prescribing of medication in low income countries.

While the World Health Organization report indicated some interest in promoting collaboration and information sharing (WHO, 2007: 23), there is to date no global networking infrastructure supported by either international health or professional organisations. This lack of global presence both reflects the dilution of mental health nursing within the broader nursing agenda, and explains the limited impact mental health nurses have in promoting their distinct contribution.

Mental health nursing leadership

This highlights a question about how leadership in mental health nursing is being actively developed, and again this falls within the broader nursing agenda. The UK Chief Nursing Officer has published *Compassion in practice*, providing a vision for the "6c" values underpinning nursing (and other care staff) of "care, compassion, competence, communication, courage and commitment" (Department of Health, 2012). While the values are sound and can be elaborated, perhaps inevitably the strategy is largely instrumental, targeted at meeting the priorities and current concerns of the NHS, as is the leadership role for delivering the "6c" values. There is little direction added from the Royal College of Nursing, whose pages on leadership are firmly placed in the context of organisational and political agendas, identifying it as a theme under clinical governance (Royal College of Nursing, 2013). More specific to mental health, leadership is absent from the focus of Mental Health Nursing Academics UK (2013), where there is no mention of developing leadership in their aims.

Looking abroad, Horatio, the European Association for Psychiatric Nurses (UK member organisations are the Royal College of Nursing and the Mental Health Nursing Association), in their Turku Declaration of "the unique contribution of psychiatric and mental health nurses", provides a strong statement about the role of mental health nurses, but this does not include anything about professional or wider leadership roles (Horatio, 2011). Other organisations, such as the European Nursing Leadership Foundation (once led by Jean Faugier) and the Foundation of Nursing Leadership, appear to be inactive. Organisations with a worldwide membership such as Sigma Theta Tau (2005) have a resource/position paper on leadership, although again this is largely theoretical. Finally the WHO encourages "outstanding nurses" to become involved through internships in the development of nursing and health policy, although there is no information about whether or not a mental health nurse has taken this opportunity.

The International Council of Nurses, which supported the WHO Atlas report in 2007, produced a position statement on mental health that disappointingly makes no particular reference to global mental health strategy, and says relatively little about mental health nursing other than urging:

> *...national nursing agencies to get nurses' involvement in policy development, support service development and improve educational programmes.*
>
> International Council of Nurses (2008)

The leadership challenge: Developing a global future

There is undoubtedly an audience eager to learn from the experience and expertise of other countries, and we are very fortunate in the UK to have addressed many of the challenges that to varying degrees our colleagues across the world face today. Mental health services in the UK can therefore have a much wider impact than just on the individuals, families and communities we work with. There will be many nurses who have had the opportunity to work abroad and this not only enriches the care provided in those countries, but also can give many insights as well as ideas to bring back to our own practice and profession. In our own work in Birmingham between the local NHS Trust and the University we have for many years worked internationally with governments, international agencies and other universities to support the development of services. This has included exchange visits for many mental health workers, including nurses, to understand and learn from the day-to-day role of nurses and, critically, the context within which that role has developed. Undoubtedly this has enriched experience and widened people's horizons about mental health nursing.

In the UK there is also a growing academic community and concomitant nursing research to provide evidence of our contribution, but there is clearly the need to develop our professional audience, and it seems that although international organisations are open to the development of mental health nursing, there is currently a lack of leadership to drive this forward. While there is a literature on leadership and nursing, the more practical concern is how leadership in nursing is realised by national or international departments, bodies and organisations. As experienced here in the UK, and evidenced by the WHO (2007), the role of nurses is defined by context and pragmatism; although that may be a threat to maintaining our identity, it creates the opportunity for promoting our relevance and value. If we do not accept the challenge then eventually evidence from other parts of the world will suggest alternatives to nursing, and this is certainly already happening in community care, with the evolution of community support workers.

Mental health nurses in the UK are particularly well placed to lead, because the achievements of our services are wholly aligned with the aims of global mental health as developed by the WHO. This includes the "de-institutionalisation" agenda of shifting care from large institutions to more local services, integrating psychiatry into general hospital and primary care services, and challenging stigma and discrimination. The concept of recovery has provided a framework for promoting person-centred care and has reinforced the core values of nursing practice. With the revolution in telecommunication, and the good fortune that

English is invariably used as the first language for international collaboration and dissemination, this creates an environment of opportunity for mental health nurses to engage and influence global mental health.

References

BCC Research (2011) *Report PHM074A: Drugs for treating mental disorders: Technologies and global markets.* BCC Research, Wellesley, MA. Available from: http://www.bccresearch.com/report/mental-disorders-drugs-phm074a.html#

Department of Health (1999a) *National service framework for mental health: Modern standards and service models.* HMSO, London

Department of Health (1999b) *Making a difference: Strengthening the nursing, midwifery and health visiting contribution to health and healthcare.* HMSO, London

Department of Health (2001) *Implementing the NHS plan: Modern matrons. Strengthening the role of ward sisters and introducing senior sisters.* HMSO, London

Department of Health (2012) *Compassion in practice.* Department of Health, London

European Commission (2013) *The European Single Market.* Available from: http://ec.europa.eu/internal_market/search_en.htm?hl=en&as_sitesearch=ec.europa.eu%2Finternal_market%2F&cx=010624300341678344703%3A_u-3r0niuzu&cof=FORID%3A9&q=nursing&sa.x=14&sa.y=6

Horatio: European Psychiatric Nurses Association (2011).= *The Turku Declaration.* Available from: http://www.horatio-web.eu/downloads/Horatio_Turku_Declaration_2011.pdf

Hoult J (1986) Community care for the acutely mentally ill. *British Journal of Psychiatry* **149**: 137–44

Hyman S (2012) Revolution stalled. *Science Translational Medicine* **4**: 155. DOI: 10.1126/scitranslmed.3003142

Insel T (2012) Next generational treatments for mental disorders. *Science Translational Medicine* **4**: 155. DOI: 10.1126/scitranslmed.3004873

Institute for Health Metrics and Evaluation (2012) *Global burden of disease: Massive shifts reshape the health landscape worldwide.* Press release. Available from: http://www.healthmetricsandevaluation.org/gbd/news-events/news-release/massive-shifts-reshape-health-landscape-worldwid

International Council of Nurses (2008) *Position statement: Mental health.* International Council of Nurses, Geneva. Available from: http://www.icn.ch/images/stories/documents/publications/position_statements/A09_Mental_Health.pdf

Lancet Global Mental Health Group (2007) Scaling up services for mental disorders – a call for action. *Lancet* **370**: 1241–52

McGorry PD (1993) Early Psychosis Prevention and Intervention Centre. *Australasian Psychiatry* **1**: 32–4

Mental Health Nursing Academics UK (2013) *Aims of the group*. Available from: http://mhnauk.swan.ac.uk/AimsoftheGroup.htm

Murray CJL, Vos T, Lozano R et al (2012) Disability-adjusted life years (DALYs) for 291 diseases and injuries in 21 regions, 1990–2010: A systematic analysis for the Global Burden of Disease Study 2010. *Lancet* **380**(9859): 2197–223

National Human Rights Commission (1999) *Quality assurance in mental health*. National Human Rights Commission of India, New Delhi

Patel V, Boyce N, Collins P, Saxena S, Horton R (2011) A renewed agenda for global mental health. *Lancet* **378**(9801): 1441–2

Royal College of Nursing (2013) *RCN Leadership Programmes*. Available from: http://www.rcn.org.uk/development/rcn_leadership_programmes

Sigma Theta Tau International (2005) *Resource paper and position statement: Leadership and leadership development priorities*. Sigma Theta Tau International, Indianapolis, IL

Stein LI, Test MA (1978) An alternative to mental hospital treatment. In LI Stein, MA Test (Eds) *Alternatives to mental health hospital treatment*. Plenum Press, New York

Stein LI, Test MA (1980) Alternative to mental hospital treatment. I. Conceptual model, treatment program, and clinical evaluation. *Archives of General Psychiatry* **37**: 392–7

United Nations (2012) *The Millennium Development Goals Report 2012*. Available from: http://www.un.org/millenniumgoals/pdf/MDG%20Report%202012.pdf

World Health Organisation (2004) *The global burden of disease: 2004 update*. WHO, Geneva

World Health Organisation (2007) *Atlas: Nurses in mental health 2007*. WHO, Geneva

World Health Organisation (2008) *mhGAP: Mental Health Gap Action Programme: Scaling up care for mental, neurological and substance use disorders*. WHO, Geneva

World Health Organisation (2010a) *Global experience of community health workers for delivery of health-related Millennium Development Goals*. WHO, Geneva

World Health Organisation (2010b) *mhGAP Intervention guide for mental, neurological and substance use disorders in non-specialized health settings*. WHO, Geneva

World Health Organisation (2010c) *Strategic directions for strengthening nursing and midwifery services 2011–2015*. WHO, Geneva

Chapter 9

Towards leadership and social inclusion

Mark Jukes

Recent major reports into service failures, both in specialist and mainstream acute general services, point to the need for sound leadership. The serious case review into Winterbourne View (Flynn and Citarella, 2012) identified failures that stemmed from a complete malaise, and demonstrated a total lack of the necessary synergy between the functions of management and leadership. This resulted in an unacceptable level of care, and systematic abuse.

However, such failings are not just attributable to poor management, they are also as a result of a lack of professional and personal values, ethics and knowledge of the quality provision agenda of how care is delivered.

There are numerous theories on management and leadership, and no one particular theory can be applied to all situations. It is not the intention of this chapter to review theories, but rather to focus on transformational leadership (Bass, 1985, 1996) as being relevant for practice leadership and to further social inclusion.

The essence of effective management and leadership, however, is to embrace them so as to ensure the right measure or balance is attained. The relationship between leadership and management continues to attract debate, and the literature certainly demonstrates the need for both. Within some organisations an over-emphasis is on management functions, which ensure compliance in the workforce through a hierarchical transactional model. As a consequence, the organisation may not be prepared or responsive to challenges to the service, whereas to apply a transformational model would be appropriate for leaders adopting a more strategic and visionary approach.

However, leadership is held by some as one of management's many functions; others maintain that leadership requires more complex skills and that management is only one role of leadership; still others delineate between the two (Marquis and Huston, 2000). Ritson and Parker (2005) quote Fayol as the originator of the classic organisation and the establishment of core management functions, which are planning, organisation, command, coordination and control. The manager is a person who brings things about, the one who accomplishes, has the responsibility and conducts. Conversely, a leader is a person who influences and guides direction, opinion and course of action. *Table 9.1* offers a comparison of how management and leadership differ. Frequent problems found in leadership

Table 9.1. Comparison of management and leadership functions	
Managers	*Leaders*
Have an assigned position within the formal organisation.	Often do not have delegated authority but obtain power through other means, such as influence.
Have a legitimate source of power due to the delegated authority that accompanies their position.	Have a wider variety of roles than do managers.
Are expected to carry out specific functions, duties and responsibilities.	May not be part of the formal organisation.
Emphasise control, decision making, decision analysis and results.	Focus on group process, information gathering, feedback and empowering others.
Manipulate people, the environment, money, time and other resources to achieve organisational goals.	Emphasise interpersonal relationships.
Have a greater formal responsibility and accountability for rationality and control than leaders.	Direct willing followers.
Direct willing and unwilling subordinates.	Have goals that may or may not reflect those of the organisation.
	Source: Marquis and Huston (2000)

development have been identified by Roebuck (2011) in a paper commissioned by the King's Fund. Roebuck cites examples of such key challenges as:

- Lack in clarity around roles and responsibility.
- Need for leadership development at all levels, not just at the top.
- Silo mentality, restricting partnership working.
- Need for better proactive communication that engages, not just "tells".
- Need for ownership.
- Responsibility, living the values, flexibility, partnership working, promotion of more coaching rather than directing people.

Contemporary theories of leadership can work towards promoting social inclusion which will be seen as applicable for the promotion of practice leadership in mental health and intellectual disability nursing.

Transformational leadership

During the 1980s, within the NHS, none of the leadership approaches offered ways of how to adapt and cope within environments which were subject to continual change, particularly between the interface of seamless services and within a culture of multi/interprofessional working.

The transactional approach, whereby followers were rewarded, or plans and targets were based around static organisations, were inadequate for leading people or services through significant change.

Burns (1978) is credited with revolutionising and creating a new paradigm and a different perception and perspective of leadership, which was best summarised by Bass and Avolio (1994) under the four "I"s whereby leaders demonstrated and exemplified:

- Idealised influence.
- Inspirational motivation.
- Intellectual stimulation.
- Individual consideration.

Transformational leaders are charismatic and, because of their positive influence, are engaging for others to work for and with. However, criticism and concerns revolve around making decisions that need to be based on facts, and for leaders not just to be inspiring and passionate about taking a vision forward (Straker, 2004; McCrimmon, 2008). Another concern is that charismatic leaders may instil dependency through their followers' reliance upon the leader's inspiration and drive, and as a consequence may dissuade them from adopting responsibility or putting forward suggestions or ideas (Doyle and Smith, 2001).

In this post-transformational or charismatic leadership age there is a growing literature about the "dark side" of leadership (Hartley and Benington, 2011), about an association with narcissism (Parry and Bryman, 2006), and additionally about leaders who are destructive (Krumm, 2001). The latter is characterised when leaders exert the charismatic element to a degree where they create a high level of dependency among followers and assume a pseudo-transformational style. The intention of the four "I"s, when internalised, is that the leader exudes a strong value base to his or her followers. However, when a leader portrays a pseudo-transformational persona the value base is seriously compromised, and the art of transformational leadership is mis-directed. Brown and Trevino (2006) also cite ethical leadership as a further relevant theory that practice leaders could consider applying. When leaders internalise an ethical value base for practice they are less likely to assume a pseudo or narcissistic persona towards their leadership style.

Integrating transformational leadership with another theory or style can allow other ideas to be expressed and decisions to be based upon facts while allowing leaders to further inspire through their passion for promoting the vision and change.

The transformational model can be seen as having influence within the NHS Leadership Qualities Framework (see *Figure 9.1*).

Figure 9.1 has at its core personal qualities, including self-awareness, personal integrity, self-belief and self-management. Surrounding the core are two segments of the outer circle: setting direction and delivering the service. The practice leader needs to know him or herself, be politically astute to what

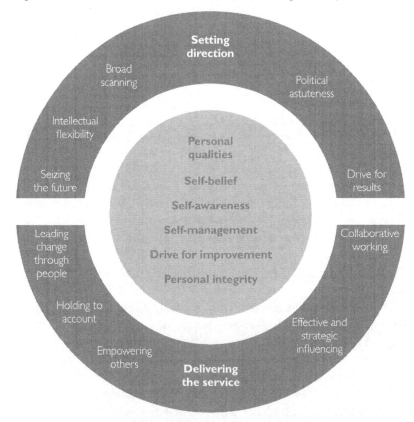

Figure 9.1. The NHS Leadership Qualities Framework. Source: NHS Institute for Innovation and Improvement (2011)

the immediate and future agenda is within the field of practice, be able to scan the horizon and lead change through people. In essence this requires practice leaders to lead themselves through their own self-belief, while being transparent and trustworthy. Leaders act to emancipate human potential through promotion of individual empowerment and the development of followers, in a similar way to how we promote these issues with people who use services.

In *Figure 9.1* these transformational qualities and influences are translated through "Leading change through people", "Empowering others", "Seizing the future", and having "Intellectual flexibility".

Bass (1985, 1996) built upon Burns' (1978) original ideas of transforming leadership, calling his revised theory "transformational leadership" which includes the four "I"s as components to this theory. *Table 9.2* further elaborates upon the four "I"s and compares these qualities with transactional leadership and a third category of leadership: laissez-faire, which, according to Avolio (1999), represents an absence of effective leadership and describes the leader who is passive or indifferent to direct instructions. Absorbed together these three categories are sometimes referred to as the Full-Range Leadership Model, (Avolio, 1999).

Table 9.2. The full-range leadership model	
Transformational leadership	*Recommendations for effective transformational leadership*
Idealised influence: Leaders serve as outstanding role models for their followers. They display conviction, emphasise important personal values, and connect those values with service/organisational goals and ethical consequences of decisions.	• Leaders do what is right, rather than what is expedient or most cost-effective. • Leaders take some time to make their decision-making more transparent and to be more consistent in their reasoning across people. • Consistently making decisions using the same criteria builds respect and trust. • Leaders who are seen by their colleagues/employees as people who can be counted on to "do the right thing" epitomise idealised influence. • Idealised influence can be encapsulated in the philosophy and ethos of the service/unit and its mission statement. The leader should ideally involve staff, families and service users in the design and implementation of these statements.

Table 9.2/cont

Inspirational motivation: Leaders articulate an appealing vision of the future and challenge followers' high standards and high expectations. Leaders provide encouragement, optimism, and purpose for what needs to be done.	• Leaders who display enthusiasm and optimism, communicating the message "I know you can do it", raise colleagues'/employees' sense of self-efficacy and inspire individuals to try harder to carry out a broader and more proactive role beyond traditional prescribed requirements. • Leaders need to support learning beyond registration courses and initiate/support in-service education and training for all levels of the care team, based upon individual needs. • All new members of staff are given an orientation period into the service, its vision, goals and expectations.
Intellectual stimulation: Leaders question old assumptions and stimulate new perspectives and innovative ways of doing things. They encourage followers to think creatively to address current and future challenges.	• Enhanced by a leader's ability to get colleagues/employees to think about work-related problems in new and creative ways. • Responding to questions by asking, "What do you think we should do?" or, "What would you advise if you were me?" engages colleagues' minds in the workplace. • This encapsulates the concept of lifelong learning and partnerships within a workplace which is resource or career-pathway limited. • Leaders enhance intellectual stimulation by providing opportunities for development by attending conferences/seminars, and encouraging employees to share their knowledge with the team, thereby enhancing the contribution towards evidence-based practice.
Individualised consideration: Leaders provide a supportive environment and carefully listen to followers' needs.	• Ability of the leader to respond to individual needs by acting as a coach, mentor, supervisor and confidant(e). • Making time to pay attention to individual concerns is one of the key behaviours.

	• Schedule time to talk to staff.
Leaders also advise, teach or coach their followers with the intention of advancing follower development.	• Encourage staff to take ownership of particular aspects of managing the care environment or specific projects to lead on, for example, reviewing care plans. • Personally thank colleagues for their efforts
Transactional leadership	*Recommendations for transactional leadership*
Contingent reward.	• Leaders offer followers rewards in exchange for desired efforts. Behaviours in this category revolve around clarifying expectations and exchanging promises.
Management by exception: active.	• Leaders observe follower behaviour and take corrective action when followers deviate from expected performance.
Management by exception: passive.	• Leaders choose not to or fail to intervene until a problem is brought to their attention.
Laissez-faire leadership	*Recommendations for laissez-faire leadership*
Laissez-faire leadership (non-leadership).	• Leaders avoid accepting responsibility and delay or even fail to follow up on requests. This type of leader behaviour also includes little or no effort to address followers' needs. It is essentially an absence of leadership.
Adapted from Bass (1997), Kellaway and Barling (2000), Northouse (2010), Doody and Doody (2012)	

So far we have concentrated on leadership perspectives and have focused on transformational leadership as compared with transactional and laissez-faire leadership as illustrated in *Table 9.2*.

Towards social inclusion

Eleven priorities were set down as a challenge by Allen et al (2009) in a paper commissioned by the Social Care Institute for Excellence. All of the priorities are relevant, but the four included in *Box 9.1* are those which are pertinent for the development of practice leadership and that clearly emphasise the relationship between a strong personal value base and a partnership with people for effective leadership.

Box 9.1. Priorities for leadership

- Develop and demonstrate leadership that tackles stigma and promotes social inclusion.
- Facilitate citizen involvement and leadership in determining the overall shape and delivery of mental health support systems.
- Facilitate effective cross-sector partnerships, including developing innovative engagement between councils and the NHS in relation to mental health.
- Lead from a strong personal value base, bringing oneself explicitly and effectively into one's leadership practice.

A plethora of reports promotes both personalisation and social inclusion for people with mental health needs and people with intellectual disabilities. These include *Putting people first* (Department of Health, 2007) and *Our health, our care, our say* (Department of Health, 2006).

Terms such as "inclusive society", "inclusion" or indeed "the big society" can become meaningless and rhetorical, particularly when repeated within reports, mission statements or operational/job descriptions. They become the "buzz" words that everyone recognises, but they are empty vessels. However, social inclusion continues to be an aspiration for many people with mental health needs and for those with intellectual disabilities (Sherwin, 2010).

For the recipient, social exclusion means a history of rejection, separation from ordinary life and relationships, loneliness, isolation and powerlessness within service systems. Social inclusion, therefore, for practice leaders is an ethical and practice issue; leaders should help people to integrate and participate within society. Practice leaders need to have a person-centred outlook and to develop person-centred thinking.

Attributes for leadership

Sherwin (2010) identifies five attributes (see below) for those in leadership roles within disability services.

A moral and ethical base

Leaders should hold deep personal values and beliefs which reflect the ethos that humanity is a construct shared by everyone. They should have a deep concern and feeling for the plight of people with mental health needs and/or intellectual disabilities who are excluded in society because their differences are negatively valued. They should have qualities of compassion, dignity and respect combined with optimism and a capacity for resilience.

Such qualities are essential in working towards inclusion. Young (1990) identifies the oppressive state of "cultural imperialism" where dominant groups in society reject and exclude people with vulnerabilities. Leaders work against these forces in the interests of people who need to be included. Therefore the moral and ethical base becomes the foundation for what is implemented at the next level, which is knowledge.

Conceptual clarity, insight, knowledge and wisdom

For mental health and intellectual disability nurses, having a combination of conceptual clarity, insight, knowledge and wisdom is about applying theoretical and practice-based knowledge which builds upon sound values and ethics.

Facilitating social inclusion is about person-centred thinking and action and evaluating therapeutic assessments or interventions which are person focused. Leaders should promote empowerment, mental capacity, the use of best interests and connection with networks and communities to encourage participation and inclusion.

Relationships with people and family members

Having authentic relationships with people and family members includes the leader having an understanding of the reality of exclusion and rejection in an individual's life and provides the leader with an impetus for action. The leader is mindful of what is at stake for people who are marginalised, and needs to be constantly aware of the extent of exclusion within mainstream services.

Appreciation of history

If we were to develop a timeline for mental health and intellectual disability services today, we can see that some contemporary services are a replication of services from the past. We are still creating new "in patient" facilities, not perhaps on hospital campuses but rather within communities. Treatment centres continue to be based on the old hospital design and private companies are still building hospitals.

For the leader, a respect for history is important as is an understanding that not everything purported to be new is, in fact, new. With regard to knowledge and theories, person-centred care and what supports personalisation, have their roots in person-centred counselling derived from Carl Rogers (1961) in the 1930s. Person-centred care therefore is an amplification of person-centred counselling. Indeed, contributors to person-centred planning include John O'Brien (O'Brien and Lyle O'Brien, 1991) who was a collaborator behind the five accomplishments which were part of normalisation and social role valorisation. Additionally, what is missing in our educational and training agenda today, is a focused exposure to relationship processes which reinforce such values. We seem to be dominated by simulation laboratories that emphasise physical skills and competencies at the expense of how we relate to patients and people. This theory has made a contribution to human service workers' development and understanding of valuing relationships with people, and to the measurement of service quality in order to stem the residual effects of institutionalisation. The Tidal Model, developed by Phil Barker (2001), is, after all, a return to what mental health nursing practice is about, and Phil Barker was influenced by both Peplau and Roy in locating mental health nursing practice as a relational process.

Putting faith and efforts in things that are likely to bring dividends

No matter how sophisticated assessments are, how many quality inspections are carried out, or how much money or training is put into place, they are not likely to be the deciding factors that make a difference in the lives of people with mental health and intellectual disabilities who are marginalised and excluded from society.

Solutions for successful social inclusion and participation are more than likely to be found among leaders and staff who have values-based qualities and work towards supporting people with their day-to-day experiences. A survey conducted by Kouzes and Posner (2007) of 75000 people regarding recommendations for leaders, found modelling expected behaviour, having and sharing a vision, challenging the process with innovative ideas and action, allowing and enabling others to take action, and being passionate about your work were key factors for success.

Such attributes are essential in applying a transformational model of leadership. Leaders not only empower and envision the team they are working with, but also form a clear relational bond between and with service users, providing connectivity and an ability to move towards social inclusion.

Relationship between leadership and management of change

Many nurses are in positions of being practice leaders in mental health and intellectual disability services, and will therefore need to work closely with their service managers. This symbiotic relationship is critical for communicating a vision for developing "best" practice initiatives between service managers and practice leaders. Both leadership and management are necessary. Leadership is about vision – being able to make sense of and communicate the bigger picture within complex situations and it is also about ensuring things happen and enabling practical innovation.

Zalzenik (1993) has suggested that managers and leaders are fundamentally different in personality and has postulated that leaders tolerate, indeed create, chaos, foster disruption, can live with a lack of structure and closure, and are actually on the look-out for change. Managers, in his view, seek order and control, which means achieving closure on problems as quickly as possible. Practice leaders may have a joint role of both team leader and manager.

As is clear in *Table 9.2,* to internalise and fulfil a transformational leadership style is clearly about articulating a vision, being able to translate and communicate the "bigger" picture to your team, for example, introducing a service innovation towards implementation of person-centred care and planning. How to make this happen will depend on how the practice leader is aligned and relates to the service manager and is able to collaborate with him or her in vision or/and innovation. This will enable them collectively to plan strategies, operations, processes, reporting, communication and perhaps further involvement of finance and human resources. Therefore, effective management of change processes and leadership are commensurate. *Chapter 10* examines the processes of management of change to achieve maximum success in the implementation of an innovation.

Both leadership and management are necessary, and organisations need to ensure that they are in the right measure and balance. As illustrated in *Table 9.1,* many aspects of leadership and management overlap. Therefore, implementing any management of change through a leadership model requires planning and requires leaders to relate closely with managers in communication and implementation of any innovation.

References

Allen R, Gilbert P, Onyett S (2009) *Leadership for personalisation and social inclusion in mental health.* Social Care Institute for Excellence, London

Avolio BJ (1999) *Full leadership development: Building the vital forces in organizations.* Sage, Thousand Oaks, CA

Barker P (2001) The Tidal Model. Developing and empowering. Person-centred approach to recovery within psychiatric and mental health nursing. *Journal of Psychiatric and Mental Health Nursing* **8**: 233–40

Bass BM (1985) *Leadership and performance: Beyond expectations.* Free Press, New York

Bass BM (1996) *A new paradigm of leadership: An inquiry into transformational leadership.* US Army Research Institute for the Behavioral and Social Sciences, Alexandria, VA

Bass BM (1997) *The ethics of transformational leadership.* Kellogg Leadership Studies Project, Transformational Leadership Working Papers. James MacGregor Burns Academy of Leadership Press, College Park, MD

Bass B, Avolio B (1994) *Improving organizational effectiveness through transformational leadership.* Sage, Thousand Oaks, CA

Brown ME, Trevino LK (2006) Ethical leadership: A review and future directions. *The Leadership Quarterly* **17**: 595–616

Burns JM (1978) *Leadership.* Harper & Row, New York

Department of Health (2006) *Our health, our care, our say: A new direction for community services.* HMSO, London

Department of Health (2007) *Putting people first. A shared vision and commitment to the transformation of adult social care.* HMSO, London

Doody O, Doody CM (2012) Transformational leadership in nursing practice. *British Journal of Nursing* **21**(20): 1212–18

Doyle ME, Smith MK (2001) *Shared leadership, the encyclopedia of informal education.* Available from: http://www. infed. org/leadership/shared_leadership. htm

Flynn M, Citarella V (2012) *Winterbourne View Hospital. A serious case review.* South Gloucester Council, Gloucester

Hartley J, Benington J (2011) *Recent trends in leadership – Thinking and action in the public and voluntary service sectors.* Commission on Leadership and Management in the NHS. The Kings Fund, London

Kellaway EK, Barling J (2000) What we have learned about developing transformational leaders. *Leadership and Organization Development Journal* **21**(7): 355–62

Kouzes JM, Posner BZ (2007) *The leadership challenge* (4th edn). Josssey-Bass, San Francisco, CA

Krumm DJ (2001) Leadership. In: DJ Krumm (ed) *Psychology at work: An introduction to industrial/organizational psychology* (pp 235–78). Worth Publishers, New York

Marquis BL, Huston CJ (2000) *Leadership roles and management functions in nursing* (3rd edn). Lippincott Williams & Wilkins, Philadelphia, PA

McCrimmon M (2008) *Transformational leadership.* Available from: http://

businessmanagement.suite101.com/article.cfm/transformational_leadership

NHS Institute for Innovation and Improvement (2011) *Leadership Qualities Framework.* NHS Institute for Innovation and Improvement, London. Available from: www. leadershipqualitiesframework.institute.nhs.uk

Northouse P (2010) *Leadership: Theory and practice* (5th edn). Sage Publications. London

O'Brien J, Lyle O'Brien C (eds) (1991) *Framework for accomplishment. Manual for a workshop for people developing better services.* Responsive System Associations, Georgia

Parry KW, Bryman A (2006) Leadership in organisation. In ST Clegg, C Harry, TB Lawrence, WR Nord (eds) *The Sage handbook of organization studies* (pp 447–68). Sage, Thousand Oaks, CA

Ritson PA, Parker LD (2005) Revisiting Fayol. Anticipating contemporary management. *British Journal of Management* **16**(3): 175–94

Roebuck C (2011) *Developing effective leadership in the NHS to maximise the quality of patient care – The need for urgent action.* Commission on Leadership and Management in the NHS, The Kings Fund, London

Rogers C (1961) *On becoming a person. A therapist's view of psychotherapy.* Houghton Mifflin, Boston, MA

Sherwin J (2010) Leadership for social inclusion in the lives of people with disabilities. *International Journal of Leadership in Public Services* **6**: 84–93

Straker D (2004) *Transformational leadership.* Available from: http://changingminds. org/ disciplines/leadership/styles/transformational_leadership. htm

Young IM (1990) *Justice and the politics of difference.* Princeton University Press, Princeton, NJ

Zalzenik A (1993) Managers and leaders: Are they different? In WE Rosenbach, RL Taylor (eds) *Contemporary issues in leadership* (3rd edn). Westview Press, Oxford

Chapter 10

Strategies for implementing and managing change

Mark Jukes, Premchunlall Mohabeersingh and Paul Allen

In mental health and intellectual disability services, practice leaders who are in positions of leading, managing and implementing change, are required to be influenced by and knowledgeable about change theories that represent a systematic, sequenced, co-ordinated and robust structure. However, any idea for innovation within complex health or social care organisations presents immense challenges, and demands a breadth in thinking and understanding about how change can be brought about at any number of service and organisational levels.

The ability to systematically orchestrate continuous change is integral to management and leadership success. Therefore, most traditional approaches to management and leadership can no longer be organised and led as discrete episodes. A state of continual flux and change in the NHS, and in particular within mental health and intellectual disability services, can now be seen as the norm and as such require a renewed approach to energise change. From our experiences as practice educators we have found that nurses' stability in hospitals and community services has lead to decline in the type of service given. Therefore, to be proactive with regard to change reduces risks rather than threats to survival. Change is driven by political, economic, social, technological, ethical and legal factors, and hence the balance between planned and unplanned change becomes an important organisational issue. The danger here is that organisations become reactive, as managers have insufficient time and skills to manage the change process, and are more liable to adopt a transactional mode of operations. While it is problematic to sustain a high level of energy in any particular change process over a period of time, it does not follow that major changes need to be achieved with speed. Given a more realistic timescale that accounts for the needs of the individuals concerned and the power and boundary issues that are raised, the chances of success could increase.

In England, the Darzi Report, *High quality care for all,* published in 2008, identified practice leadership as an essential component for delivering improvement and setting out the role of the clinician as practitioner, partner and leader. Therefore, the impetus for practice leadership to align reforms with the needs of the service user has never been greater. The Care Quality Commission has at its heart the measurement of quality of the experiences of the patient within healthcare.

Leadership and management have attracted a variety of negative responses, the most negative being for professionals to adopt such roles. A culture of "anti-managerialism" has been fuelled by a "management by targets" attitude and the claim that some clinicians, by becoming managers, have gone over to the "dark side". In addition, leadership is seen by others as being unproven; that is, in our evidence-based practice culture, leadership is regarded as unscientific.

Darzi claims that his review provides a diagnosis of where we currently are, a unified vision of where we want to be, and a common language framework to get us there. He further claims that leadership will make this happen.

A radical change to the organisation of the NHS has now been delivered since 2008, by way of the introduction of the Health and Social Care Act (Department of Health, 2012), which faced a barrage of criticism and opposition, mostly from doctors, who would be required to take the lead as consortia of general practitioners across England and charged with the task of commissioning healthcare.

A key policy area includes making the NHS more accountable to patients and the public by introducing and establishing Healthwatch, a new independent body that can investigate and scrutinise the performance of local health providers. Another key area is to improve public health by establishing a new body, called Public Health England, with an aim to reduce health inequalities between the richest and poorest in society. It will be interesting to monitor progress; when GP fundholding was introduced in 1994, the then Community Health Council found that GPs struck off 40000 patients from their lists, mainly those with disabilities, mental ill-health or who were deemed too expensive to treat (Brindle, 1994). Halstead (2010, cited in Flatchett, 2012) has suggested that most doctors would rather spend time dealing with patients' medical problems than wrestling with "the latest number crunching exercise".

Approaches to change

The NHS reformed agenda demands transformational change with service improvements. To endure this process of transformation, the relationship between the leader and follower will require trust and commitment. The dynamics of such change can evoke undesirable (intolerable) frustration for the followers, making them vulnerable and eager to accept the leader of change (personal concrete) agenda without a purpose. Followers choosing to participate in the relational process of improvement can be exposed to the consequential dynamics of confusion and ambiguity. If leaders are to succeed in implementing change, then trust is imperative, and they require integrity. With current NHS reforms it is essential to identify a variety of change approaches. Iles (2011) categorises these approaches into planned or deliberate change, spontaneous change and emergent change. Change leaders can apply these approaches when planning strategies for implementation and reflective practice as detailed in *Table 10.1.*

Table 10.1. Approaches to change		
Planned or deliberate change Example: An element of reform from the NHS Health and Social Care Act (2012) or the Equality Act (2010). Analysis followed by plan and implementation.	*Spontaneous change* Example: An element of risk behaviour which has impacted upon your service, and has resulted in an investigation/inquiry. Events, actions and behaviours emerge spontaneously from interactions in a complex adaptive system.	*Emergent change* Example: To introduce in real terms person-centred planning and care in a specialist in-patient facility. Foster, craft, discover things, detect patterns. Patterns of behaviour that indicate the direction of change are already under way, are identified and encouraged.
Prospective: Thinking ahead		
Undertake a rigorous analysis that leads to a list of critical issues that need to be addressed, and some form of implementation programme. *Key skills*: analytical and computational. Force-field analysis. Change management model.	Engage with a wide range of people, encouraging them to contribute their perspective and to take responsibility for playing their part in shaping the analysis and the design. *Key skills*: listening, being comfortable with ambiguity.	Work with the people with "tacit" knowledge, authentic and intuitive understanding of the organisation. Experiment with different ideas and look for patterns in the experience of the organisation. *Key skills*: spotting patterns, identifying authenticity.
		Table 10.1. cont/

Real time: Implementing		
Manage the programme or project using sound, proven methods for monitoring progress. Language used: critical path, compliance, milestone, progress reports, contingency plans, performance management.	Keep in mind, and voice for others, the spirit of the programme of change; help others to behave in the spirit of this plan. Attributes required: dynamic poise, attentiveness, flexibility and responsiveness.	Make all your usual everyday decisions that appear to have little connection with the implementation plan. Take opportunities as they arise, fostering and crafting choices to make the best of each unforeseen situation. Interpret all sorts of knowledge and information, tacit as well as explicit, and bring meaning to events as they unfurl.
Retrospective: Reflecting		
Compare actual events and outcomes with those of the plan, and with the analysis that led to the plan. In practice, this can have a developmental intent (enabling better analysis and planning in the future) or a judgemental one (performance management).	Try to understand what actually happened and how, by considering the events and processes, behaviours and relationships that emerged as time went on. This gives a better understanding of the dynamics of the system and enables the design of development programmes that will influence the way people respond in the future. *Tools used*: Facilitated reflection, informal reflection, non-blame feedback, systems thinking.	Tell stories: help people make sense of what has happened, by selecting some events and decisions and not others. Stories woven here are not accurate pictures of reality but simplified, coherent versions of reality that can be told to multiple stakeholders. This engenders a sense of meaning and of belonging to a longer narrative, which can become part of the history of the service or organisation.
		Adapted from: Iles (2011)

The chapter focuses on planned or emergent change, in terms of implementing change, and from the common themes identified in *Table 10.1*. The influences on strategy choice for practice leaders can lead to success if leaders and staff teams:

- Are involved in proposing and designing the change.
- Feel that opinions are heard and contribute to a new reality (rationale vs. reality).
- Ultimately benefit from the change: the organisation, patients, wider community also benefit from the change.
- Understand the reasons for change.
- Dislike the present status quo.
- Believe the change is important and necessary.
- Are involved in reflective activities and discussion on progress.
- Can see the big picture and how the change contributes to it.

Development of change theory

Lewin (1951), whose origins were in social psychology within the human relations movement, posited that to understand behaviour requires an in-depth knowledge of the person as well as a knowledge of what surrounds the person. As a result of this analysis his "force-field" model was developed (Schwering, 2003), which used psychological terms to understand what keeps an individual or organisation in equilibrium. Lewin described behaviour in an organisation as being a dynamic balance between driving and restraining forces. Driving forces facilitate change and lead people within an organisation in new directions and towards new goals, while restraining forces impede change and work towards maintaining the status quo. A leader/manager has to analyse these forces and ultimately shift the balance between them via force-field analysis. Lewin further suggested that this change is brought about by a three-stage process encompassing unfreezing, moving and refreezing (see *Table 10.2*).

In the unfreezing stage, the change agent unfreezes forces that maintain the status quo. Thus, people become discontented and aware of a need for change. Unfreezing is necessary because people must believe that change is required.

Unfreezing occurs when the change agent coerces members of the group to change. For effective change to occur, the change agent needs to conduct a thorough subjective and objective assessment of the current state, the nature and depth of motivation and the environment in which the change will occur.

Table 10.2. Lewin's three-step process of planned change	
Phase 1: Unfreezing	
Change leader's role: Create a felt need for change by preparing self and others before the change and ideally create a situation in which there is a desire for change. Unfreezing and getting motivated for the change is all about weighing up the "pros" and "cons" and deciding if the "pros" outnumber the "cons" before taking action. This is the basis of what Kurt Lewin called "Force-field analysis".	*By:* • Establishing a good relationship with the people involved. • Helping others realise that present behaviours are not effective and there is a need for change. • Making people believe change has benefits to patients, team and organisation.
Phase 2: Moving or transforming	
Change leader's task: Implement change. Use of the new levels for change in the system positively and creatively. Support is important here and can be in the form of training, coaching and expecting mistakes as part of the process. Use role models and allowing people to develop their own solutions. Keep communicating a clear picture.	*By:* • Identifying new, more effective ways of working • Choosing changes in tasks, people, culture, technology, structures. • Taking action to put these changes into place • Minimising resistance to change
Phase 3: Refreezing	
Change leader's role: To stabilise change and establish stability once changes have been made. To support the desired change.	*By:* • Creating acceptance and continuity for new behaviours • Providing any necessary resource support • Integrating within services

The second phase of planned change is movement. In movement, the change agent identifies, plans and implements appropriate strategies, ensuring that driving forces exceed restraining forces. Because change is such a complex process, it requires a great deal of planning and intricate timing. Recognising, addressing and overcoming resistance may be a lengthy process. Any change of human behaviour, or the perceptions, attitudes and values underlying that behaviour, takes time. Therefore, any change must allow enough time for those involved to be fully assimilated in that change.

The last phase is refreezing. During the refreezing phase, the change agent assists in stabilising the system so it becomes integrated into the status quo. If refreezing is incomplete, the change will be ineffective and the pre-change behaviours will be resumed. This final phase of refreezing can perhaps sit uncomfortably in terms of new change within modern health services, where change can be only weeks away, and therefore does not perhaps fit with contemporary thinking that change is a continuous chaotic process. More modern models of change, such as the ADKAR model (see *Table 10.3*) (Hiatt, 2006), are more explicit about this refreezing phase and include reinforcement so that changes during this phase are maintained and new outcomes can be measured.

Table 10.3. The ADKAR model of change management	
A	Awareness of the need for change – understanding why change is necessary. Reasoning and thought that underpins a required change.
D	Desire to support and participate in the change – the individual makes a personal commitment to support change and participate. Addressing incentives and creating a desire to be part of the change.
K	Knowledge of how to change – providing knowledge about the change achieved through training and coaching, forums and mentoring. Knowledge on how to change and knowledge on how to perform once change is implemented.
A	Ability to implement the change – the difference between theory and practice, or actual performance of the individual needs to be supported. Can take some time but achieved through practice, coaching and feedback.
R	Reinforcement to sustain the change – ensuring that changes stay in place and that individuals do not revert to old ways. Can be achieved through positive feedback, rewards, recognition, measuring performance and taking corrective actions.
	Source: Hiatt (2006)

The practice leader as change agent acts as a diagnostician in assessing the readiness of teams. Broom (1998) identifies a variety of human responses to change which can be similar to the symptoms of bereavement and shock. Three further levels of resistance are identified:

- *Level 1*: resistance relates to information: lack of, confusion or disagreement with key information.
- *Level 2*: resistance is an emotional and physiological reaction to change based on fear of loss, incompetence or abandonment.
- *Level 3*: resistance goes beyond the immediate situation. It may be deeply entrenched and can encompass personal, cultural and racial differences.

Transforming levels of resistance into commitment is required if planned change and improvements are to have maximum chance of success. When dealing with resistance, the strategy must match the level of resistance you are facing.

The touchstone test is to see if your strategies address level 2 concerns:

- Build strong working relationships – involve people.
- Maintain a clear focus.
- Embrace resistance – get to the root of concern.
- Use action conflict management strategies.
- Listen with an open mind.
- Maintain a neutral zone.
- Stay calm to stay engaged.

Navigating the change process

Thomas (2006) explores a model that attempts to frame a breadth of understanding through the adoption of a matrix which helps teams to reflect on the different domains of learning that are required for the success of a proposed innovation (see *Table 10.4*).

Across the top of the matrix in *Table 10.4* are the headings: experience, attitude, skills, knowledge, and tangible outcomes. These reflect the different domains of learning that are needed for the success of a proposed innovation. An example here could be within planning and implementing person-centred care, an innovation which includes practitioners having the experience of facilitating person-centred reviews, valuing the contribution of this process, having skills of initiating person-centred plans and knowledge about where such tools can be sourced.

Table 10.4. Towards a breadth of understanding: Domains of learning					
	What changes will be seen				
	Experiences Includes all experiences, irrespective of whether people learn from them, e.g. visiting other organisations	Attitudes Includes values and beliefs – the ways in which people think and judge others	Skills Includes the things people can practically do, e.g. listen	Knowledge Includes the things people know, both as facts and deeper understandings	Tangible outcomes Includes organisational and service developments such as team meetings and new clinics
Where change will be seen					
Individual change Change in individual people					
Organisational change Change in individual organisations					
Inter-organisational or system change Including communication systems and networks					
Wider change Not in the local system					

Down the side of the matrix are different headings to indicate places where learning and change are needed: individual change, organisational change, inter-organisational or system change, and wider change. With the example above, it could be an innovation which results in improved understanding among service-users in how this process benefits them individually, better understanding of how organisations can benefit from person-centred thinking about how the service is organised, better inter-organisational understanding about person-centred processes, and better communication across sectors and professionals about person-centred care. As a mapping exercise this approach can ultimately improve

131

a broader understanding into how such innovations can move forward involving organisations, individuals and the wider community.

Boddy and Buchanan (1992) identified that change agents face core tasks which challenge the uncertainty that surrounds the change situation. To promote a more positive outcome they propose a five-point plan which the change agent pursues.

1. Identify and manage stakeholders, thereby gaining visible commitment.
2. Work on objectives, making them clear, concise and understandable.
3. Set a full agenda. Take a holistic and "helicopter" view and highlight potential difficulties.
4. Build appropriate control systems. Communication is a two-way process; feedback is required.
5. Plan the process of change. Pay attention to:
   • establishing roles – clarity of purpose
   • building a team – do not leave it to chance
   • nurturing coalitions of support – fight apathy and resistance
   • communicating relentlessly – manage the process
   • recognising power – make the best use of supporting power bases
   • handing over – ensure that the change is maintained.

Practice leaders who work introspectively and are isolated from each other will fail. By working together they can develop communities of practice (Wenger, 1998) with a shared vision based on the "triple aim" to: "improve the health of the population, enhance patient experience of care, and control the cost of care". This collective clinical/practice voice is vital to make the case for service rationalisation and service transformation across health and social care sectors.

John Kotter (1996) is widely regarded for his thinking and action around change management, where his belief is that organisational change can be managed through a dynamic eight-step approach. However, to fully appreciate Kotter's work it is important to understand the emotional content associated with achieving change, particularly with employees and colleagues, who faced with feelings of complacency, pessimism, arrogance, anger and anxiety. These are all emotions that can be identified in staff teams across mental health and intellectual disability and which can and do undermine any attempts at promoting change. Therefore, the challenge for the practice leader is to turn negatives into positive feelings such as trust, optimism, urgency and enthusiasm that can lead to change. When employees and colleagues are motivated it is something they actually feel in their hearts rather than something based on statistics or related to targets to be achieved, or as lessons to be learned from the Francis Report (2013). So, to instil a feeling of action in colleagues, Kotter recommends that a leader or manager adopts a "see–feel–change" approach and uses this approach at every stage in the model (Campbell, 2008).

When behaviour is fuelled by emotion, it is more likely to last longer and become sustainable. As an example, if staff teams can be introduced to visual educational resources about poor routinised care, then be introduced to a visual model of "best practice" which epitomises person-centred care, this exposure to positive processes and outcomes will have more of an impact on how person-centred care works for individuals. This will ultimately have a significant influence in altering staff perceptions about their practice. Kotter organises each of the eight steps into three distinct phases. The first phase is "creating a climate for change" and includes:

- *Creating a sense of urgency.* This is the kind of urgency that Kotter calls for managers/leaders to instil in their employees, "making sure that sufficient people act with sufficient urgency, with behaviour that looks for opportunities that energise the team – that beams a sense of let go". The key to developing urgency is to help employees see first hand what and why a change needs to occur.
- *Building guiding teams.* As the sense of urgency grows among employees, managers must turn their attention to the development of a guiding team. Selecting the right members for a team is imperative because these individuals will guide the change management project throughout the remaining steps. Guiding team members who are perceived as credible will bring a sense of trust to the team, and with trust comes believability.
- *Getting the vision right: Compassionate care.* Communicate this compelling vision to win the hearts and minds of staff. The vision should promote continuous dialogue in the change effort. A good vision statement will consider the options that are available when answering the question: What does it mean to create a quality sensitive culture within a healthcare organisation? To develop a vision statement, Kotter recommends that the guiding team identify six or seven broad visions of the future.

The second phase is "engaging and enabling the organisation" and consists of three stages:

- *Communicate for the "buy in"*: Chart/map the journey ahead by engaging others in planning and implementing the changes. Appoint clinical champions.

- *Enable action*: To succeed, Kotter advises the guiding team to achieve visible, meaningful and unambiguous progress quickly.
- *Create short-term wins*. Make the change stick. Continue to use systems when a new supportive, strong organisational culture is in place that reminds staff of the new ways of working.

The final phase is "implementing and sustaining the change" and engages with the final steps.

- *Do not let up*: Ensure coherence with performance management.
- *Make it stick*: Institutionalise the changes. Formalise the process through the formulation of a written strategy. This will help establish a safe and sustainable healthcare delivery paradigm for the future. Reliable, safe healthcare should become an integral part of the health and social care service culture.

In its document *Compassion in practice*, the Department of Health (2012) has published its vision for nursing, midwifery and care staff and has proposed and embodied a visionary culture in the form of six fundamental values – the six "c"s: care, compassion, competence, communication, courage and commitment.

To drive these values through are six areas of action including "building and strengthening leadership", where it is proposed that the Department of Health will lead work to implement and embed the Leadership Qualities Framework for Adult Social Care and roll this out.

If mental health and intellectual disability nurses are to renew public confidence in services, managers and leaders will need to internalise these values. Also instilled by the NHS constitution (HM Government, 2013) are:

- *Respect and dignity*: treating people as individuals, not symptoms or resources.
- *Commitment to quality of care*: earning others' trust by insisting on quality and getting the basics right.
- *Compassion*: finding the time to listen and understand.
- *Improving lives*: striving to improve health and well being in the NHS through excellence and professionalism.
- *Everyone counts*: using our resources for the benefit of the whole community.

- *Working together for patients*: putting patients first in everything we do by reaching out to staff, patients, carers, families, communities and professionals outside the NHS.

Two strategies often enacted for managing change are prescriptive and participative.

Prescriptive strategies have a strong directive approach. They highlight a manager's use of power to impose change. The advantage of these strategies is that change can be undertaken quickly but the disadvantage is that they do not take into consideration the views or feelings of those involved in or who are affected by the imposed change. They may stifle creativity and innovation as valuable information and ideas may be missed and there is usually strong resentment from staff when changes are imposed rather than discussed, debated and agreed.

Participative strategies include: participative strategies in action, educative strategies and negotiating strategies.

Conclusion

How does a practice leader unfreeze a healthcare organisation? A provocative problem or event needs to be presented to the team to enable members to recognise the need for change and search for new solutions. This problem acts as the catalyst that creates the movement for new thinking and for the change to occur. People's willingness to change is key. People generally need to see for themselves the need for change for the catalyst to occur and to provoke them to "unfreeze". Following on from that, practice leaders can begin to highlight gaps between the current and desired states and present a vision for developing a culture of compassionate and safe care.

- Present compelling rationale for change, the "why?"
- Discuss the benefits of the proposed change to patient/client, team and organisation.
- Maintain regular, open communication to influence and inform (two-way communication).
- Remain focused, open, transparent and honest with feedback to staff to build cohesiveness among groups affected.
- Build a coalition and support from senior management and pay attention to key stakeholders.

- Conduct a situational analysis to add value.
- Define a clear case for change. Be transparent about the reasons.
- Challenge the data: Do they really describe current performance?

The role of practice leaders in transforming services is to pose the question: What does it take to transform a service to promote excellence in care? Before embarking on any change or transformation programme, it is essential to review the following key steps for success:

- Paint an inspiring vision for the future.
- Use the vision to motivate change and maintain momentum.
- Identify a model in which to manage short-term action while maintaining the visionary and sustainable picture of the future.
- Use collaborative leadership skills to promote joined-up thinking at all levels.
- Anticipate conflicts and deal with resistance.
- Take the lead within the matrix management in setting ground rules.
- Engage the team in this model of transformation.
- Constructively challenge the team to innovate.
- Identify the change champions and equip them with the necessary leadership and relationship skills.

The role of practice leaders in refreezing or reinforcing change is imperative so as to effect change at the practice level, which directly involves service users in attempts to transform person-centred care and environments. The appropriate use of staff will bring out the best in people and will identify options and embed the change. A requirement for practice leaders therefore is to be effective in challenging attitudes and practices that promote open and transparent communication and to aim to stabilise new change. Ultimately, this will pave the way for mental health and intellectual disability services to be invigorating environments in which to work, which will stimulate creativity and vitality in staff teams.

References

Boddy D, Buchanan DA (1992) *Take the lead: Interpersonal skills for project managers.* Prentice Hall, London

Brindle D (1994) GP's rid lists. *The Guardian* 11 **July**: 6

Broom A (1998) *Essentials of nursing management: Managing change* (2nd edn).

MacMillan Press, Basingstoke

Campbell RJ (2008) Change management in health care. *The Health Care Manager* **27**(1): 23–39

Darzi A (2008) *High quality care for all. NHS next stage review. Final report.* Department of Health, London

Department of Health (2012) *Compassion in practice – Nursing, midwifery and care staff. Our vision and strategy.* Department of Health, London

Flachett A (2012) *Social policy for nurses.* Polity Press, Cambridge

Francis R (2013) *Mid-Staffordshire NHS Foundation Trust public inquiry. Francis Report.* Mid-Staffordshire NHS Foundation Trust Public Inquiry, London

Halstead J (2010) GPs may not want to hold the purse strings. *Nursing Standard* **24**(47): 28

Hiatt J (2006) *ADKAR: A model for change in business, government and our community: How to implement successful change in our personal lives and professional careers.* Prosci Learning Center Publications, Loveland, CO

HM Government (2013) *The NHS constitution. The NHS belongs to us all.* Department of Health, London

Iles V (2011) Leading and managing change. In T Swanwick, J McKimm (eds) *ABC of clinical leadership* (pp 19–23). BMJ Books, Oxford

Kotter J (1996) *Leading change.* Harvard Business School Press, Boston, MA

Lewin K (1951) *Field theory in social science.* Harper & Row, London

Schwering RE (2003) Focusing leadership through Force Field Analysis: New variations on a venerable planning tool. *Leadership and Organization Development Journal* **24**(7): 361–70

Thomas P (2006) *Integrating primary health care – leading, managing, facilitating.* Radcliffe Publishing, Abingdon

Wenger E (1998) *Communities of practice: Learning, meaning and identity.* Cambridge University Press, Cambridge

Chapter 11

Better care in hospitals: Care adjustments for equal treatment

Jim Blair

Going into hospital can be a frightening experience. Imagine what it is like for someone with an intellectual disability who finds it hard to interpret and navigate such a frenetic environment. Add to this an individual who has some behaviours considered challenging or distressing, for example, screaming or head banging, and it is no wonder that such behaviours can be viewed as being part of the person's disability rather than the result of his or her ill health or general level of distress. This is known as diagnostic overshadowing (Gates and Barr, 2009) and occurs where no attempt is made to explore an underlying health problem or to consider another potentially treatable cause. When a new behaviour or an existing one escalates, it is essential to examine the causes behind the changes. A biological reason to explain differences in an individual's normal functioning should always be explored (Blair, 2012).

People with an intellectual disability are more likely to experience major illnesses that necessitate hospital admission (Disability Rights Commission, 2006) (see *Box 11.1*). The Department of Health (2001) in its document, *Valuing people*, reported that people with intellectual disabilities get a "worse deal" from health services than the rest of the population. *Death by indifference* (Mencap 2007)

Box 11.1. People in England with an intellectual disability and admissions to hospital

- There are 1 191 000 people with an intellectual disability.
- Of these, 285 000 are children (180 000 boys and 106 000 girls) aged 0–17 years.
- There are 905 000 adults aged over 18 (530 000 men and 375 000 women), of whom only 21% are known to intellectual disability services.
- The number of admissions to general hospitals which happen as emergencies is considerably higher for people with intellectual disabilities than for non-intellectually disabled people (50% compared to 31%).

Emerson et al (2012)

---

detailed the case histories of six individuals with intellectual disabilities who Mencap and the families felt died in healthcare settings from avoidable conditions.

The quality of care in the NHS and social services for people with learning disabilities is at best patchy, and at worst an indictment of our society.
(Parliamentary and Health Ombudsman, 2009)

Health service staff, particularly those working in general healthcare, have very limited knowledge about learning disability. They are unfamiliar with the legislative framework, and commonly fail to understand that a right to equal treatment does not mean treatment should be the same.
(Independent Inquiry into Access to Healthcare for People with Learning Disabilities, 2008: 7)

This lack of knowledge and insight is in part due to the paucity of learning opportunities related to people with intellectual disabilities within most health professional programmes.

Ensuring equal treatment does not mean that all treatment should be the same. For people such as those with intellectual disabilities it is necessary to make reasonable adjustments to care, as required by law under the Equality Act 2010, so that they can access the healthcare they need, thereby enhancing their health outcomes.

In 2012 Mencap published *Death by indifference: 74 deaths and counting.* This document provided a bleak reminder of the effect that healthcare inequalities continue to have on people with intellectual disabilities. In the report, Mencap highlights common failings such as ignoring vital advice from families and an inability of staff to meet basic care needs. Diagnostic overshadowing has led to individuals' untimely deaths.

This chapter uses examples from practice in leading change that illustrate how reasonable care adjustments can improve care and treatment experiences. Change is difficult because we often overestimate the value of what we have and underestimate the value of what we may gain by altering the way things are done. It is necessary to involve those who are to be affected by any change to be involved in its in planning, shaping, delivery and evaluation. An example of this is the Learning Disability: Our Health Our Hospital group set up at St George's Hospital in 2010 and chaired by people with an intellectual disability along with family carers and local charities.

Ensuring that the capacity to consent to treatment is appropriately assessed is vital, however, it is not the purpose of this chapter to go into depth about consent but rather to provide a guide using practical examples. This chapter mainly focuses on adults with intellectual disabilities but many of the issues and solutions can be applied to children as well as many other groups in society who experience health inequalities.

Getting it right: Improving care and experience

A change in attitude and value base is necessary to improve care and experience. This can be through using and demonstrating the efficacy of reasonably adjusted care that enables people to receive the care and treatment they need.

Reasonable adjustments

For care and treatment to be equitable reasonable adjustments are required to reduce inequalities. In health terms this means adjusting care so as to ensure everyone can access and receive the treatment they need in a way that suits their individual requirements (Blair, 2011). *Boxes 11.2, 11.3* and *11.4* demonstrate how making reasonable adjustments to how care is provided improves a person's experiences and health outcomes.

Box 11.2. Example from practice:
One-to-one support to ensure treatment

Earl has a mild intellectual disability as well as autism. He has poor vision and significant hearing loss. Earl requires dialysis that takes four hours. He understands why he needs dialysis and is able to make a capacitated decision to have it. However, after about 30 minutes of having the treatment he pulls the tubes out and decides he has had his treatment and it is time to go. Other healthcare colleagues suggest to me that since he has removed the tubes he does in fact lack capacity.

However, what Earl lacks is a concept of time, which does not equate with him lacking capacity but rather an inability to tell the time. In order for Earl to have the treatment he needs, a reasonable adjustment is put in place. This adjustment is to have a care assistant with him for the whole four-hour period to provide him with reassurance, distraction and conversation to encourage him to continue to have treatment. Over a period of sessions the length of time the care assistant is with him is reduced until he is able to have the treatment like anyone else. This adjustment means that Earl can now receive the care and treatment he needs.

Box 11.3. Example from practice: Changing the service to fit the person

Rosa has a mild intellectual disability and requires dialysis. She is refusing to have treatment, not because she did not want it or understand, but because the dialysis machine is making a noise that she finds disturbing. The solution found is to provide her with headphones, a side room and for her mother to be present.

This care adjustment is easy for the service to put in place and means that she has her treatment. Rosa now has her dialysis without her mother or her headphones and sleeps through the procedure because she is no longer worried about the noise. This adjustment to her treatment means that her quality of life is much improved.

Box 11.4. Example from practice: Understanding the person

Tariq has a severe intellectual disability and has limited verbal language. He came into hospital because he has fractured his hip. He finds the setting very noisy and interacting with ward staff difficult. However, he particularly likes Michael Jackson and once ward staff know this and that Tariq can express his feelings and mood through uttering a few words and sounds from songs in differing tones, they begin to feel comfortable engaging with him, and him with them. After a while many of the ward staff become fluent in Michael Jackson songs and highly skilled at interpreting Tariq's mood, pain levels and general well-being by the tone of the words of the songs he uses. This greatly enhances his care experience and reduces his and his family's anxieties.

The hospital passport

Hospital passports are completed by the individual and/or their family/carers prior to or during a hospital admission, and come in various forms. An example of the front page of a typical hospital passport is shown in *Figure 11.1*. People can acquire a hospital/health passport from their GP, community learning disability team, day services, the staff that support them, or when coming into hospital. These passports provide core information and ensure that people are at the heart of the care they receive. When they have been read and acted on, improvements in care have taken place. For example, a patient was bubbling up liquids and regurgitating food, which can be an indication of dysphagia. The medical consultant reading this acted on the information and made an immediate referral for a dysphagia assessment. In another case, the hospital passport helped

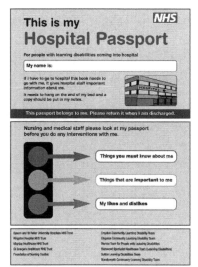

Figure 11.1. Example of the front page of a hospital passport.

one individual to receive a place in a rehabilitation service. This was because staff members in that service could see from the passport how the person usually functioned and were able to build achievable and measurable rehabilitation goals for the person. The information on a passport may also assist in addressing issues of diagnostic overshadowing.

Hospital passports can assist in enhancing health professionals' assessment of a person's capacity to consent. Over 85% of people with an intellectual disability who come into St George's Hospital have a hospital passport which staff find essential in providing tailored care. A dementia version, based on the intellectual disability hospital passport, has been introduced illustrating how changes can assist many other people.

Consent in practice

The Mental Capacity Act states that everyone is assumed to have capacity unless assessed as not having capacity regarding particular decisions. Decisions are time, location and decision-specific and it is essential to ensure that just because someone may lack capacity in one area of their life at a certain time this does not equate with a general lack of capacity. Capacity needs to be assessed and reassessed depending on the circumstances of the decision to be reached. The individuals must always be involved along with people who know them well who necessarily should be consulted.

Assessing capacity is a core part of practice and one that frequently requires clinicians to think and act creatively. A helpful tool to support the assessment of an individual's mental capacity to consent is the CURB BADLIP approach (Hoghton and Chadwick, 2010). See *Box 11.5*. *Box 11.6* uses an example from practice regarding a person, Martha's, capacity to agree to an operation. *Box 11.7* illustrates how to assess capacity by ensuring there are no leading questions, and

---

Box 11.5. CURB BADLIP assessment of capacity

CURB is used to assess and document capacity:
C   *Communicate.* Can the person communicate his or her decision?
U   *Understand.* Can he or she understand the information you are giving?
R   *Retain.* Can he or she retain the information given?
B   *Balance.* Can he or she balance or use the information?

If an individual does not have capacity, move onto BADLIP to consider if a decision can be made following a review of best interests:
B   *Best interest.* If the person lacks capacity can you make a best interest decision?
AD *Advanced Decision.* Is there an Advanced Decision to refuse treatment?
L   *Lasting Power of Attorney.* Has Lasting Power of Attorney been appointed?
I   *Independent Mental Capacity Advocate.* Is the person without anyone to be consulted about his or her best interest. In an emergency involve an Independent Mental Capacity Advocate.
P   *Proxy.* If unresolved conflicts exist, consider local ethics committee of the Court of Protection appointed deputy.

Hoghton and Chadwick (2010)

Box 11.6. Example from practice: Agreeing to an operation

Martha has a mild intellectual disability and a condition that is not curable. She understands that the proposed operation would not make her completely better but it would improve the quality of her life. Martha is able to respond clearly to questions and relay back information given to her to demonstrate she knows what she has been told.

When asked if she wanted the operation she responded, "I don't want the operation but I know I need it." This clearly illustrates that she has capacity.

Box 11.8 demonstrates how people can at times refuse treatment because they have not been given information in a manner they can understand.

**Box 11.7. Example from practice:
Assessing capacity and not leading the answers**

Karchi has a mild intellectual disability and has not been eating or drinking for a while. When asked what options have been offered to him to help him get better he says, "a tube". When asked what this is for he says, "food and drink". When asked where the tube for food and drink is to be placed he says, "in my tummy". Following this he is asked what happens if you do not have the "tube" put into your tummy for food and drink and Karchi replies, "I will fade away". Because fade away is an abstract term it was important to ascertain, as part of the Mental Capacity Act capacity assessment, whether or not he realises that without this he would die, thereby illustrating or otherwise a clear appreciation of what is at stake. Karchi breaks down in tears when told he would die if he did not have the tube put into his tummy. This shows he understands the gravity of the situation. He is then asked what he is going to do, to which he replies, "Give it a go". This clearly demonstrates his understanding but also, if he had said he did not want it, he would have been making a capacitated decision, however unwise others might think it.

This example sets out how a capacity assessment should be done. At no time was Karchi led into responses he did not wish to make and he provided the information at each turn without being given it beforehand. As a result it is a useful example of how to assess capacity.

**Box 11.8. Example from practice:
Refusing treatment because you do not understand**

Peter has a mild intellectual disability and a chronic breathing condition. He comes into the accident and emergency department with difficulty breathing. He is frightened and anxious. None of the doctors or nurses speaks to him about his condition in a way that he understands. The result is that Peter refuses to be treated and becomes very tearful. He asks to see the consultant learning disability nurse working in the hospital. When the nurse explains what can be done for him in a way Peter understands he agrees to receive the treatment.

This demonstrates the need to take time to break down information into a form that is tailored to the person receiving it to enable that individual to make a decision.

In order to improve the care and experiences of people with intellectual disabilities in hospitals it is imperative to involve them in planning, developing and delivering services in partnership with families, carers and professionals.

Learning Disability: Our Health Our Hospital

The group Learning Disability: Our Health Our Hospital was set up by the author to help improve care experiences and outcomes at St George's Hospital. The group is made up of six people with an intellectual disability, five parents and two chief executives of local intellectual disability charities. There are two co-chairs, both of whom have an intellectual disability and two co-vice chairs, one a parent and the other a chief executive of a local charity. The panel meets every six to eight weeks. The focus is on knowing what is happening in the hospital, what needs to be changed and what is going well. Members are on the hospital's Access Committee. Achievements include a member who has an intellectual disability ensuring that a changing places toilet will be created (to ensure that adults with severe physical disabilities can be changed in a dignified safe manner). The group has ensured that all information is presented in an accessible format and that the hospital has beds for carers of people with intellectual disabilities so they can stay overnight. Members of the group have also assisted in adapting and rolling out the hospital passport, teaching healthcare professionals, speaking at conferences, creating a patient experience evaluation tool, sitting on patient experience and interview panels in the hospital, and bringing their experiences to shape the services to meet their requirements. Practice can be improved by remembering the following:

- Talk and engage with the person directly as well as the carers, if present. It is imperative to find out who the carer is in relation to the person with intellectual disability and how well they know them.
- Remember people with an intellectual disability do become physically unwell and feel pain.
- Ensure that possible biological reasons for behaviour changes are explored.
- Always be aware that an adult has capacity unless assessed otherwise and that decisions are time, location and topic dependent. It is important to follow the Mental Capacity Act and always practice within it.
- Use a range of aids to assist communication, e.g. photos, symbols, the hospital communication book.
- Find out about the person's previous hospital experience(s), what worked and what did not work.

- Reduce stress for the person by finding out if he or she has favourite items.
- Use a hospital plan, such as a hospital passport or guidance of how the person behaves when in hospital or faced with a stressful situation, if it is available.
- Remember how individuals appear may not be how they really are.
- Remember to take time. If assessments and interactions are conducted properly the person's journey in the hospital as well as the diagnostic process will be much improved (Bradley, 2002).

Conclusion

Endless discussions about change can often be a barrier. Actively committing to undertaking something and then acting is what is required. This chapter has shown that we cannot change the future if we keep thinking as we do today. It is vital to reflect on the past while addressing the issues of the present in order to build for the future.

To provide effective and efficient change leadership it is important to articulate a compelling case for the change that is being sought. It is essential that leaders of change are trusted, proactive and involve those who are to be affected by change in a facilitative and strategic manner.

Reasonable adjustments to how care is delivered should ensure a significant reduction in the episodes of diagnostic overshadowing and assist in reducing health inequalities. Having skilled staff in senior positions within hospitals to be responsible, accountable and provide vision and leadership is not a luxury but essential if we are to avoid future deaths by indifference and subsequent investigations into appalling care practices.

In order to enhance the quality of care and treatment experiences it is vital that health professionals see the person rather than the disability and make sure they engage with and involve people with intellectual disabilities, their families and carers. Health professionals must also acknowledge that the experts are not them but rather those with intellectual disabilities and their families (Blair, 2010). Once this mindset has really taken root then the care and treatment of people with intellectual disabilities and their families will be much improved.

References

Blair J (2010) Service quality. In P Talbot, G Astbury, T Mason (eds) *Key concepts in learning disabilities* (pp 219–24). Sage, London

Blair J (2011) Care adjustments for people with learning disabilities in hospitals. *Nursing Management* **18**(8): 21–4

Blair J (2012) Caring for people who have intellectual disabilities. *Emergency Nurse* **20**(6): 15–19

Bradley E (2002) *Guidelines for managing the patient with intellectual disability in accident and emergency.* Available from: http://www.intellectualdisability.info/how-to../guidelines-for-managing-the-patient-with-intellectual-disability-in-accident-and-emergency?searchterm=hospital

Department of Health (2001) *Valuing people.* HMSO, London

Disability Rights Commission (2006) *Equal treatment: Closing the gap.* Disability Rights Commission, London

Emerson E, Baines S (2011) *Health inequalities and people with learning disabilities in the UK: 2010. Improving health and lives.* Learning Disability Observatory supported by Department of Health, London

Emerson E, Hatton C, Robertson J, Roberts H, Baines S, Evison F, Glover G (2012) *People with learning disabilities in England 2011. Improving health and lives.* Learning Disability Observatory supported by Department of Health, London. Available from: http://www.improvinghealthandlives.org.uk/securefiles/120524_0859//IHAL2012-04PWLD2011.pdf

Gates B, Barr O (2009) *Oxford handbook of learning and intellectual disability nursing.* Oxford University Press, Oxford

Hoghton M (2010) *A step by step guide for GP practices: Annual health checks for people with a learning disability.* Royal College of General Practitioners, London

Hoghton M, Chadwick S (2010) Assessing patient capacity. Remember CURB BADLIP in the UK. *British Medical Journal* **340**: C2767

Independent Inquiry into Access to Healthcare for People with Learning Disabilities (2008) *Healthcare for all?* Aldridge, London

Mencap (2007) *Death by indifference.* Mencap, London

Mencap (2012) *Death by indifference: 74 deaths and counting.* Mencap, London

Parliamentary Health Service Ombudsman (2009) *Six lives: The provision of public services to people with learning disabilities.* Parliamentary Health Service Ombudsman, London

Chapter 12

Learning disability intensive support teams

Jonathan Beebee

This chapter discusses Periodic Service Review as a leadership and management tool and describes in detail the elements of it. Many of these elements can be seen in other leadership and management initiatives. Comparisons are made with two of these initiatives, the National Leadership Framework (www.nhsleadership.org. uk) and Productive Community Services (www.institute.nhs.uk), the latter being a model from the Productive Series available from the NHS Institute for Innovation and Improvement.

Introduction

Applied behaviour analysis is the most evidence-based science in learning disability practice. The science began in 1968 (Baer et al, 1968) and has been the founder for many contemporary psychological behavioural therapies, such as cognitive behaviour therapy, acceptance and commitment therapy, and dialectic behaviour therapy.

The term "behaviour" is used to describe anything that people may do. When describing what people do, behaviour is described in observable terms that can be clearly understood and consistently used by everyone. Consider the descriptions in *Table 12.1* which are used with carers to improve the clarity of behaviour recordings.

Table 12.1. Descriptions of behaviours	
Vague terms	*Description of behaviour*
Anna is disruptive	Anna shouts loudly when a teacher talks to another pupil
Philip is obsessional	Philip replaces any ornaments that have been moved in his bedroom
Jane is attention seeking	Jane throws toys at her carers
Peter is upset	Peter is crying and pacing around the room
Bill is paranoid	Bill often asks if people are talking about him

In learning disability practice, positive behaviour support (Donnellan et al, 1988) has evolved from applied behaviour analysis. Practitioners of positive behaviour support aim to identify what function/purpose the target behaviours serve for the person and then address this in a non-aversive manner, such as teaching the person a more functional way to achieve what they want. A key principle of this is that, by positively promoting an equivalent behaviour, the target behaviours will reduce naturally as a positive side effect.

Applied behaviour analysis in management

As with many other sciences, applied behaviour analysis requires three levels of scientific enquiry: description, prediction, and control (Cooper et al, 2007). First the behaviour is described in clear behavioural terms, then it is measured to see when and where it occurs, which leads to the ability to predict when behaviours are more or less likely to happen. In the final stage, control is achieved by manipulating variables to make behaviours we aim to increase more likely and behaviours we want to reduce less likely.

The use of applied behaviour analysis is not restricted to healthcare. Other fields where it has been used include:

- Education
- Sports
- Retail
- Military
- Parenting
- Criminal justice
- Management.

The use of applied behaviour analysis in management is not new and the Journal of Organisational Behaviour Management has been published since 1977. The terms "manipulating variables" and "control" described above are scientific and may not sit comfortably with our humanistic approaches to leadership and management. But how can we lead or manage other people without influencing some form of "control" over the behaviours of others? Other authors have highlighted similar issues.

"Management" within services for people with intellectual disability frequently does not manage. There is a strong tradition of allowing autonomy of decision *making by front-line staff, often bolstered by the asinine arguments that they "know the person best". In effect, as a "management" style, failure to direct front-line staff typically conceals a poverty of skills and ideas on the part of managers about what should be done.*

(Kiernan, 1997: 250)

Those who don't know how to manage are managing those who don't know what to do.

(LaVigna et al, 1994: 4)

Periodic Service Review

Periodic Service Review (LaVigna et al, 1994) is a model for leadership and management that combines organisational behaviour management (www.obmnetwork. com) with total quality management (Deming, 1986). It then frames this with the same values as positive behaviour support. If we are using this approach to manage the behaviours of people we care for why should we not use this for managing our teams? If we can change people's behaviours using positive non-aversive methods, why would we not use these positive approaches with our staff?

As leaders and managers we may have performance issues with team members. We may use vague terms to describe these difficulties, such as lazy, lacks motivation, under-achiever. Deming famously said that 94% of performance issues are the responsibility of management (1994: 33). Periodic Service Review begins with the unquestionable belief that all staff want to do their very best. Where staff are under-performing 94% of the time this will be the result of management not giving a clear description about what is expected, or the organisational systems not supporting the person effectively to perform well. The aims of Periodic Service Review are to provide managers and leaders with the tools to address these issues.

Periodic Service Review has four key areas: performance standards, performance monitoring, feedback, and staff training.

Performance standards

In practice, when we assess service users' behaviours we develop clear operationalised definitions of what the target behaviours look like so anyone who sees them will know exactly whether the person has or has not shown these behaviours before. For Periodic Service Review we try to do the same for staff behaviours. We develop performance standards that describe exactly what would be seen if the job were done well. In this way, staff know clearly what is expected of them.

There is a true bottom-up approach to developing standards, and staff should be asked what standards the service they provide should be measured upon. The guidance on selecting standards is to start by asking what is important to the people we serve? How would the people who receive our service know we are doing a good job? Secondly, what standards should we set to show that we are meeting our administrative demands? What are the important administrative tasks that support us in doing our jobs well? And finally, what standards do we want to set to measure that we are meeting external demands, such as Care Quality Commission standards (Care Quality Commission, 2010), NHS trust standards, or professional standards.

A truly person-centred service that sets good quality person-centred standards will generally be meeting administrative and external standards (LaVigna et al, 1994). For example, the following is a standard used by Southampton Intensive Support Team to review files:

> *The paper file contains a copy of an accessible care plan that has been signed by the service user, or it is clearly documented that the person is unable to consent.*

The Intensive Support Team strives to ensure that service users are involved in their care as much as possible, and in so doing inadvertently meets Care Quality Commission standards relating to service user involvement, and the legal requirements of consent.

If we set standards relating to everything the team does, the list would be endless. The following advice should support the development of high impact standards and keep monitoring manageable:

- *Identify the essential element in a process.* If this standard is met, other standards will be met too, for example, a signed care plan reflects information is understood by service users, the principles of the Mental Capacity Act 2005 have been followed, and the person has been involved in care planning.
- *Group similar standards.* For example, if the team has a standard about accessible information it may be fair to assume that communication needs have been considered, person-centred approaches used, and advocacy sought where required.

- *Monitor end products.* For example, a good quality care plan should be the product of a good quality assessment. If auditing care plans shows that a good quality assessment has taken place you may be able to avoid the necessity to audit the assessment.
- *Randomly sample pieces of work.* It would be impossible to review all care plans every week. A selection of files can be randomly selected to be audited. If the sample is genuinely random the team is motivated to maintain high standards for all.

When standards are being developed for the team it is vital that they reflect team outputs and do not publicly single out one individual's performance. Individual standards should be reflected in the individual's own Periodic Service Review and should be reviewed in individual supervision (LaVigna et al, 1994)

When deciding how challenging to make the standards, it can be appealing to set them at the team's average performance. This, however, will only lead to an average team. The targets will be too easy to meet and will provide no motivation for the team to strive to do its best. Another attractive option may be to set the standards at the level when the team achieved its best. This may have been just before a planned inspection when the team strived to get everything in good order. This would be a good option. However, the recommended option is to ask team members what they think the service should strive to achieve. Team members who set the standards themselves will have better ownership of them and more drive to achieve them. Teams will often set standards higher than the expectations of the team leader (LaVigna et al, 1994).

Performance monitoring

Annual audits, inspections or benchmarks give a snap-shot of how a team is performing at a particular moment. Reactive corrective actions may be taken as a result of these checks. However, as time passes people may forget the importance, and performance will slip into established poor practice. Periodic Service Review proactively monitors performance on a continuous basis. To begin with Periodic Service Review is carried out weekly and frequent monitoring leads to rapid improvement (LaVigna et al, 1994). When scores reach 85%, monitoring can change to monthly.

A key aspect in monitoring is team involvement. The team sets the standards, takes part in monitoring these standards, and then identifies opportunities for improvement. Monitoring also permits staff comments to be heard and Periodic

Service Review score sheets have space for comments. There may be a valid reason why standards have not been met. It is important to stay faithful to the standards and say whether or not they were met, but reasons for not meeting them need to be acknowledged as this can help to identify solutions in the future. Staying faithful to Periodic Service Review standards ensures the team knows that a good review score means good performance and not lenience. The same score should be achieved whoever performs the review.

In keeping with team ownership of the Periodic Service Review it is vital that new standards are not added unless the team agrees. If standards are added by management, the team will feel the review has been imposed upon it. If the team owns the standards and goals it will be keen to address them.

Standards that are monitored regularly will be well known and available to everyone. This is preferable to the team leader raising concerns at random with the team. It may not be necessary for the team leader to raise concerns as these will be transparent.

Feedback

Similar to positive behaviour support, Periodic Service Review strives to provide only positive feedback. When scoring a Review, standards are not marked with ticks or crosses. A "+" is given if the standard has been met, and "O" for Opportunities is given where there are opportunities for improvement. This is to reflect that the Review is not used to persecute team members for what they have not done, it is looking for where there are opportunities for improvement. (See *Appendix 2*.)

Periodic Service Review results are measured, analysed, summarised and displayed in the team office as a graph. Visual feedback is one of the most powerful tools in behaviour change (LaVigna et al, 1994). When discussing the results it is vital that the team leader gives only positive feedback. This sets the tone for how the team is expected to interact with people who use the service.

Feeding back to the team a low review score, such as 30%, may appear challenging, but if you were not using Periodic Service Review (or similar system) you would not know what you had achieved and what needed to be done. The team will at least know that 30% of the standards are being achieved and the 70% not achieved will be clearly defined so the team can easily identify which standard they would like to focus their attention on.

The target is to achieve 85% of the standards. Achieving 100% indicates the standards are not stretching the service enough and there is no motivation to strive to do better. In this situation, it is likely that team members would not see the need to check quality, and standards would start to slip. When service review is first implemented scores are expected to be between 25% and 35%.

When feeding back results to the team it is important to remember the responsibility for not meeting the standard sits with the team leader; 94% of performance is the responsibility of the manager. It may be that the standard has not been clearly explained to the team or set too high or needs to be reworded for clarification. The standards are a platform for discussing performance targets and do not need to be set in stone. There may also be an aspect of the service delivery that inhibits achievement of a standard that the manager can address.

There may be occasions when an individual's performance is causing concern. Individual Periodic Service Reviews related to job descriptions can help identify what the challenges are for the person. In the same manner as the team review, a supportive approach to improving standards can be adopted. If this is not successful following support for the person, disciplinary action may be instigated. This would be the very last resort. By using a Periodic Service Review system for individual performance management, disciplinary procedures are less personal. If a person needs to face disciplinary action this may be due to a mismatch between the person and the job, and not due to failings of the individual.

Staff training

Sending staff on training is an easy option for improving staff performance. However, the competencies the person will gain from attending training, and the impact this will have on practice are frequently not clearly expressed or monitored.

Staff training in Periodic Service Review is mainly focused on in-house or self-directed learning opportunities. Specific competency-based criteria are set to measure how the person's work practice will look if the training has been effective and this is monitored with a competency-based criterion-referenced checklist – a brief Periodic Service Review in its own right.

Competence is measured on three levels: the ability to display oral competence (verbally describe the skill), the ability to role play competence (demonstrate skills in a simulated situation), and the ability to show "*in vivo*" competence (demonstrate skills in real-life settings). For example, a care plan may be developed relating to responding to aggressive incidents. Firstly, you would ask the person to describe verbally the content of the care plan, then you would ask the person to role play how he or she would implement the plan, and finally you would observe the person putting the plan into practice. The observations in practice can be regularly reviewed to monitor consistency.

Using one system to monitor all

In practice, many different forms of auditing and monitoring are usually in place. These can include supervision and appraisal, benchmarks, meeting key performance indicators, incident reporting, managing budgets, service user feedback, and many more. Information from these different forms of monitoring are usually scored in different ways. For example, some may be scored as a percentage, some by ranking out of five, some using a red, amber, and green scale, some reflecting on qualitative comments, and some on whether or not the standard has been met.

When using Periodic Service Review to monitor team performance it makes sense to transform all monitoring systems to Periodic Service Reviews, which in effect serve as sub-reviews. These sub-reviews can then feed into the overall team review. For example, in the Southampton Intensive Support Team there is a Periodic Service Review to monitor the quality of paper health records. In the team review there is a standard that states, "The sampled file scores 85% or greater on the secondary paper file Periodic Service Review standards".

By adopting all forms of audit and monitoring to Reviews, one system is achieving total quality assurance. Information on how the team is performing in general and in specific areas is easily accessible.

Comparisons with other leadership and management initiatives

Interest in using a behaviour-based approach to performance is growing. Many services now use staff behaviours for appraisal purposes (for example, see the appraisal policy of Southern Health Foundation NHS Trust, 2011). The key elements of Periodic Service Review can also be seen in national leadership initiatives.

The Productive Series (www.institute.nhs.uk) is a recent NHS initiative to reduce waste and improve output. Many of the modules within this series have elements related to Periodic Service Review. The clearest link is the "Knowing how we are doing" module, where the team decides what standards it wants to be monitored against. It sets monitoring systems and the results are publicly displayed and frequently discussed. The "Standard care procedures" module is highly relevant too. Here standardised processes are established so that everyone is clear how procedures should be done and what the quality indicators are.

The NHS Leadership Framework (www.nhsleadership.org.uk) sets out a single set of competencies that can be applied to anyone working in an NHS setting. There are five domains, and an additional two aimed at staff in senior positions. Each domain has four descriptors for the behaviour, knowledge, skills and attitudes expected for each element. These can be used to evaluate the competence of leaders. The "Managing services" domain is particularly relevant, and using Periodic Service Review demonstrates how the competencies within this are achieved. For example, under "Managing performance" one competency states, "Competent leaders analyse information from a range of sources about performance". In a Periodic Service Review, information is collected frequently from a range of sources and this information is shared with the team to identify areas for improvement.

Summary and reflections on practice

The model of intervention used in intensive support teams is positive behaviour support, which has evolved from the science of applied behaviour analysis. Periodic Service Review has been described as a method for applying the science of applied behaviour analysis to management while utilising the positive philosophies of positive behaviour support for team leadership.

Many comparisons can be made with Periodic Service Review and other initiatives for leadership and management. Periodic Service Review is a system that can be used in contemporary practice to lead the delivery of high quality healthcare, which reflects the positive principles used with service users to staff members.

At the time of writing the Southampton Intensive Support Team has been using Periodic Service Review for total quality management for six months. The team Review score sheet and graph can be seen in *Appendices 2* and *3*, respectively. From first using the Review the standards have significantly changed as it has provided a platform for discussion between what the standards initially were and what is achievable in practice. The graph in *Appendix 3* demonstrates the improvements achieved by its implementation.

At 20 weeks the team agreed to move from weekly monitoring to monthly, although they were only at 76%. The reason for this was that the remaining opportunities could not be addressed quickly and therefore continuing to be regularly reminded of these opportunities was of no further benefit.

Despite the team leader's efforts to keep feedback positive, some team members had a long history of feedback that was not positive and struggled to see there was no aversiveness imposed by the review, other than the natural tendency to be critical of self. These team members found adapting to a culture of regular monitoring and feedback difficult. There is ongoing support to help adaptation to this process.

Overall, the team speaks highly of Periodic Service Review and can clearly see the benefits. The team is also able to describe clearly how quality and outcomes are being reviewed to the trust and commissioners. The team continues to use the Periodic Service Review monthly and to make additions and amendments as practice changes.

References

Baer DM, Wolf MM, Risley TR (1968) Some current dimensions of applied behaviour analysis. *Journal of Applied Behaviour Analysis* **1**(1): 91–7

Care Quality Commission (2010) *Essential standards of quality and safety: Guidance about compliance.* Care Quality Commission, London

Cooper JO, Heron TE, Heward WL (2007) *Applied behaviour analysis* (2nd edn). Merrill Publishing, New York

Deming WE (1986) *Out of the crisis.* Massachusetts Institute of Technology Press, Massachusetts

Deming WE (1994) *The new economics for industry, government and education.* Massachusetts Institute of Technology Press, Massachusetts

Donnellan AM, LaVigna GW, Negri-Shoultz N, Fassbender LL (1988) *Progress without punishment.* Teachers College Press, New York

Kiernan C (1997) Future directions. In RSP Jones, CB Eayers (eds). *Challenging behaviour and intellectual disability: A psychological perspective.* BILD, Cleveland

LaVigna GW, Willis TJ, Shaull JF, Abedi M, Sweitzer M (1994) *The periodic service review: A total quality assurance system for human services and education.* Paul H Brookes, Baltimore

Organisational Behaviour Management Network (2012) *About organizational behavior management (OBM).* Available from: http://www.obmnetwork.com/what_is_obm/definition_description_common_applications

Southern Health Foundation NHS Trust (2012) *Appraisal policy.* Available from: http://www.southernhealth.nhs.uk/hr/myjob/appraisals/

Appendix I

Periodic Service Review for Southampton Intensive Support Team

Operational definitions

1. *Administrative and general*
A. Job performance standards
   i. Each member of staff is evaluated monthly in a supervision session using individual performance standards and these are documented on an individual performance graph. To achieve this target 85% or greater of performance graphs will be submitted to the team leader, and graphs will not be more than one month old.
   ii. 85% or more of staff members are maintaining performance levels of 85% or better (maintaining is defined as three consecutive scores at this level).
   iii. A randomly sampled file has a protocol that documents verbal competence has been assessed for non-registered practitioners in the team who are identified on the case weighting tool as coming into contact with that person. The + is given if the non-registered practitioner and the checking registered practitioner has signed the protocol.
   iv. The randomly sampled file has a Periodic Service Review that reflects the protocol and a registered practitioner has used this to give feedback to a non-registered practitioner or a direct carer. The + is given if a scored review (protocol-related) is in the file and there is evidence of its use.
B. Team performance standards
   i. 85% or greater of team members have an up-to-date appraisal and workforce planning has received signed confirmation of this. The + is not achieved if the team leader receives notification of appraisals being out of date for more than one team member. A 30-day window is acceptable.
   ii. 85% or greater of team members have attended a minimum of one external training event in the last 12 months that is linked to their appraisal and Intensive Support Team practice. This is evidenced on the team training log. This is to exclude team members who, for whatever reason, are not working in the team for more than 3 months.

iii. 85% of team members' statutory and mandatory training is up to date as evidenced on the training and development website. A 30-day window is acceptable.

iv. The "training delivered" log is reviewed at the monthly extended team meeting and is up to date with training that has been delivered to direct carers. The training log provides evidence that assessments and interventions have been presented to others.

v. The spot check of the office environment finds no confidential information on display and the office is clean and well kept to at least 80% of the office standards.

vi. There are no position vacancies in the intensive support team and all posts are recruited to whole time equivalents as specified in operational policy.

vii. The previous periodic service review was done on time and the current review graph is displayed in Intensive Support Team office

C. Client case files

i. Team secondary paper files are neat, organised, and up to date, meeting Trust and professional standards for record keeping. Evaluation will be based upon a random sample of one file checked against the secondary paper file standards and achieving 85% or more of these standards.

ii. The same person's electronic case record is checked against the electronic case record standards checklist and meets 85% or more of these standards.

2. *Team meetings*

A. Attendance

i. Team meetings for the last four weeks have been attended by 80% or more of the current working team. Working team is defined as the team that is in post, not on annual leave, not on study leave, not on sick leave, and not on maternity leave. This will be evident in the team meeting minutes. A + is given if all meetings in the last four weeks have 80% attendance or greater.

ii. 100% of the last four Community Learning Disability Team meetings have been attended by an Intensive Support Team representative. This will be evidenced by the Community Learning Disability Team attendance sign off sheet.

B. Client reviews

    i.   At the last team meeting 90% of people's reviews were performed within the four week standard. This is evaluated by reviewing Intensive Support Team meeting minutes. A + is scored if client feedbacks for all people in the last week are in client feedbacks in any of the preceding four team meetings. An exception for this domain are new referrals who were fed back in the last two meetings who have not been previously discussed.

    ii. All client feedbacks at the Intensive Support Team team meeting have a progress note within the last four weeks evidencing that the Community Learning Disability Team named healthcare professional has received an update from the Intensive Support Team on the work with the service user.

3. *New referrals*
A. Criteria

    i.   All new referrals accepted by the team meet the team's agreed criteria. This will be evidenced on the referral agreement form. A random sample of one new referral in the last four week period will be used to review this. If there are no new referrals the score from the last review will be carried forward.

B. Process

    i.   Using a randomly sampled file, a qualified team member will have met with the Community Learning Disability Team referrer within two working days of verbal agreement to complete the referral agreement form. This timescale will be documented on the referral agreement form by documenting the date the verbal request was made and the date signed by the Community Learning Disability Team member.

    ii. The initial face-to-face contact is made within five working days of the signed referral agreement form as evidenced by progress note on the client's electronic record.

    iii. The new referral will be discussed at an Intensive Support Team meeting within two weeks of the referral agreement form being completed. This is documented on Intensive Support Team meeting minutes.

    iv. An assessment care plan is available on the client's electronic record.

    v. The assessment care plan is available within two weeks of referral.

     vi.   The initial care plan will be shared with the person or carers within four weeks if appropriate. A paper copy of the shared care plan will be available in the secondary paper file indicating the date shared and agreed. If this is not appropriate the best interest box on the consent form will be ticked and the reason for this will be clearly documented on the client's electronic record.

    vii. A multi-agency meeting is arranged within six weeks of referral to share information on assessment to date and to develop an agreed formulation of need. This will be evidenced by a progress note on the client's electronic record detailing attendance at a multi-agency meeting.

4. *Behaviour assessments*
      i.   A completed behaviour assessment is available in the randomly sampled file. This is not applicable if the file is less than eight weeks old or the process form indicates a behaviour assessment is not required.
      ii. There is a behaviour assessment report Periodic Service Review completed and filed behind this report.

5. *Interventions*
   A. Intervention plans
      i.   An intervention plan based upon positive behaviour support is available in a random sample of client electronic record files. This is not applicable if the file is less than eight weeks old or the process form indicates that a positive behaviour support plan is not required.
      ii. There is a positive behaviour support Periodic Service Review completed and filed behind this report.
   B. Delivery
      i.   There is evidence in the secondary paper file of how protocols have been shared with carers and competence has been assessed.
      ii. The client's electronic record progress notes describe how protocols have been delivered by Intensive Support Team staff alongside carers to role model or support care delivery.
   C. Monitoring
      i.   Data gathering procedures are in place to monitor the effect of intervention on target behaviours and there is a graph of this data available in the secondary paper file. The + is given if graphed data is

available. This is not applicable if the process form indicates a graphed baseline is not required.

ii. Graphs demonstrate that for at least one behaviour there is a reduction in frequency or severity, or an increased achievement of functional alternative behaviours consistently for the last three data points.

iii. The person has an active Care Programme Approach evidenced by a Intensive Support Team progress note of attendance, or minutes being available.

6. *Evaluation*

A file closed in four to eight weeks before the Periodic Service Review is chosen randomly. If no files have been closed, the score from the last available review will be carried forward. Use the Team's files spreadsheet to pick a closed file.

i. The file contains a discharge summary sheet that has been submitted to admin and completed within two weeks of last client contact. Pre and post outcome measure scores are included in this and show that intervention has reduced the individual's level of need.

ii. The discharge summary sheet documents quality of life improvements that the person has achieved during team involvement.

iii. Keeping track, or alternative engagement assessment, scores have been updated and demonstrate an increase in activity levels or the person is in employment.

iv. The individual's Periodic Service Review has been shared with care providers more than four weeks before the person was closed. Carers were taught how to carry this out. Intensive Support Team staff conducted fidelity checks on care providers completing individual Periodic Service Reviews and fidelity checks scored 85% or more on three occasions. This information is in the secondary paper file.

v. Feedback forms received in the last month contain positive feedback on 80% or more forms. Feedback is discussed at team meetings, minuted and considerations for service improvements are contained in the minutes. If no feedback has been received in the last four weeks the previous score is carried forward.

vi. A discharge report and letter has been sent to the person, referrer, carer, GP and any other key individuals and details maintenance procedures for the carers and Community Learning Disability Team and a date is stated when a three month follow up has been arranged.

Appendix 2

Periodic Service Review for Southampton Intensive Support Team

	Score Sheet		
	Date of evaluation:		
	Evaluator:		
Item	*Responsibilities*	*+/O*	*Comments*
I.	*Administrative and general*		
A.	Job performance standards		
i.	Monthly individual reviews		
ii.	85% performance level		
iii.	Protocol verbal competence		
iv.	Periodic service review to check protocol		
B.	Team performance standards		
i.	Appraisals		
ii.	External training		
iii.	Statutory and mandatory training		
iv.	Training log		
v.	Staff environment		
vi.	Recruitment		
vii.	Last periodic service review		
C.	Client case files		
i.	Secondary paper file standards		
ii.	The client's electronic record standards		
2.	*Team meetings*		
A.	Attendance		
i.	Intensive Support Team present		
ii.	Intensive Support Team at MDT		
B.	Client reviews		
i.	Within four weeks		
ii.	Progress not updated to Community Learning Disability Team		

3.	*New referrals*		
A.	Criteria		
B.	Process		
i.	Referral agreement form two days		
ii.	Face-to-face within five days		
iii.	Intensive Support Team discussion within two weeks		
iv.	Assessment care plan		
v.	In two weeks		
vi.	Shared care plan		
vii.	Multi-agency meeting		
4.	*Behaviour assessments*		
i.	Behaviour assessment available		
ii.	Behaviour assessment Periodic Service Review available		
5.	*Intervention*		
A.	Intervention plans		
i.	Positive behaviour support plan		
ii.	Positive behaviour support Periodic Service Review		
B.	Delivery		
i.	Protocol training checklists completed		
ii.	Role modelling/shadowing		
C.	Monitoring		
i.	Graphs		
ii.	Descending behaviour trends/ascending functional behaviours		
iii.	Active Care Programme Approach		
6.	*Evaluation*		
i.	Discharge summary		
ii.	Qualitative quality of life		
iii.	Keeping track		
iv.	Fidelity checks		
v.	Feedback scores		
vi.	Discharge letter and three month follow up		

Total score possible:	Total score achieved:
Percentage score:	
Comments/issues/recommendations:	

Appendix 3

Southampton Intensive Support Team: Periodic Service Review results graph

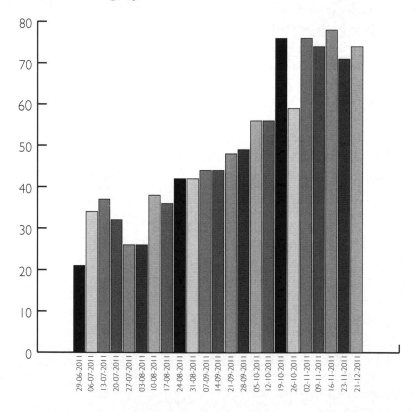

Note: On 23 November monitoring changed from weekly to monthly.

Chapter 13

Practice leadership in community forensic learning disability services

Carl Benton and Rachael Garvey

Introduction

Learning disability ideology has changed considerably over recent years from a hospital to a more community-focused agenda. Social policy has set out how people with learning disabilities can be empowered to exercise their rights and supported to live fully integrated lives within their own communities (Department of Health, 2001, 2009a). Consequently, this group is now more likely to become involved in the criminal justice system, both as victims and perpetrators, with Department of Health figures estimating that 3% of the learning disabled population living in the community have a conviction (Department of Health, 2007a).

Alongside social policy is recognition that learning disabled offenders are a homogenous group within the wider definition of mentally disordered offenders that require specialist intervention. Policy documents have highlighted the need to recognise learning disability within the criminal justice system due to the complex needs of this group (Department of Health and Home Office, 1992; Department of Health, 1993, 2007a, 2009b, 2011; Prison Reform Trust, 2008). These documents acknowledge the need for greater collaboration between health professionals and the criminal justice system. A new specialist multi-professional role and specialist service provision have been created as a consequence (Benton and Roy, 2008). Many challenges are recognised that require careful balancing, such as risk, individual rights and therapeutic interventions. To confound these challenges are the legal frameworks of the criminal justice system, the Mental Health Act 1983 as amended in 2007, the Human Rights Act 1998, the Mental Capacity Act 2005 and the Deprivation of Liberty Safeguards 2008. To ensure a progressive, quality service there is a need for effective leadership.

This chapter reflects on a specialist integrated multi-professional service for people with a learning disability who offend. It explores how leadership enables the balance between risk and autonomy, rights and responsibilities and considers staff qualities and their needs.

Rights and responsibilities

Since the 1990s there has been a greater emphasis on community living and inclusion for people with learning disabilities. While this move may have had a positive impact on the recognition and upholding of service users' rights and autonomy; it also brings about the expectations of accepting responsibility as a citizen within the wider community (Carson, 1993; Greig, 2007). Therefore, behaviours that may have previously been informally managed by clinical teams within institutionalised settings may now be present within a community setting and directly affect the public (Benton and Roy, 2008). Consequently, this has a direct impact on how risks are managed which are now more likely to receive attention from criminal justice agencies (Murphy and Clare, 1998).

In view of this it is believed that there has been an evolving clinical response from practitioners in forensic services supporting people with learning disabilities, which is underpinned by theoretically derived knowledge, practice and social policy. This response is not necessarily echoed within mainstream learning disability services and can lead to divergence regarding intervention if service users access support from a number of services.

Historically, there is evidence to suggest that practitioners have had an extremely high tolerance towards offending behaviour, including hesitance in reporting offences (Lyall et al, 1995) and protecting service users from experiencing the negative consequences of socially unacceptable behaviour (Seaward and Rees, 2001). However, more current guidance recognises that contact with the criminal justice system may be appropriate to aid the learning disabled offenders to understand consequences, take responsibility for actions and make more appropriate choices in future about their behaviour (Greig, 2007).

Balancing person-centred approaches and autonomy within a clinical practitioner's duty of care, legal restrictions, beneficence and non-maleficence is complex and requires a reflective model of practice (Smith et al, 2010). Indeed Mohabeersingh and Jukes (2007) suggest that to embed person-centred approaches requires substantial changes away from service-led and paternalistic approaches to care provision. Practitioners therefore are often faced with both ethical and legal dilemmas that require frequent supervision and support from the multi-professional team.

A challenge for services in the support and management of learning disabled offenders is the impact of legislative developments and interagency working. The impact of individuals' impairments and diagnosis on their ability to proceed in criminal justice processes must also be considered.

Legal tests, such as fitness for interview and fitness to plead, require interagency collaboration between health and criminal justice agencies, with assessment outcomes often determining the future management of learning disabled individuals who may have offended. Current literature (Jacobson and Talbot, 2009) questions whether existing legal tests and subsequent actions safeguard an individual's rights under legislation such as the Human Rights Act 1998 and the Equality Act 2010, for example, the use of reasonable adjustments to uphold an individual's right to a fair trial.

Within the criminal justice system there is a requirement to ensure safeguards for vulnerable persons, such as appropriate adult requirement for police interviews (Police and Criminal Evidence Act 1984). Compliance with this guidance and legal requirements is dependent on the recognition of a person's learning disability in the first instance. Evidence suggests that a number of learning disabled individuals pass through the criminal justice system without being recognised and there are no consistent evidenced-based screening procedures (Jacobson and Talbot, 2009; Department of Health, 2009b, 2009c). However, recent developments can be observed in practice with the development of the Learning Disability Screening Questionnaire being piloted and used in the prison population (Prison Reform Trust, 2010).

Where an individual who has capacity accepts responsibility for an offence, police may seek an outcome such as a caution or local community victim resolution. In practice, health service professionals can consider such resolutions less significant than a conviction through the courts, thereby allowing the minimising of the offence by either the individual or services when reviewing the offence in the historical context for future offence-specific work. Community treatment orders imposed by the courts can provide a structure for both the offender and professionals. Once applied, such orders can enable health practitioners to concentrate on an individual's rehabilitation rather than being responsible for the application of restrictions. Once applied, such orders can enable health practitioners to concentrate on an individual's rehabilitation rather than being responsible for the application of restrictions. However, in our experience service users may not fully understand the impact of the legal orders on their liberty, including future consequences of a criminal record. There may be hesitation in applying the same legal outcomes to this service user group as their mainstream counterparts by professionals in criminal justice agencies, even when the seriousness of the offence would warrant such action.

Given such complexity, the practitioner has an important role in communication, as from experience it is more often people with mild to moderate learning disabilities that access forensic services, and communication difficulties can go unrecognised. The offender may be able to verbalise and so communication difficulties may not be apparent. An essential requirement of a learning disability forensic practitioner is to identify communication difficulties and to provide support to develop effective communication channels. Unless effective communication occurs, engagement into a therapeutic relationship may be unattainable and affect future outcomes. Issues of suggestibility and acquiescence (Clare and Gudjohonsson, 1993) should also be considered when people with a learning disability are interviewed.

Observation skills and the analysis of observational data are considered crucial to establishing differences between challenging and offending behaviour. The practitioner's skills will be required in analysing causation to identify behaviours that are exhibited to communicate a need, or seek evidence of criminogenic risk factors that predispose, lead and maintain offending behaviour. This can often be a consultative role to generic learning disability services to support the development of future intervention strategies, balancing the observed need while considering the service user's views.

In the case where a person is convicted and a sentence received, learning disabled offenders may have difficulties upholding or achieving requirements of their sentence. This scenario again requires collaborative working to ensure an individual's behaviour is not criminalised due to unrecognised or unsupported impairments.

Risk and autonomy

Balancing risk and autonomy is always a challenge when working with offenders with learning disabilities in the community. Managing this within the Mental Health Act (1983, as amended in 2007) or community criminal justice legal framework is difficult; managing without is fraught with risk for the practitioner and the multi-professional team, organisation and wider community. It requires open discussions with the service user and the multi-agency team, resulting in clear risk assessments, care plans and relapse-management plans, communicated effectively to service users and the professionals involved in their care. The dichotomy of person-centred care and imposed restrictions within forensic practice requires practitioners to allow the maximum level of service user involvement given changes within their medico-legal status. Upholding the ethos of person-centred care can be difficult for practitioners within the field to manage, however, more recent frameworks have been developed to support this.

Recent theorists have suggested the Good Lives Model as a way of working with offenders (Ward and Brown, 2004). This model highlights the importance of a positive approach to treatment, how good lives affect risk management, causal conditions to engage meaningfully in treatment, motivating offenders, and forming a positive therapeutic relationship. The Good Lives Model suggests rehabilitation aimed at giving people the skills to lead fulfilling lives thereby reducing recidivism. It has been argued that the Good Lives Model lacks empirical research (Bonta and Andrews, 2003; Ogloff and Davis, 2004), and a Risk–Need–Responsivity Model based on management and a reduction of the dynamic risk factors has been suggested as an alternative. Both models appear to add value in managing this service user group and clear and effective leadership will provide a focus in individual cases. Adopting the Good Lives Model enhances person-centred approaches reinforcing the notion of rights, responsibility and autonomy.

Best practice guidance published by the Department of Health (2007b) advocates that practitioners seek to support service users in a culture of positive risk taking with defensible decision making, rather than being risk averse, which potentially can lead to excessively restrictive management and protracted lengths of detention in care settings. It has been suggested that risk aversion can lead to increased dependency and disability for some service users (Koubel, 2012). Positive risk taking requires an understanding of the benefits, for a service user, in taking an identified risk, with multi-agency consideration of risk assessment in the aid to rehabilitation for the individual while developing both proactive and reactive strategies (Morgan, 2004).

Developments with risk assessment tools used within specialist forensic services offer clinicians a method to collate and consider empirically derived risk factors using a structured clinical judgement model, for example, the Historical-Clinical-Risk-20 (HCR-20; Webster et al, 1997), the Sexual Violence Risk-20 (SVR-20; Boer et al, 1997), and the Risk for Sexual Violence Protocol (Hart et al, 2003). While these identified methods of risk assessment were initially derived for mentally disordered offenders generally, research has addressed the validity of their use within the learning disabled offender population (Blacker et al, 2011; Lindsay et al, 2011). Boer et al (2010a, 2010b) identified "qualifiers" for additional consideration when applying the HCR 20 and the SVR-20 to offenders with learning disabilities.

More recently the ARMIDILO (Assessment of Risk and Manageability of Intellectually Disabled Individuals who Offend; Boer et al, 2004) has considered not only risk factors but also protective factors in the management of learning disabled offenders. Initial research findings indicate a good predictive measure

171

of recidivism (Blacker, 2009) and also a framework which can be used for regular review to identify changes in risk. We feel this approach can support a clinical team in positive risk taking, by recording and reviewing the data used in making decisions about a service user's care and assessing the effectiveness of interventions adopted. Care needs to be taken that the goals of interventions are not seen in the first instance as public protection to the detriment of therapeutic outcomes for the service user (Coffey and Hewitt, 2010). Practitioners therefore need to develop effective therapeutic alliances to involve service users in this process, and link it in with their aspirations to achieve a balance between risk and autonomy.

Nursing skills, personal qualities and leadership

Research (Mason, 2002; Bowring-Lossock, 2006; Kettles and Woods, 2006; Mason et al, 2009) has identified skills, knowledge, competencies and desirable personal qualities that the forensic mental health nurse role demands (*Boxes 13.1* and *13.2*).

Box 13.1. Skills, knowledge and competencies needed by forensic mental health nurses

- Ability to assess and manage risk with knowledge of actuarial and clinical evidence-based risk assessments.
- Observation skills for the supervision of patients and monitoring of behaviour.
- Communication skills including written, verbal, listening and non-verbal.
- Interpersonal skills such as self-awareness, reflection and the ability to forge and maintain therapeutic relationships.
- Planning and delivering therapeutic interventions such as behavioural and cognitive therapies in addressing unacceptable behaviour and developing self-control, social skills training and maintaining independent living skills.
- Management of violence, aggression and security breaches.
- Knowledge, not only of mental well-being and ill health but also an understanding of forensic theory, offending behaviour and recidivism.
- Knowledge of wider legal context, including criminal justice processes, criminal law and relevant case law alongside understanding of mental health law and other health legislation

Adapted from Mason, 2002; Bowring-Lossock, 2006; Kettles and Woods, 2006; Mason et al, 2009

Box 13.2. Personal qualities needed by forensic mental health nurses

1. Ability to manage own emotions effectively, including being able to appear relaxed and calm.
2. Ability to make decisions effectively.
3. Ability to understand and set therapeutic boundaries.
4. Ability to not personalise negative events.
5. Ability to have a non-judgemental attitude irrespective of the patient's background.

Adapted from Mason, 2002; Bowring-Lossock, 2006; Kettles and Woods, 2006;
Mason et al, 2009

There is also consideration of the desirable personal qualities of the nurse practising within the forensic field and these reflect an emotional intelligence approach (*Box 13.2, Table 13.1*).

It is discussed within the literature that some of the identified skills, knowledge and qualities may be relevant to various nursing fields, however Bowring-Lossock (2006) concludes that there are areas that are unique to forensic mental health nursing. It is recognised that while the above literature relates to mental health forensic nurses, the competencies are pertinent for working within the field of

Table 13.1. Four elements of emotional intelligence	
Personal/self-awareness	Insight into your thoughts, feelings and emotions and how they may affect others. Strengths and limitations. Effective listening and communication skills. Motivate self.
Conscious filters/self-management	Understand personal motives, regulate behaviour, self-confidence, take initiatives, be creative, optimistic about outcomes, manage change.
Context/social awareness	Sensing and understanding others' thoughts, feelings and emotions. Perceive how others relate to each other.
Relational skills/relationship management	Motivate others to achieve professional and personal goals. Inspire others, manage interpersonal and team/agency relationships.
	Adapted from Goodwin (2006)

forensic learning disabilities. In addition, Inglis (2009) concluded that it was important for nurses not to attribute an individual's offending behaviour solely to a person's learning disability. The study also identified trustworthiness, genuine concern, empowerment and caring as good nurse characteristics. This was echoed by Clarkson et al (2009) who identified that the above qualities made service users feel safe within residential forensic settings; however, immaturity, inexperience and a short temper were unhelpful qualities that gave a feeling of discontent.

It has been suggested that staff working in forensic services are at risk from both stress and burnout (Coffey and Coleman, 2001; Dickinson and Wright, 2008). The importance of leadership within community forensic services is therefore essential to ensure staff are appropriately supervised and supported. Forensic multi-professional teams require robust and thorough processes to ensure an honest and open culture where all staff members can confidently communicate their opinions to facilitate care pathways that may carry some risk to individuals, the team and the organisation. We advocate regular individual and group clinical supervision, protected time for team meetings, openness, and flexible access to support networks. Clinical supervision is an important aspect that allows individuals and teams to engage in critical reflective practice for complex situations. Working with high risk complex caseloads can impact on the thoughts, feelings and emotions of staff within this field and can contribute to stress. Therefore, supervision is an essential requirement for staff and it has been indicated that Heron's Six Category Intervention Analysis has some value as a supervision model (Sloan and Watson, 2001). Heron (1983) also discussed emotional competence which has influenced the development of emotional intelligence as a leadership model. Goleman (1998, cited in Jasper and Jumaa, 2005) suggested emotional intelligence can facilitate effective leadership, and Goodwin (2006) postulates that people with increased emotional intelligence are likely to make better leaders and advises the four elements shown in *Table 13.1*.

Goodwin's (2006) four elements mirror some of the skills, knowledge, competencies and desirable personal qualities suggested by Mason (2002), Bowring-Lossock (2006), Kettles and Woods (2006) and Mason et al (2009). We believe that these elements are important in a forensic setting and enable a supportive environment for an integrated multi-professional team.

Conclusion

This chapter set out to identify how leadership within a forensic community service can lead to choice, inclusion and empowerment for people with learning disabilities and forensic needs. It has been suggested that finding a perfect balance between rights, risks and responsibilities is to achieve the impossible (Koubel, 2012). However, there are processes and models available, as described throughout this chapter, which can be embedded within a forensic service to facilitate robust critical thinking and reflective practice and to enhance clinical practice and service user outcomes. We have found that at the heart of leadership in forensic practice is a value base of person-centred approaches alongside a multi-professional team that is open and supportive to all team members. Staff knowledge, skills and qualities need to be considered and reflected upon throughout the practitioner's career within a forensic setting. Positive risk taking has been embraced, which we believe has led to enhanced positive outcomes for service users. Engagement and the therapeutic relationship have proved to be paramount, especially within a community setting where the service user often has no medico-legal restrictions.

The landscape of learning disability services, and in particular forensic services, appear to be in a constant state of flux, ever changing and evolving. There is a need for robust and effective leaders to improve quality (Griffiths et al, 2010). Therefore, practitioners at all levels need to embrace leadership.

References

Benton C, Roy A (2008) The first three years of a community forensic service for people with a learning disability. *British Journal of Forensic Practice* **10**(2): 4–12

Blacker JE (2009) *The assessment of risk in intellectually disabled sexual offenders.* Thesis submitted to the School of Psychology, University of Birmingham

Blacker JE, Beech AR, Wilcox DT, Boer DP (2011) The assessment of dynamic risk and recidivism in a sample of special needs sexual offenders. *Psychology, Crime and Law* **17**(1): 75–92

Boer DP, Hart SD, Kropp PR, Webster CD (1997) *Manual for the sexual violence risk – 20: Professional guidelines for assessing risk of sexual violence.* Mental Health Law and Policy Institute, Vancouver BC

Boer DP, Tough S, Haaven J (2004) Assessment of risk manageability of intellectually disabled sex offenders. *Journal of Applied Research in Intellectual Disabilities* **17**: 275–83

Boer DP, Frize M, Pappas R, Morrissey C, Lindsay WR (2010a) Suggested adaptations to the HCR-20 for offenders with intellectual disabilities. In LA Craig, WR Lindsay, KD Browne (eds). *Assessment and treatment of sexual offenders with intellectual disabilities: A handbook.* John Wiley and Sons, Chichester, UK

Boer DP, Frize M, Pappas R, Morrissey C, Lindsay WR (2010b) Suggested adaptations to the SVR-20 for offenders with intellectual disabilities. In LA Craig, WR Lindsay,

KD Browne (eds). *Assessment and treatment of sexual offenders with intellectual disabilities: A handbook.* John Wiley and Sons, Chichester, UK

Bonta J, Andrews DA (2003) A commentary on Ward and Stewart's model of human needs. *Psychology, Crime and Law* **9**: 215–18

Bowring-Lossock E (2006) The forensic mental health nurse – a literature review. *Journal of Psychiatric and Mental Health Nursing* **13**: 780–5

Carson D (1993) Disabling progress: The law commission's proposals on mentally incapacitated adults' decision-making. *Journal of Social Welfare and Family Law* **15**(5): 304–20

Clare I.C, Gudjonsson GH (1993) Interrogative suggestibility confabulation and acquiescence in people with mild learning disabilities (mental handicap): Implications for reliability during police interrogations. *British Journal of Clinical Psychology* **32**(3): 295–301

Clarkson R. Murphy G, Coldwell J, Dawson D (2009) What characteristics do service users with intellectual disability value in direct support within residential forensic services? *Journal of Intellectual and Developmental Disability* **34**(4): 283–9

Coffey M, Coleman M (2001) The relationship between support and stress in forensic community mental health nursing. *Journal of Advanced Nursing* **34**(3): 397–407

Coffey M, Hewitt J (2010) Ethical issues in forensic community work. In M Coffey, R Byrt (eds). *Forensic mental health nursing: Ethics, debates and dilemmas* (pp 59–69). Quay Books, London

Department of Health (1993) *Services for people with learning disabilities and challenging behaviour or mental health needs.* (Chairman Professor Jim Mansell). HMSO, London

Department of Health (2001) *Valuing people: A new strategy for learning disability in the 21st century.* The Stationery Office, London

Department of Health (2007a) *Services for people with learning disabilities and challenging behaviour or mental health needs.* (Revised edn) (Chairman Professor Jim Mansell). HMSO, London

Department of Health (2007b) *Best practice in managing risk.* National Mental Health Risk Management Programme, London

Department of Health (2009a) *Valuing people now: A new three-year strategy for people with learning disabilities.* The Stationery Office, London

Department of Health (2009b) *The Bradley report. Lord Bradley's review of people with mental health problems or learning disabilities in the criminal justice system.* Department of Health, London

Department of Health (2009c) *Improving health and supporting justice.* Department of Health, London

Department of Health (2011) *Positive practice positive outcomes: A handbook for professional in the criminal justice system working with offenders with a learning disability.* Department of Health, London

Department of Health and Home Office (1992) *Review of health and social services for mentally disordered offenders and others requiring similar services* (The Reed Report) HMSO, London

Dickinson T, Wright KM (2008) Stress and burnout in forensic mental health nursing: A literature review. *British Journal of Nursing* **17**(2): 82–7

Goleman D (1998) *Working with emotional intelligence.* Bloomsbury, London

Goodwin N (2006) Leadership and emotional intelligence. In N Goodwin (ed) *Leadership in health care. A European perspective* (pp 101–5). Routledge, Oxford

Greig R (2007) *Positive practice, positive outcomes: A handbook for professionals in the criminal justice system working with offenders with learning disabilities.* Care Services Improvement Partnership; Health and Social Care in Criminal Justice and Valuing People Support Team, London

Griffiths D, Sheehan C, Debar S, Ayres B, Colin-Thome D (2010) Clinical leadership – the what why and how. In E Stanton, C Lemer, J Mountford (eds). *Clinical leadership. Bridging the divide* (pp 1–14). Quay Books, London

Hart SD, Kropp PR, Laws DR, Klaver J, Logan C, Watt KA (2003) *The Risk for Sexual Violence Protocol (RSVP).* The Mental Health Law and Policy Institute of Simon Fraser University, Burnaby, BC

Heron J (1983) Education of the affect. In M Jasper, M Jumaa (eds). *Effective healthcare leadership* (pp 159–76). Blackwell, Oxford

Inglis P (2009) *Forensic nursing and the good nurse characteristics presentation.* Proceedings of Learning Disabled Offenders Network 8th Conference 2009. University of Central Lancashire, Lancaster

Jacobson J, Talbot J (2009) *Vulnerable defendants in the criminal courts: A review of provision for adults and children.* Prison Reform Trust, London

Jasper M, Jumaa M (eds) (2005) *Effective healthcare leadership.* Blackwell, Oxford

Kettles A, Woods P (2006) A concept analysis of 'forensic' nursing. *British Journal of Forensic Practice* **8**(3): 16–27

Koubel G (2012) Critical reflections on balancing rights, risks and responsibilities. In G Koubel, H Bungay (eds). *Rights risks and responsibilities.* Palgrave Macmillan, Hampshire

Lindsay WR, Hastings RP, Beech AR (2011) Forensic research in offenders with intellectual and developmental disabilities. 1: Prevalence and risk assessment. *Psychology, Crime and Law* **17**(1): 3–7

Lyall I, Holland AJ, Collins S (1995) Offending by adults with learning disabilities and the attitudes of staff to offending behaviour: Implications for service development. *Intellectual Disability Research* **39**(6): 501–8

Mason T (2002) Forensic psychiatric nursing: A literature review and thematic analysis of role tensions. *Journal of Psychiatric and Mental Health Nursing* **9**: 511–20

Mason T, King L, Dulson J (2009) Binary construct analysis of forensic psychiatric nursing in the UK: High medium and low security services. *International Journal of Mental Health Nursing* **18**: 216–24

Mohabeersingh P, Jukes M (2007) Managing change innovation and leadership. In M Jukes, J Aldridge (eds). *Person-centred practices. A holistic and integrated approach.* Quay Books, London

Morgan S (2004) *Positive risk-taking: An idea whose time has come. HealthCare Risk Report.* Available from: http://practicebasedevidence.squarespace.com/storage/pdfs/OpenMind-PositiveRiskTaking.pdf

Murphy G, Clare CH (1998) People with learning disabilities as offenders or alleged offenders in the UK criminal justice system. *Journal of the Royal Society of Medicine* **91**: 178–82

Ogloff JRP, Davis MR (2004) Advances in offender assessment and rehabilitation: Contributions of the risk-needs-responsivity approach. *Psychology, Crime and Law* **10**(3): 229–42

Prison Reform Trust (2008) *No one knows. Report and final recommendations. Prisoners' voices. Experiences of the criminal justice system by prisoners with learning disabilities and difficulties.* Prison Reform Trust, London

Prison Reform Trust (2010) *Bromley briefings prison factfile.* Prison Reform Trust, London

Seaward S, Rees C (2001) Responding to people with a learning disability who offend. *Nursing Standard* **15**(37): 36–9

Sloan G, Watson H (2001) John Heron's six-category intervention analysis: Towards understanding interpersonal relations and progressing the delivery of clinical supervision for mental health nursing in the United Kingdom. *Journal of Advanced Nursing* **36**: 206–14

Smith I, Addo M, Ninnoni J (2010) The promotion of autonomy in clients with learning disabilities. In M Coffey, R Byrt (eds). *Forensic mental health nursing: Ethics, debates and dilemmas* (pp 59–69). Quay Books, London

Ward T, Brown M (2004) The good lives model and conceptual issues in offender rehabilitation. *Crime and Law* **10**(3): 243–57

Webster CD, Douglas KS, Eaves D, Hart SD (1997) *HCR-20: Assessing risk for violence (Version 2).* The Mental Health Law and Policy Institute of Simon Fraser University, Burnaby BC

Statute

Deprivation of Liberty Safeguards (2008) HMSO, London

Equality Act (2010) HMSO, London

Human Rights Act (1998) HMSO, London

Mental Health Act (1983) HMSO, London

Mental Capacity Act (2005). HMSO, London

Mental Health Act (2007) HMSO, London

Police and Criminal Evidence Act (1984) HMSO, London

Chapter 14

Practice leadership and child and adolescent mental health

Paul Millwood, Jon Stringer, Josh Millwood and Mike Jenkins

The emotional health and well-being of children and young people is of fundamental importance. Unmet mental health needs during childhood lead to difficulties in adolescence and problems in adulthood. The need to develop comprehensive prevention, early recognition and timely intervention services is essential. Despite this, many mental health problems go unnoticed or are only treated when advanced. Late intervention can often be associated with severe impairments for children and young people as well as their families
(McDougall 2011: 48)

Introduction

In setting out to consider key factors that have influenced the leadership agenda within child and adolescent mental health services, it is important to recognise the fundamental importance, expressed by McDougall (2011), of providing preventative, responsive and user-friendly community and in-patient services. Nevertheless, as this chapter will demonstrate, it has only been within recent decades that child and adolescent mental health services have developed. This suggests a growing acknowledgement socially, politically and professionally of the detrimental effects of unrecognised, undiagnosed and untreated child and adolescent mental health problems, and their potentially long-term aversive effects (Health Advisory Service, 1995; Rutter and Smith, 1995; Kurtz, 1996; Audit Commission, 1999; Bradford and Cohen, 1998; Williams and Kerfoot, 2005; Thompson et al, 2012).

Although this chapter focuses on child and adolescent mental health services as a specific service provision, it acknowledges that it is part of the government's vision for improving the physical, mental and emotional health of all children. The re-emphasis on the needs of children and young people with a learning/intellectual disability is pursued actively across child and adolescent mental health service teams.

Towards this endeavour there is still a need to embed quality commissioning and provider services for all children and young people, and in particular those who have learning and/or intellectual disabilities. As an additional resource it is recommended that readers access *Developing mental health services for children and adolescents with learning disabilities – A tool kit for clinicians* by Bernard and Turk (2009).

Child and adolescent mental health: Service transformation and the four tier framework

Within the wider context of mental health provision, child and adolescent mental health services have undergone significant transformation. Arguable, the most significant strategic influence on this process was the NHS Health Advisory Service Report, *Together we stand* (1995), which identified the need to develop a comprehensive tiered approach to service provision, commissioning, and coherent leadership of mental health provision for young people (McDougall et al, 2008; Health Advisory Service, 1995).

Thompson et al (2012: 1) state:

> *…it is becoming increasingly clear to government ministers, planners and the adult services, that child and adolescent mental health is everyone's business.*

However, this has not always been the case. Key reports, including *Together we stand* (Health Advisory Service, 1995) and the Audit Commission's (1999) *Children in mind*, identify poor service availability, inconsistencies in provision, and fragmented services. Furthermore, poor communication between health practitioners and other statutory services, unclear referral systems, inadequate staff training, and a lack of clear leadership and accountability contribute to a lack of quality in young people's and families' experiences of mental health resources.

In response to the findings of the Health Advisory Service and Audit Commission reports, child and adolescent mental health services were designed into what became known as the Four Tier Framework (Health Advisory Service, 1995; Audit Commission, 1999). This framework sought to improve communication between health and other statutory and non-statutory services engaging young people and families. It was also envisaged that the establishment of coherent, transparent and structured referral and care pathways would improve partnership and seamless working, accountability and leadership across services. It is worthwhile listing the roles and responsibilities of the range of clinicians engaged within child and adolescent mental health services, which we believe highlights the fundamental roles that nursing, child psychiatry, social work, education, youth justice and other resources play in co-ordinating and leading services currently accessed by young people and families.

Tier 1 resources comprise primary first contact services, including child health, paediatrics, midwifery, health visitors, school nurses, teachers, social workers and general practitioners. These are considered frontline key tier 1 roles responsible for assessment, intervention and timely referral to other services when the needs of the child and young person require more specialist mental health care. The development of primary mental health worker roles has also been established to promote prompt access, screening, risk assessment and seamless referral into child and adolescent mental health services.

Tier 2 resources include clinical psychologists and other independent professionals who provide assessment, intervention and joint working with frontline services. These clinical roles are frequently subsumed within tier 3.

Tier 3 services are predominantly made up of community-based multidisciplinary child and adolescent mental health teams, including nursing, child psychiatry, social work, youth justice, and other specialist roles that engage those young people who present complex mental health needs.

Tier 3.5 consists of multi-disciplinary community-based teams whose structures vary but essentially consist of medical and nursing staff. Their remit is to engage with young people and their families pre- and post-admission, to divert from admission, or reduce admission duration through intensifying existing community-based intervention, and rehabilitate back into the community post-admission.

Tier 4 primarily accounts for in-patient resources for young people who are deemed to be experiencing significant mental health problems, and who are considered to meet Mental Health Act criteria. This includes in patient child and adolescent mental health services and, in some cases, referral to specialist forensic resources.

More recently, Tier 5, specialist forensic provision, has also been developed and provided by adult mental health services or private sector providers.

The choice and partnership approach

There is an increasing need for comprehensive and competent commissioning of child and adolescent mental health services underpinned by strategic leadership and evidence-based practice that focuses on the provision of preventative and responsive services, positive outcomes and efficiency improvements (McDougall et al, 2008; Department of Health, 2011; Thompson et al, 2012). Furthermore, a Department of Health (2010) report, *Equity and excellence: Liberating the NHS* draws attention to the increasing application of payment by results, audit, and efficiency measures within healthcare services.

In relation to child and adolescent mental health services, Kingsbury and York (2006) note the benefits of developing clear referral pathways, service criteria, and effectiveness targets to measure outcomes of evidence-based care packages. Kingsbury and York emphasised the need to identify demand and capacity issues within the commissioning and provision of child and adolescent mental health services, and designed the "choice and partnership approach" framework. More specifically, they coined the "seven helpful habits", which they suggest improve practice leadership efficiency, effectiveness, and overall service quality. These consist of:

1. *Handle demand*: Eligibility criteria, levels of priority and service level agreements.
2. *Extend capacity*: Know your capacity, set activity standards and focus on follow-ups.
3. *Let go of families*: Clear and consistent service referral pathways following initial assessments/interventions, care plans and plans for long-term conditions.
4. *Process map and redesign*: Understand the patient journey, identify bottle-necks and enhance user-friendly perspective.
5. *Flow management*: Analyse bottlenecks, screen referrals daily and reduce waiting lists.
6. *Use of care bundles*: Identify current best practice approaches, local agreement of care bundles. Implement and monitor use of care bundles.
7. *Look after staff*: Plan roles, appraise annually, value staff, and promote team-working practices.

Nevertheless, austerity measures impacting on all areas of public services have also influenced the provision and development of mental health services for young people and their families. Furthermore, the commissioning of child and adolescent mental health services equally demands improvements in efficiency, performance and outputs, underpinned by evidence-based interventions, quality and throughput. The growth of such services with mental health grant monies, now in demise, had resulted in a dedicated commitment to services that sought to address the diagnosis of and intervention strategies for neurodevelopmental disorders as a broader dimension of child and adolescent mental health services. This has in part changed the orientation of the services to psychological and developmental well-being rather than services that traditionally responded to formal psychiatric illness presentations. Leadership in a time of growth can often be unimaginative and generous in its scope of planning services as there appears to be enough for all. This can promote a "silo" mentality where services grow parallel to each other rather than across service boundaries. However, in a time of constricting budgets, leadership itself is called on to be more dynamic and imaginative to safeguard essential services while driving for improvements in care through a more collaborative strategy.

Involving young people

Government policy set the target date of 2006 for all areas to have designated community and in patient services capable of responding to the mental health needs of children and young people (Department of Health, 2002). Emphasis was also placed on the need to deliver flexible and creative services encouraging greater user choice, involvement and empowerment, and recognition of young people's views and rights. This chapter falls short of suggesting that this has been fully achieved. However, the positive experiences of one of us suggest that young people's views are beginning to be heard and valued within the process of local and national policy design. This includes young people being elected to patient governor roles, implementing and steering Youth Advisory Panels and becoming involved in Youth Ambassador roles across educational and clinical domains. This offers the opportunity for young people to be consulted and to represent their views, which contributes to the leadership and commissioning of services. However, it is our opinion that progress achieved in areas of service user involvement may be at risk in view of the current culture of cutbacks evident across the child and adolescent mental health services and other healthcare resources.

Education and training

In setting out to consider the multidisciplinary nature of child and adolescent mental health provision and the diversity of clinical roles that are integral to the development of quality services and their leadership, the remainder of this chapter focuses on meeting nurses' educational needs and the role of the nurse consultant.

The growth in community, in patient and forensic child and adolescent mental health services demonstrates the specialist nature of nursing and other health-related clinical roles within this area of mental health. Child psychiatry, psychology and social work disciplines play significant roles in assessing, planning, implementing and evaluating service provision. The role of nursing within child and adolescent mental health is equally pivotal to the identification of and response to the comprehensive needs of young people and families across a range of settings. Nursing clinicians remain as frontline practitioners engaging children and families. However, Nolan (2012) suggests that historically the role of the nurse has been absent from the literature, which has failed to recognise the value of nurses in the provision of comprehensive care, and their role in service development and leadership.

Developments in pre-registration education and "learning beyond registration" programmes have contributed to the identification and mapping of the learning needs of nurses responsible for the provision of child and adolescent mental health services. Significantly, the establishment of the BSc (Hons) Mental Health Studies nursing degree programme and the additional child and adolescent mental health services award (formerly the ENB603) spotlights the fundamental importance nursing plays within the provision of high quality care for young people, and its central position within the multi-agency approach to child and adolescent mental health service development, leadership, innovation and change. This part-time BSc (Hons) Mental Health Studies nursing degree programme, usually offered by local universities, enables nurses and allied health clinicians working in child and adolescent mental health to access a structured framework of enquiry-based learning opportunities, knowledge, and supervision, which seek to underpin evidence-based practice. Arguably, this has contributed to the child and adolescent mental health nurse becoming a more visible and equal partner within multidisciplinary service provision, leadership and development. The course has also highlighted the needs of young people, and instilled and developed professional attitudes, skills and competencies, including leadership, of registered nurses completing this programme of studies.

Nevertheless, Thompson et al (2012) caution that austerity measures and cut-backs introduced within the NHS are likely to impact on child and adolescent mental health services, including the scaling back of learning beyond registration programmes, which may impact on the overall quality and standard of care provision. It is evident that the current economic crisis has brought the funding review of public services to the forefront of political attention. However, the increasing incidence of emotional, behavioural, and serious mental health problems experienced within childhood and adolescence suggests that policy makers must be cautious of the consequences of squeezing child and adolescent mental health services education. In addition there may be an increase in referrals of young people to inappropriate services and a drop in standards of care provision.

Nevertheless, more optimistically, at times of austerity there is also an opportunity to re-visualise the importance and flexibility of nursing. An example of this is the development practitioner roles in child and adolescent mental health services/youth offending services that offer comprehensive care packages to young people at the interface of the mental health and criminal justice systems. Nurse-led services for young offenders has allowed nursing to assert its influence in areas of development through delivery at a clinical level, building in an awareness of, and taking into consideration, the strategic position of child and adolescent mental health provision. Establishing and building up service frameworks from the platform of clinical practice endorses the importance of the nurse leadership role.

McDougall (2011:49) reflects on the sentiments of the recent Department of Health (2011) report, *No health without mental health*, which recommends "invest to save" and preventative approaches to the provision of mental health services in the future. McDougall goes on to explain that the report recognises the clear link between childhood mental health disorders and a range of psychosocial problems in adolescence and adult life. This document highlights childhood and adolescence as key developmental periods in the individual's life, and seeks to focus the leadership and reform of mental health services in the direction of prevention and prompt intervention.

It is therefore crucial that nurses engaging with children and families across community and in patient child and adolescent mental health services continue to be enabled to access suitable and high quality education, which equips them with appropriate knowledge, skills and competencies to provide highest standards of assessment, interventions and compassionate care. This will also enable and empower clinicians to develop effective leadership and decision making skills and qualities. Arguably, a failure to invest in the provision of child and adolescent mental health services and in appropriate specialist education may contribute to a crisis of care, which must be prevented at all costs.

The nurse consultant role

Rowden (2000) suggests that nursing is littered with hierarchical baggage from Florence Nightingale up to the present day and adds that the profession has often been saddled with so-called leaders who have merely maintained the status quo. Nevertheless, Rowden notes that the late 1990s saw the development of the nurse consultant role across the NHS following the political perspective that nursing lacked practice leadership. This role encouraged senior clinical nurses to take a more active position within leadership agendas, clinical decision making and development of NHS services.

Nurse consultants were identified as being central to the process of health modernisation, spending at least 50% of their time working directly with patients. The aim was that they would also become significantly involved in research, education, training and service development with the goal of promoting a more evidence-based approach to service provision (Rowden, 2000). However, since their inception, there has been a lack of clarity about their direct clinical roles, leadership and managerial responsibilities. Franks and Howarth (2012) point out that effectiveness and efficiency within the nurse consultant role requires managerial support and supervision, to enable and empower participation within strategic planning, commissioning and implementation of policy. Hawkins and Shohet (2006) underline the importance of establishing a robust framework of clinical supervision, which promotes improvements in service and supports clinicians in their roles.

Leadership in any context has been considered in relationship to attributes, attitudes, behaviours and qualities of an individual and his or her ability to encourage others within a team or organisation (Pearce and Conger, 2002). Within the context of child and adolescent mental health services greater emphasis has been placed on the application of training, knowledge and technology to facilitate autonomous clinical practice and multidisciplinary team working. Pearce and Conger (2002) add that a significant element of any successful organisation must include shared leadership, which they define as a dynamic and interactive influencing process among key stakeholders, including nurse consultants, within any team with the shared vision or aims to meet individual and organisational needs.

The Department of Health (2008) document, *High quality care for all: NHS next stage review*, also recognises the importance of encouraging and enabling greater involvement of clinicians in the leadership agenda which is inclusive of all grades of clinicians, including nurse consultants, other key stakeholders and people accessing services. More specifically, there is also acknowledgement of the need to further embed the development of leadership skills, qualities and attitudes within the foundation and principles of the nurse education curriculum. This must be evident both at pre-registration and post-registration levels and should include greater joint working between clinical and university domains. Furthermore, key clinical nursing personnel, including nurse consultants, should be included in the development of high quality educational programmes to ensure the preparation of nurse leaders of the future.

Conclusions

This chapter has considered the relatively brief history of developments within child and adolescent mental health services. These have recognised the need to establish clear referral systems, accessibility and equity of services received by young people and their families. The development of the Four Tier Framework and the Capacity and Partnership Approach have contributed to the development of comprehensive and structured commissioning of evidence-based care packages.

Political and professional parties have spotlighted the need for improved practice leadership within the provision of health services. In relation to child and adolescent mental health services, it is evident that central to this philosophy is the provision of the highest quality and standards of care underpinned by mental health promotion, prevention, early detection and intervention. Effective and efficient leadership must seek to sustain and develop the involvement of young people at all levels of service development and leadership. An example of this is where one of us was elected to a patient governor role representing the views of young people accessing local health services.

Finally, we have also sought to emphasise the integral role nurse education plays in equipping the current and future workforce with the requisite knowledge, skills, attitudes and values. Future developments within these education programmes must take account of the need to develop management and leadership skills and qualities. We remain cautious of the impact cutbacks in NHS funding are likely to have on pre- and post-registration education programmes for clinicians engaging with children and families accessing child and adolescent mental health services.

References

Audit Commission (1999) *Children in mind. A guide for parents and professionals.* Jessica Kingsley Publishers, London

Bernard S, Turk J (2009) *Developing mental health services for children and adolescents with learning disabilities.* Royal College of Psychiatry Publications in collaboration with the National CAMHS Support Service, London

Bradford DL, Cohen AR (1998) *Power up: Transforming organisations through shared leadership.* John Wiley, New York

Department of Health (2002) *Improving, expansion and reform: The next three years: The priorities and planning framework.* Available from: www.doh.gov.uk/planning

Department of Health (2008) *High quality care for all: Next stage review.* Department of Health, London

Department of Health (2010) *New horizons: Towards a shared vision for mental health –*

consultation. Department of Health, London

Department of Health (2010) *Equity and excellence: Liberating the NHS.* Department of Health, London

Department of Health (2011) *No health without mental health: Cross government mental health outcomes strategy for people of all ages.* Department of Health, London. Available from: www.dh.gov.uk/mentalhealthstartegy

Franks H, Howarth M (2012) Being an effective nurse consultant in the English National Health Service. What does it take? A study of consultants specializing in safeguarding. *Journal of Nursing Management* **20**(7): 847–57

Hawkins P, Shohet R (2006) *Supervision in the helping professions* (3rd edn). Open University Press, Maidenhead

Health Advisory Service Document (1995) *Together we stand: A thematic review of mental health services in England and Wales.* Department of Health, London

Kingsbury S, York A (2006) *The 7 helpful habits of effective CAMHS and the choice and partnership approach: A workbook for CAMHS.* camhs network Surrey

Kurtz Z (1996) *Treating children well. A guide to using the evidence base in commissioning and managing services for the mental health of children and young people.* The Mental Health Foundation, London

McDougall T (2011) Mental health problems in childhood and adolescence. *Nursing Standard* **26**(14): 48-56

Meltzer H, Gatward R, Goodman R, Ford T (2000) *Mental health of children and adolescents in Great Britain.* HMSO, London

McDougall T, Worrall-Davies A, Hewson L, Richardson G, Cotgrove A (2008) *Tier 4 Child and Adolescent Mental Health Services (CAMHS) – Inpatient care, day services and alternatives: An overview of Tier 4 CAMHS provision in the UK.* Child and Adolescent Mental Health **13**(4): 173–80

Nolan P (2012) Reviewing the history of mental health nursing. *British Journal of Mental Health Nursing* **1**(2): 78–80

Pearce CL, Conger JA (2002) All those years ago: The historical underpinnings of shared leadership. In CL Pearce, JA Conger (eds). *Shared leadership: Reframing the hows and whys of leadership* (pp 1–18). Sage Publications, Thousand Oaks, CA

Rowden R (2000) Is leadership in nursing more myth than substance? *Nursing Times* **96**(30): 18

Rutter M, Smith DJ (1995) *Psychosocial disorders in young people: Time trends and their causes.* John Wiley & Sons, Chichester

Thompson M, Hooper C, Laver-Bradbury C, Gale C (2012) *Child and adolescent mental health theory and practice* (2nd edn). Hodder Arnold, London

Williams R, Kerfoot M (2005) *Child and adolescent mental health services: Strategy, planning, delivery, and evaluation.* Oxford Press, Oxford

Chapter 15

Crisis resolution and home treatment

Tom Casey

Introduction

The National Service Framework for mental health (Department of Health, 1999) made it clear that there should be 24-hour access to community psychiatric services and this led to the nationwide adoption of crisis resolution and home treatment team. The National Audit Office report (2007) highlighted the general success of these teams as both cost and clinically effective. The cost of mental health problems is estimated at £110 billion annually, more than the cost of crime, and likely to double in the next 20 years (McCrone et al, 2008; Department of Health, 2011). The continuing loss of acute psychiatric beds (Holmstrom, 2011), and the growing acceptance that timely community-based interventions are generally more acceptable to service users (Hopkins and Niemiec, 2007; Winness et al, 2010) and can reduce recovery time and therefore costs (Sjolie et al, 2010), places these teams at the forefront of current and future care provision.

Those who are tasked with leading this service are faced with an array of challenges; some are common to all NHS leaders, others are more specific.

Two of these areas are examined in more detail with regard to the specific needs of the crisis resolution and home treatment service, firstly the clinicians themselves and the qualities of leadership most relevant to their position, and secondly the team leaders and their need to provide a specific service, maintain a skilled workforce and reconcile the duality of their role as manager and leader.

Team members

Crisis resolution and home treatment teams are not dissimilar in structure to other community teams. The majority of the members are nurse trained but there is often a multi-disciplinary representation. Occupational therapists, healthcare workers, social workers and psychologists are often directly employed or closely associated with the service. The challenges associated with leading a multi-disciplinary, and often multi-generational, multi-demographic team (Chang et al, 2006; Sherman 2006) will be common to the majority of community mental health workers. The essential differences lie in the need to have clinicians who are able to manage crises on a daily basis and provide intensive, almost hospital, levels of care and support in a domestic environment.

The clinicians employed in crisis resolution and home treatment need to be able to use a range of interventions in order effectively to manage care at a time when their clients are by definition in crisis and not necessarily willing or able to cooperate. These include psychosocial interventions (Morgan and Hunte 2008), the use of medication (Sreenath et al, 2010), carer support, information sharing and effective communication (Hopkins and Niemiec, 2007; Boschart, 2009), at a time of increase in service uptake (NHS Information Centre, 2011) and decrease in bed provision (Holmstrom 2011). They must also have the ability to assess and manage risk.

Their assessments and interventions take place outside of the controlled environment of the hospital and team members need to be able to act with confidence and purpose at times of minimal support. They must embody the definition of the autonomous practitioner able to work independently and decisively, making informed decisions with the client's needs central to the process.

While it is important that the teams are well led it is equally important that the individual members are themselves able to perform a leadership role. Leaders are recognised and defined more by their personal attributes and abilities than by their hierarchical position. They are seen as having many different qualities such as focus, integrity, energy, visibility in the workplace and ability to advocate and problem solve (Daly et al, 2004; Tweedell, 2007). As an example:

The crisis resolution and home treatment clinician has identified a client who needs to be assessed for admission to hospital under the Mental Health Act from an A and E department at 02.00 hrs. He will not have access to his usual administration, medical or managerial support. There is a need to act as the focal point of the event, the conduit of information for the different agencies involved, as well as advocate for the client and support the carers.

Figure 15.1 illustrates some of the leadership skills required.

Good leaders are able to act on their own initiative, essential for crisis resolution and home treatment clinicians. When this is done successfully it provides a visible demonstration to colleagues that the leader is a competent, skilled individual in whom others can trust. When tasks are delegated to colleagues or carers they can take direction from what they have seen modelled and feel able to complete the task.

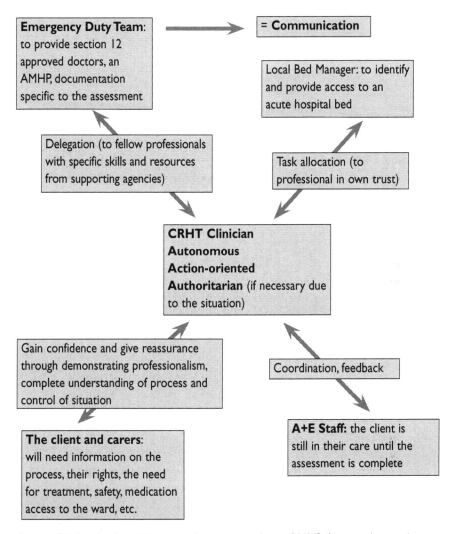

Figure 15.1. Leadership skills required in crisis resolution. AMHP: Approved mental health professional. CRHT: Crisis resolution and home treatment

Crisis resolution and home treatment clinicians must recognise that they can only lead if others are prepared to follow (Goffee and Jones, 2006) and that this relationship will only exist if co-workers agree to follow because they have been given reason to have confidence in the ability of the individual to bring satisfactory resolution to the crisis. The ability to inspire and enable others to work at a higher level is a core component of leadership (Marquis and Huston, 2009) that dovetails into the framework of the crisis resolution and home treatment clinician.

Team leader/manager

Managers are defined by their role within an organisation. They will have formal responsibilities and duties, including leadership, and while the two roles of manager and leader often overlap (Tappen et al, 2004) they do not always meet comfortably in the same person. The position of manager is attained mechanically by the process of application and interview, while acknowledging the inclusion of the word leader in the job description; it would seem the position of leader is achieved via a less well-defined path. Leadership does not always have or require a formal structure (Kelly, 2007); the person who leads is not necessarily the one in the boss's chair.

The crisis resolution and home treatment manager must deal with the same level of bureaucracy as all the other community mental health team managers, including the need to meet key performance indicators, maintain budgets, attend policy meetings, adhere to targets, etc. Some 35 agencies audit or monitor the activity of the NHS (NHS Confederation, 2009a) and the team manager's day-to-day activities are often tied to the need to produce data that synchronises with that scrutiny. The crisis resolution and home team manager has the added responsibility of "gatekeeping" the acute admissions process and providing a rota that contains the essential skill mix to cover the specific 24-hour service requirement.

The majority of teams are nurse-led and this must inevitably lead to some sense of moral and professional conflict with the management role, since there is a need to balance increasing budgetary constraints with the demands of a client-centred service (Jooste, 2011). The two roles must sometimes appear to be at odds but there is an obvious need for the person in charge of a crisis resolution and home treatment team to recognise and resolve any such conflict. This could be achieved by acknowledging the differences in the two roles and that both need the success of the other. The manager needs to "caretake" the everyday financial and organisational requirements of the team and the leader needs to inspire and drive the team forward. Nurses in charge of teams can seek to resolve the conflict they might experience by accepting the essential interdependence and allocating their time to both roles with improved service provision as the reward (Barr and Dowding, 2010).

Team leaders should spend time investing in the social capital (Foote et al, 2011) within the team, building resilience, moving early to resolve conflict, keeping team members up to date with organisational and clinical developments and working to realise their own and the team's potential. There is an obvious need for leaders to be perceived as confident and capable, perhaps even charismatic, but essentially they must be seen as someone who can be relied upon to make good decisions that bring benefit to the team and to provide guidance, especially at times of uncertainty.

There should be no manager/leader role conflict when recognising the need continually to update the skill base of the team, since this is beneficial to both roles. Leaders should be actively engaged in continuous practice development (McCormack et al, 2004) providing and facilitating training which is not simply adequate to meet minimum standards but specific and meaningful to the role. Seeking to improve the clinical competence and performance capabilities of team members is essential since they represent a service that is on the frontline of mental healthcare provision.

Individuals leading/managing a team need to foster and promote a working environment in which the team members feel able to work in the way described in the earlier example (see *Figure 15.1*) knowing that they will be supported and facilitated in their actions. To be effective these individuals require an understanding of their own role as a leader, an ability to identify and develop the leadership qualities of others and the willingness to give them "room to lead" (King's Fund, 2011). So it would seem that this is not a role where ego can play any significant part. In such a critical area where the everyday activity is the preparation for and management of crises, individuals appointed to lead need to recognise their own limitations and assemble a team whose members are skilled in disciplines that complement their own (Useem et al, 2011). To sum it up they must set the "direction of travel" (King's Fund, 2011) but allow for the primacy of others with specific abilities when navigating parts of the "route".

Similarities and differences

The need for leadership and the exact nature of what that term means has been discussed and written about at enormous length and there would seem to be no one answer as to who should lead in what situation. As mentioned earlier, someone can only lead if someone else is following and the original need for a group leader may go back as far as our cave dwelling ancestors and their need to be organised and led in defence against a rampaging mammoth, leaving a genetic imperative that is still with us today (Van Vogt and Ahuja, 2010). However, the person who can lead an army into battle may have no place trying to lead in a call centre.

To put that into nursing terms, a nurse leader who works in a long-term residential rehabilitation unit may well have the necessary leadership skills to excel in that environment but be unable to work effectively in crisis resolution. Practice leaders in the latter area have a different skill set and perhaps a different set of personal attributes. They may well be attracted to the urgency of the work, the need to be actively involved with client, carer and worker interactions that focus on the immediacy of the situation. They will focus their skills acquisition and specialist knowledge requirements on what is best suited to short-term intensive working.

Leaders in rehabilitation settings are possibly less involved with the medical model and more closely aligned with a model of care based around long-term recovery. They are more likely to encourage their team members to form collaborative relationships as companions in recovery with their clients; in contrast to the short-term, risk-management focused, authoritative relationships of acute care (Onyett, 2003; Norman and Pyrie, 2009).

There must always be one eye on the long-term implications of any plan of care, but the crisis resolution and home treatment team will not be involved for long and do not need to build up the long-term therapeutic relationship that needs to be formed by those involved in the recovery phase of the client's illness.

Style choices

Much has been written about different leadership styles – autocratic, democratic, toxic and so on (Elliot, 2006; Kelly, 2007; Barr and Dowding, 2010), with no one particular style seeming to stand out as the universal solution to the problems found in NHS leadership.

The principles of transformational leadership can be seen as desirable within the NHS where there have been, and will continue to be, great changes. A style based on leading people forwards towards new ways of working would seem to have merit. Transactional leadership is often shown as the counterpoint to transformational leadership (Harms and Crede, 2010) and we can examine how the two styles might fit in with crisis resolution and home treatment and how they may be developed and used in both day-to-day working and in long-term realisation of strategic goals.

On the face of it, the NHS team leaders of today, and the foreseeable future, would seem to have little to offer an employee should they choose to adopt a transactional approach to motivating their staff towards greater efficiency.

The current economic climate is unlikely to offer up many opportunities for increased financial reward or promotion, the obvious tools of the transactional relationship. This leaves them with the need to consider other alternatives when negotiating with team members and seeking to motivate them to greater productivity and efficiency. They might propose additional training, which allows clinicians to invest in their own human capital, and so offer a chance to improve their own employability in an increasingly competitive environment. There may also be room to allow a degree of flexibility in work hours, offering longer shifts and thereby reducing the person's frequency of travel and the associated costs. Such tokens will need to be appropriate to the individuals and their motivational needs, and identifying those is the occupation of the skilled transactional leader.

Transformational leaders are those who inspire, encourage and alter people's perceptions. They reveal their vision and move their employees willingly towards it (Marriner Tomey, 2004; Kotter 2007). They empower those they lead and this is perhaps their most important function in healthcare leadership (Ning et al, 2009). There does not appear to be any one specific way of empowering people (Bradbury Jones et al, 2008) but there are several things that the transformational team leader can do to encourage crisis resolution and home treatment team members to move towards this state. They can identify through individual supervision where clinicians place themselves in the team and their perception of their own role as a leader, if indeed they even perceive that as a part of their job. Team members may identify more with collectivist working or may hold the view that the emphasis placed on being an autonomous practitioner necessitates that they lean more towards individualism. Either way the team leader will need all of them actively to participate in moving towards a shared goal. This can only be achieved if they are fully aware of their role within the team, the authority and autonomy within that role, and accept the inherent need to act as a leader.

Whichever leadership style they favour, their naturally dominant style or one they have voluntarily adopted, they also need to be emotionally intelligent (Winship, 2010). They should be aware of the need to avoid displays of negative behaviour and foster a positive emotional climate in their workplace (Sy et al, 2005; Stanley, 2006), have an ability to sense the differing emotional states and needs of their colleagues, and a willingness to adjust and compensate. This is an important skill at times of change when it can be easy for team members to feel their opinions have not been heard or their needs fully considered.

Changes to come

Change is something that would seem to be looming large in the present and future of the NHS, financially driven for the greater part (Appleby et al, 2009), and mental health services will not escape the need to make savings (NHS Confederation, 2010) as the NHS learns to disinvest. Crisis resolution and home treatment teams are bound to come under pressure to accept changes to their workloads and practices when the burdens of bed closure and increased referral take hold. These changes must occur without impeding the quality of the care that is delivered (NHS Confederation, 2009b). The care of people in crisis is delicate work, it must be client-centred and requires clinicians to be focused on the person and his or her carers and not distracted by concerns over organisational restructuring or financial governance.

Clinicians who perceive themselves to be overburdened and poorly supported are likely to feel that changes are being forced upon them rather than made with their consent and cooperation. This may lead to conflict and delays to successful completion (Parkin, 2009; Baker et al, 2010). They will need a clear definition of the changes, some justification of the necessity, and a transparent outline of the work required to fulfil their role within those changes (Kitson, 2008). Such changes may, on the surface at least, appear to be a function of management but will require leadership skills to gain acceptance from the clinical workforce so that the changes to service provision occur in a meaningful way and not just on a printed page.

What comes next?

Historically, the NHS seems to have failed to recognise the need for promotion of the concept of leadership at all levels or to provide a properly defined pathway for clinicians to recognise and improve on existing or dormant skills (Department of Health, 2009). There is evidence that clinicians who receive leadership training do seek to actively incorporate it into their work (Snell and Dickson, 2011) and that an investment in leadership training is justified (Martin et al, 2011). Crisis resolution and home treatment teams would seem to need leaders who are able to employ a range of skills and adopt differing styles, and there does not appear to have been a nationally, or even widely, adopted mechanism to provide these skills at team leader level.

The National Leadership Council was created in 2009 and has set in motion a number of workstreams to address the way in which leadership is incorporated into the future NHS. The NHS Institute for Innovation and Improvement (2011) has also set out a Leadership Qualities Framework detailing the requirements and expectations of NHS employees at all levels with regard to incorporating leadership as an integral part of their job. The NHS Future Forum report (2011) recommends the support of clinicians in leadership development. So it would appear that the future development of the NHS will include leadership as in integral part of workforce development. A common theme that runs through these and other reports and initiatives is the idea of a new paradigm of shared leadership moving away from the "lone hero" (NHS Institue for Innovation and Improvement, 2010; King's Fund, 2011), being the one key person on whom a team, service or organisation relies and looks towards for direction. The new way of working will see leadership as a collaborative function within the NHS (Royal College of Psychiatrists, 2009; Department of Health, 2012). Service leaders, team leaders and team members will network and share knowledge, recognising the specialist knowledge and expertise of the individuals and incorporating them into the function of leadership.

Taking some active part in the leadership of the crisis resolution and home treatment service will become the responsibility of every member. Preparing and guiding the service towards this will be the work of leaders with a degree of visionary thinking (Finkelman, 2012) to be able to see the long-term advantages of such a model, and a strong sense of their own value to be able to share the position of leader with others.

References

Appleby J, Crawford R, Emmerson C (2009) *How cold could it be? Prospects for NHS funding 2011–17*. Institute for Fiscal Studies/The King's Fund, London. Available from: www.King'sfund.org.uk/publications

Baker R, Camosso-Stefinovic J, Shaw E, Cheater F, Flottrop S, Robertson N (2010) *Tailored interventions to overcome barriers to change: Effects on professional practice and health care outcomes (Review)*. Cochrane Database of Systematic Reviews 3: Art. No.: CD005470. DOI: 10.1002/14651858.CD005470.pub2

Barr J, Dowding L (2010) *Leadership in health care*. Sage, London

Boschart V (2009) A communication intervention for nursing staff in chronic care. *Journal of Advanced Nursing* 65(9): 1823–32

Bradbury Jones C, Sambrook S, Irvine F (2008) Power and empowerment in nursing: A fourth theoretical approach. *Journal of Advanced Nursing* 62(2): 258–66

Chang E, Daly J, Hancock K, Bidewell J, Johnson A, Lambert V, Lambert C (2006) The relationships among workplace stressors, coping methods, demographic characteristics, and health in Australian nurses. *Journal of Professional Nursing* **22**(1): 30–8

Daly J, Speedy S, Jackson D (2004) *Nursing leadership*. Churchill Livingstone, London

Department of Health (1999) *The national service framework for mental health*. HMSO, London

Department of Health (2009) *Inspiring leaders: Leadership for quality*. Department of Health Workforce Directorate, London. Available from: www.dh.gov.uk/health

Department of Health (2011) *No health without mental health: A cross government mental health outcomes strategy for people of all ages*. Department of Health, London. Available from: www.dh.gov.uk/mentalhealthstrategy

Department of Health (2012) *Liberating the NHS: Developing the workforce – from design to delivery*. Department of Health, London. Available from: www.dh.gov.uk/health/2012

Elliot J (2006) *Leadership scaffolding*. Chandos, Oxford

Finkelman A (2012) *Leadership and management for nurses – Core competencies for quality care*. Pearson, New Jersey

Foote N, Eisenstat R, Fredberg T (2011) The high ambition leader. *Harvard Business Review* **89**(9): 94–102

Goffee R, Jones G (2006) *Why should anyone be led by you?* Harvard Business School Press, Boston Massachussetts

Harms P, Crede M (2010) Emotional intelligence and transformational and transactional leadership: A meta-analysis. *Journal of Leadership and Organizational Studies* 17(5). DOI: 10.1177/1548 051809350894. http://jlo.sagepub.com/cgi/content/refs/17/1/5

Holmstrom R (2011) Involuntary admissions on rise yet fewer beds available. *Mental Health Practice* **15**(1): 6–7

Hopkins C, Niemiec S (2007) Mental health crisis at home: Service user perspectives on what helps and what hinders. *Journal of Psychiatric and Mental Health Nursing* **14**(3): 310–18

Jooste K (2011) Current nursing practices: Challenges and successes. *Journal of Nursing Management* **19**: 833–6

Kelly K (2007) Power, politics and influence. In S Yoder Wise (Ed) *Leading and managing in nursing* (4th edn). Mosby, St Louis

King's Fund (2011) *The future of leadership and management in the NHS: No more heroes*. King's Fund, London. Available from: www.Kingsfund.org.uk/publications

Kitson A (2008) The need for systems change: Reflections on knowledge translation and organisational change. *Journal of Advanced Nursing* **65**(1): 217–28

Kotter J (2007) *Leading change: Why transformations fail*. Harvard Business Review. Available from: www.hbrreprints.org

Marquis B, Huston C (2009) *Leadership roles and management functions in nursing*.

Lippincott Williams and Wilkins, London

Marriner Tomey A (2004) *Guide to nursing management and leadership* (7th edn). Mosby, St Louis

Martin J, Mccormack B, Fitzsimons D, Spirig R (2011) Evaluation of a clinical leadership programme for nurse leaders. *Journal of Nursing Management* **20**(1): 72–80

McCormack B, Manley K, Garbett R (2004) *Practice development in nursing.* Blackwell, Oxford

McCrone P, Dhansari S, Patel A (2008) *Paying the price: The cost of mental health care in England to 2026.* The King's Fund, London

Morgan S, Hunte K (2008) One foot in the door. *Mental Health Today* **March**: 32–5.

National Audit Office (2007) *Helping people through mental health crisis.* National Audit Office, London. Available from: www.tso.co.uk/bookshop

NHS Confederation (2009a) *What's it all for? Removing unnecessary bureaucracy in regulation.* NHS Confederation, London. Available from: www.nhsconfed.org/Publications/Documents/

NHS Confederation (2009b) *Dealing with the downturn.* NHS Confederation, London. Available from: www.nhsconfed.org/leadership

NHS Confederation (2010) *Quality and productivity in mental health: A shared framework.* Available from: www.nhsconfed.org/NETWORKS/MENTALHEALTH/

NHS Future Forum (2011) *Clinical advice and leadership: A report from the NHS Future Forum.* Department of Health, London. Available from: www.dh.gov.uk/prodfuture

NHS Institute for Innovation and Improvement (2011) *Leadership Qualities Framework.* NHS Institute for Innovation and Improvement, London. Available from: www.leadershipqualitiesframework.institute.nhs.uk

Ning S, Zhong H, Wang L, Li Q (2009) The impact of nurse empowerment on job satisfaction. *Journal of Advanced Nursing* **65**(12): 2642–8

Norman I, Pyrie I (2009) *The art and science of mental health nursing: A textbook of principles and practice* (2nd edn). Open University Press, Maidenhead

Onyett S (2003) *Teamworking in mental health.* Palgrave McMillan, Basingstoke

Parkin P (2009) *Managing change in healthcare: Using action research.* Sage, London

Royal College of Psychiatrists (2009) *Mental health and the economic downturn: National priorities and NHS solutions.* Royal College of Psychiatrists Mental Health Network NHS Confederation and London Scool of Economics and Political Science. RCP reference Occasional Paper OP70.

Sherman R (2006) Leading a multi-generational workforce: Issues, strategies and challenges. *Online Journal of Nursing* **11**(2): Ms 2

Sjolie H, Karlsom B, Kim S (2010) Crisis resolution and home treatement: Structure, process and outcome – a literature review. *Journal of Psychiatric and Mental Health Nursing* **17**: 881–92

Snell A, Dickson G (2011) Optimizing health care employees' newly learned behaviours. *Leadership in Health Services* **24**(3): 183–95

Sreenath S, Reddy S, Tacchi M, Scott J (2010) Medication adherence in crisis? *Journal of Mental Health* **19**(5): 470–4

Stanley D (2006) Recognizing and defining clinical nurse leaders. *British Journal of Nursing* **15**(2): 108–11

Sy T, Cote S, Saavedra R (2005) The contagious leader: Impact of the leader's mood on the mood of group members, group affective tone and group processes. *Journal of Applied Psychology* **90**(2): 295–305

Tappen R, Weiss S, Whitehead D (2004) *Essentials of nursing leadership and management* (3rd edn). F.A. Davis, Philadelphia

Tweedell D (2007) Selecting, developing and evaluating staff. In S Yoder Wise (ed). *Leading and managing in nursing* (4th edn). Mosby, St Louis

Useem M, Jordan R, Koljatic M (2011) How to lead during a crisis. *MIT Sloan Management Review*. Available from: http://sloanreview.mit.edu/the-magazine/2012-winter/

Van Vogt M, Ahuja A (2010) *'Selected' – Why some people lead, why others follow, and why it matters.* Profile Books, London

Winness MG, Borg M, Hesook SMK (2010) Service users' experiences with help and support from crisis resolution teams. A literature review. *Journal of Mental Health* **19**(1): 75–87

Winship G (2010) Is emotional intelligence an important concept for nursing practice? *Journal of Psychiatric and Mental Health Nursing* **17**: 940–8

Chapter 16

Role of the matron in a medium secure service

Stuart Guy, Lorraine Conlon and Sophia Nuala Fletcher

Introduction

In 2002 matrons returned to the NHS after an absence of 36 years in reply to the NHS Plan (Department of Health, 2000), which acknowledged the need for a senior, authoritative nursing presence throughout clinical areas. Initially the role encompassed:

- Attaining higher standards of care and practice leadership.
- Ensuring that administrative and support services could deliver high standards of care.
- Providing a visible, accessible and authoritative presence in ward settings.

(Department of Health, 2002)

Since the reintroduction of matrons, the function and purpose of the role have varied hugely between different trusts and within and across different clinical specialties (Gould, 2008). The role has continued to become more complex as new targets across the NHS have been introduced in respect of regulating healthcare provision (Health and Social Care Act, 2008). An example of this can be found in the practice leadership role of the matron, in respect of ensuring compliance with the Care Quality Commission's essential standards (2012) (see *Box 16.1*).

The recently published Francis Report (2013) has provided a contemporary critique of standards of professional nursing practices in the UK. The public magnification of these standards lays down another significant layer of challenges for matrons within the NHS.

Relatively little has been written on the matron's role within mental health and forensic mental health services. Shanly (2004) published findings of measuring the impact of modern matrons within mental health wards at the South Essex Partnership NHS Trust. Using a postal survey, clinicians and managers working alongside the matrons were asked to consider the impact of the role on service delivery. The findings from the respondents demonstrated some of the tensions that exist within the development of this role in its infancy, which still has congruence today. Respondents noted that matrons were felt

---

Box 16.1. Care Quality Commission's essential standards

- Respecting and involving people who use services.
- Consent to care and treatment.
- Care and welfare of people who use services.
- Meeting nutritional needs.
- Cooperating with other providers.
- Safeguarding people who use services from abuse.
- Cleanliness and infection control.
- Management of medicines.
- Safety and suitability of premises.
- Safety, availability and suitability of equipment.
- Requirements relating to workers.
- Staffing.
- Supporting workers.
- Assessing and monitoring the quality of service provision.
- Complaints.
- Records.

---

not to be visible enough because of the amount of meetings they needed to attend. Also, because the modern matrons had no formal direct management responsibilities respondents felt that the role was seen as not possessing authority to change things. Setting standards was viewed as an essential part of the role but it was recognised that other competing demands took them away from this activity. Overall the findings suggested that modern matrons were having a positive impact.

The matron's role described in this chapter is linked centrally to the Nursing Directorate of the Birmingham and Solihull Mental Health NHS Foundation Trust. Between the director of nursing and the matrons sits a lead nurse who is responsible for a group of matrons within the medium secure services. The matron role within the Mental Health NHS Foundation Trust has similarities to those described by Shanley (2004), in that they are essentially non-operational, focusing on improving standards around quality of care and improving service user and carer experience. Under the clinical lead nurse for secure services, the matron's remit is to drive up standards of leadership and practice across the medium secure unit and to make the clear connection from policy and standards into practice.

Box 16.2. Corporate objectives of the matron's role

- Professional and practice leadership (including nursing strategy, nursing metrics essence of care and productive ward).
- Practice development (including shared care pathways, physical health and supervision).
- Education and training (risk assessment).
- Organisation and the environment (including infection control and cleanliness).

The corporate objectives of the matron's role fall into the four broad categories shown in *Box 16.2*.

This chapter explores the contextual drivers framing the agenda for how matrons function within a 90-bedded male medium secure service of Birmingham and Solihull Mental Health NHS Foundation Trust. It further describes how the role is being used to develop effective practice leadership across all bands of nurses within the medium secure unit to enhance the care pathways of mentally disordered offender service users.

Context

In order to operationalise the development of an effective forensic nursing leadership and care strategy within the medium secure service, attention was paid to the work of McCormack et al (2002) on the meaning of context in relation to practice development to provide a framework of understanding. McCormack et al (2002) argue that understanding context plays a significant role in the development of practice and practice leadership in clinical settings. They operationalise context as the boundaried settings in which nurses and service users give and receive healthcare, which in this case is a 90-bedded male medium secure service. This context influences how the nurses working within the unit, and service users who are recipients of care, experience the local NHS Trust and the wider political machinations which shape secure care policy from the Department of Health. Context, as described by McCormack et al (2002), also requires an understanding of the influences of distal and proximal contemporary culture and leadership styles of the healthcare organisation. This understanding is being utilised to underpin and frame the development of strategies to improve practice leadership and care as led by matrons.

Context: Forensic mental health nursing

Forensic mental health services have undergone massive policy (Department of Health, 2007) and legislative changes within recent years, including a revision of the Mental Health Act (1983 as amended in 2007), the introduction of the Mental Capacity Act (Department of Health, 2005) and the Deprivation of Liberty Safeguards (Department of Health, 2008). Alongside policy and legislative changes there have also been positive and welcome changes to the culture of treatment within secure services through the introduction of recovery-orientated philosophies (Drennan and Alred, 2012). These changes set some unique challenges for nurses working in secure services in being able to balance the autonomy and risk of service users' recovery against the restrictive limitations of Mental Health Act legislation. Further changes in the commissioning of forensic mental health services have also been significant, such as the introduction of payment by results through the Commissioning for Quality and Innovation payment framework (Garvey et al, 2012). All of these changes present significant challenges in the development of an effective forensic nursing workforce with the required practice leadership and capabilities.

Context: The Nursing Directorate

The Nursing Directorate of Birmingham and Solihull Mental Health NHS Foundation Trust provides a solid professional platform to assist matrons across secure services in developing localised practice leadership strategies. To enable this the Nursing Directorate has developed a four-year nursing strategy (Birmingham and Solihull Mental Health Foundation Trust, 2011) that is being implemented by lead nurses and matrons across the Trust. The strategy is being delivered through the Trust's Nursing Advisory Council with six focused strategic nursing work streams (*Box 16.3*).

Box 16.3. Nursing strategy work streams (adapted from Birmingham and Solihull Mental Health Foundation Trust, 2011)

- Service user, carer and family experience.
- Nursing governance.
- Clinical effectiveness.
- Research and innovation.
- Leadership and professional standards.
- Workforce development and education.

Table 16.1. Nursing values (adapted from **Birmingham and Solihull Mental Health Foundation Trust, 2011**)	
Respect	For the dignity of service users, carers and families premised on confidentiality and acceptance of each person's worth.
Sensitivity	To each person's beliefs and values, which requires compassion, responsiveness and self-awareness.
Integrity	The need for reflective practice and continuing professional support in order to maintain professional standards.
Recovery	Respect for the individual and for the person's expertise in their own life journey, requiring active listening, caring and helping to identify the next steps forward.

The strategy is also underpinned by the set of values shown in *Table 16.1.*

The context offered by the Trust's nursing strategy and values is firmly embedded in the change strategies being utilised by matrons in secure services across the Trust to drive practice leadership and standards.

Strategy to develop effective practice leadership and care pathways

The role of matrons at the 90-bedded male medium secure unit in South Birmingham was introduced at a time when all secure services were undergoing significant change. This change involved commissioning a new medium secure service in the northeast of Birmingham alongside the development of a new service delivery model.

In consultation with the lead nurse a four-phase strategy was developed to lay foundations for the development and introduction of effective forensic nursing leadership and care pathways to support the new service model. This involved the matrons taking identifiable practice leadership responsibilities across the acute and rehabilitation wards within the medium secure unit.

Phase 1: Mental health nursing metrics

Phase 1 of the strategy was to develop ward-based leadership and care skills to support the introduction of the Trust metrics for mental health care. The metrics developed were informed by national guidance on hospital-acquired infection, lessons learnt from serious incidents, nursing-related complaints, examination

Table 16.2. Mental health metrics indicators (adapted from Dean, 2012)	
Ward-based indicators	Medication, storage and administration
Patient-related indicators	Has the named nurse coordinated a patient's discharge? Have risk and nutrition assessments been completed? Have the service user's weight and physical observations been completed?
Patient experience indicators	Do service users know their named nurse? Do service users feel listened to? Do service users feel that they are treated with dignity and respect?

of ward environments, and input from carers and service users. The process was supported by the introduction of fortnightly quality meetings with ward managers and the introduction of weekly ward-based quality meetings to shape nursing staff awareness of key patient safety and experience issues. These meetings also dovetailed with the essential standards for compliance required by the Care Quality Commission to continue registration for the wards in the service (*Table 16.2*).

In this first phase, the matron's role also linked in with Trust service development leads who had been commissioned to introduce the Productive Mental Health Ward (NHS Insititute for Innovation and Improvement, 2008) as a structured leadership and service improvement model across secure services. The focus of the model was to release time to care and to increase the time staff have to engage meaningfully with service users. The programme offers a framework for quality and assurance, targeting the four core areas of patient safety, reliability of care, patient and carer satisfaction, and staff well-being and safety.

The philosophy of the Productive Mental Health Ward is strongly associated with the principles of transformational leadership and afforded the opportunity for matrons to adopt and role model this style of leadership in supporting the development of mental health nursing metrics and the requirements for ensuring ongoing compliance with Care Quality Commission essential standards. Burns (1978) describes the process of transformational leadership as the motivation of followers through appealing to their higher ideas and moral values where the leader has a deep set of internal values and ideas and is persuasive at motivating followers to act in a way that sustains the greater good rather than their own interests (Burns, 1978). The Productive Mental Health Ward makes it safe for staff to extend their boundaries of thinking, promoting and creating innovation.

206

Research by Corrigan et al (2000) has indicated that teams led by transformational leaders had greater positive service user feedback regarding quality of life where team members who delivered care viewed their leader as charismatic and inspirational. These results suggest that transformational leaders appear to have a direct impact on the clinical management skills of team members.

Phase 2: Forensic mental health service model

As the Trust's strategies were bedding down, the second phase of the strategy was embarked upon whereby the lead nurse and matrons contributed to the development of the Service Model (Garvey et al, 2012). In essence the model of care developed explicitly describes a care journey for mentally disordered service users that for many is long, complex and distressing. It acknowledges the difficult work that is necessary on that journey in order for the individual concerned to make significant positive changes in a way that supports their recovery and well-being. The model acknowledges the stages that many individuals have to work through and the specific type of interventions that need to be available to support this work.

Further distilling of ideas within the model led to the concept of SCALE as a descriptor of the service user's journey and the identification of eight intervention programmes aimed at assisting each client on that journey.

The SCALE stages (*Figure 16.1*) described in the document are: Stabilisation, Collaborative responsibility, Active intervention, Learning and consolidation, and Exit planning.

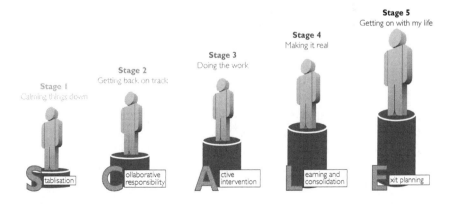

Figure 16.1. SCALE stages (adapted from Garvey et al, 2012).

The eight programmes of SCALE are:

- Mental illness and associated distress programme.
- Psychological well-being programme.
- Risk-reduction programme.
- Substance-misuse programme.
- Home and care environment programme.
- Physical health and well-being programme.
- Family and relationships programme.
- Community integration and life skills programme.

Phase 3: Home care environment programme

Following the development of the Model of Care (Garvey et al, 2012), phase three of the strategy has just begun to be implemented. In this stage, the matron is practice lead on the forensic nursing implementation of the home care environment programme.

The home care environment programme is ward-based and nurse led. It acts as a hub to support the care journey and recovery of mentally disordered service users as they progress from acute care to rehabilitation. It is also designed to equip nursing staff with the requisite practice leadership and care skills to deliver meaningful care to mentally disordered offender service users (*Box 16.4*).

The current implementation of the home care environment programme involves the matrons spending quality clinical time on wards utilising direct supervision (Guy et al, 2007) in supporting nurses to work with service users on the implementation of the programme. The matron also acts as a senior nurse on multidisciplinary team meetings ensuring that the home care environment programme becomes embedded within the nursing contribution to the care programme approach.

Phase 4: Enhanced clinical forensic nurse training programme

The final phase of the implementation strategy is to enhance forensic nursing leadership and care pathways within the medium secure unit through clinical education and skills training. This involves matrons taking the lead in researching, identifying and updating forensic nursing competencies and skills. This is required in order that forensic mental health nurses working in the Trust are brought up to date with the required managerial, clinical and leadership skills to be able to deliver and significantly enhance the nursing care of mentally disordered service

---

Box 16.4. Aspirations of the home care environment

- A service-user person-centred approach to providing individualised care and a risk management plan, tailored to the individual which is least restrictive.
- To be recovery focused, to facilitate people to recover to maximise their potential to rebuild their lives.
- To support the well-being of service users and strive to ensure that the care environment is free from harm.
- To support social inclusion, assisting with other aspects of people's lives such as employment, housing, education and maintaining family and carer involvement.
- To create an environment that optimises the physiological, physical and mental well-being of service users.
- The unit will be organised to facilitate opportunities for service users to meet their health and social needs, and to facilitate easy and prompt access to programmes, interventions and activities to support their recovery.
- To create opportunities for service users to develop learning and new skills as well as maintaining existing skills.
- To create ward-based communities that foster positive social interaction utilising pro-social modelling.
- The wards will be clean and safe. All service users will respect and be encouraged to participate in maintaining the standards as appropriate

Adapted from Garvey et al (2012)

---

users. Without this updating and provision of new training, forensic nurses will struggle to keep up with the rapid changes that are taking place within the speciality of forensic mental health. For nurses to be able to fully participate and utilise the home care programme it is acknowledged that a competency-based forensic nurse education programme is required to be developed in partnership with Birmingham City University. This would further enhance the effectiveness of nurses in contributing and supporting service users' recovery in relation to clinical targets for clinical care and offending behaviour.

Conclusion

This chapter has considered some of the key contextual policy and practice drivers at a national and local level that frame the agenda of matrons working in secure services.

Of significance, the chapter identifies the need for the upgrading of forensic nursing competencies and skills to meet the demands of the new NHS. The rapid developments of forensic mental healthcare and policy in recent years turn the observations of Burrow (1993) into truisms in that more than ever forensic mental health nurses continue to require an impressive knowledge base in order to deliver therapeutic interventions across the range of mental disorders and offending behaviours. Clinical nursing leaders in forensic mental health who fail to address these requirements will diminish further the unique contribution that forensic mental health nurses bring to the care and treatment of mentally disordered offender service users. Ultimately, this will lead our multi-disciplinary colleagues to view our contribution within the narrow domains of delivering the bulk of structural and procedural security roles within medium secure services.

The role of the matron, as described in this chapter, personifies the transformational leadership skills required for the development of the four phase strategies identified to increase forensic nurses' practice leadership skills and the development of nurse-led care pathways within a 90-bedded medium secure unit. The existence of a robust nursing strategy with a clear value base within Birmingham and Solihull Mental Health NHS Foundation Trust also serves to enhance the matron's role within secure services.

The role of the matron in medium secure services is to some degree still in its infancy and, because of this, unique opportunities exist to evaluate formally the impact of the role on the development of effective forensic nursing leadership and care pathways within such settings.

References

Burns JM (1978) *Leadership*. Harper Row, New York

Burrow S (1993) The treatment of security needs of special hospital patients: A nursing perspective. *Journal of Advanced Nursing* **18**(8): 1267–78

Birmingham and Solihull Mental Health Foundation Trust (2011) *Nursing strategy*. BSMHFT, Birmingham

Care Quality Commission (2012) *The essential standards*. Available at: www.cqc.org.uk/organisations-we-regulate/registering-first-time/essential-standards

Corrigan PW, Lickey SE, Campion JF, Rashid F (2000) Mental health team leadership and consumer satisfaction and quality of life. *Psychiatric Services* **51**(6): 781–5

Dean E (2012) Metrics initiative to boost mental health care. *Nursing Management* **19**(3): 7

Department of Health (2000) *The NHS plan: A plan for investment, a plan for reform.* Stationery Office, London

Department of Health (2002) *Modern matrons in the NHS. A progress report.* Stationery

Office, London

Department of Health (2008) *Deprivation of Liberty Safeguards*. Stationery Office, London

Department of Health (2009) *The Bradley Report. Lord Bradley's review of people with mental health problems or learning disabilities in the criminal justice system.* Stationery Office, London

Drennan G, Aldred D (2012) Recovery in forensic mental health settings: From alienation to integration. In G Drennan, D Aldred (eds). *Secure recovery: Approaches to recovery in forensic mental health* (pp 1–23). Routledge, London

Garvey K, Clarke J, Conlon L (2012) *Secure services clinical model of care*. Birmingham and Solihull Mental Health Foundation Trust, Birmingham

Gould D (2008) The matron's role in acute National Health Service trusts. *Journal of Nursing Management* **16**: 804–12

Guy S, Fyffe S, Iffil W (2007) Low conflict, high therapy nursing in a psychiatric intensive care unit. In A Kettles, P Wood, R Byrt, M Addo, M Coffey, M Doyle (eds). *Forensic mental health nursing: Forensic aspects of acute care* (pp 136–56). Quay Books, London

McCormack B, Kitson A, Harvey G, Rycroft-Malone J, Titchen A, Seers K (2002) Getting evidence into practice: The meaning of context. *Journal of Advanced Nursing* **38**(1): 94–104

NHS Institute for Innovation and Improvement (2008) *The Productive Mental Health Ward Module Boxed Set*. NHS Institute for Innovation and Improvement, Coventry

Shanley O (2004) Measuring the impact of modern matrons in the wards setting. *Nursing Times* **100**(44): 28–9

Chapter 17

Education and leadership

Paul Illingworth

Introduction

Leadership is a vital element of any organisation as previous chapters have shown. Indeed you can go further to say that it is a vital element of any group within an organisation, especially where the organisation is changing. There can be fewer organisations in the world with more groupings and sub-groupings than the health service in the UK and in which so much change occurs on a regular basis. It is not surprising then, that leadership can be found in the curricula of all professions working in the NHS. It is also unsurprising that the NHS has invested heavily in developing a national framework for leadership and a central website to go with it (http://www.nhsleadership.org.uk/). From the national framework was developed a National Leadership Competency Framework (http://www.nhsleadership.org. uk/framework-theframework.asp). One project within this has been practice leadership, which is based on the concept of shared leadership.

Additionally, a vast amount of money is spent every year in the UK on leadership. This is because of the need for change. Whenever change is happening, good leadership is needed. The context in which this happens currently is one of major cultural changes within health and social care, which has being triggered by the current government on the grounds of economic austerity. It also comes at a time of increasing challenges to professionals' power from service users, carers, the government, voluntary and private sectors and the increasing inter-professional means of health and social care delivery. Nurses, as the largest group of staff, are, therefore, at the centre of many of the cost-cutting measures and NHS reforms being introduced by the current coalition government. Nurses need, therefore, to be not only able to deliver high quality care, but to also give good practice leadership and be sufficiently politically astute to challenge any measures being introduced that would compromise care quality.

Mental health and intellectual disability nurse leaders are in a difficult position, as are nurse leaders within all fields, for while they are required to share their organisation's collective responsibilities and be accountable to their employer, they are also, as individual nurses, professionally accountable to the Nursing and Midwifery Council. This often causes a conflict of interest for the nurse.

The importance of practice leadership and nurses' participation in leadership and management was shown in a King's Fund report (2011). The report asserted that any deficiency in clinical nurse leaders' involvement was a failing, and called for leadership that paid attention to systems and two-way relationships.

This chapter explores whether "leadership" can in fact be taught. The underpinning knowledge is no doubt important to enable students to reflect on it and develop a better understanding before they are able to use that information to transform the care delivered and the organisation they work in.

In the UK there have been several recent accounts of nurses', and other professionals', failure to care for service users, particularly older people, but also those with mental health problems and those with intellectual disabilities. These failures are not acceptable and urgent attention is needed to address the issue. Nurse leadership has been seen to be a significant factor in these and other failures. However, such "crises" are not new. Following the Griffiths Report (Department of Health and Social Security, 1983), general managers and new administrators began working in the NHS. The "traditional" ward sisters or charge nurses were replaced by ward managers. The issue was that something that service users and carers valued and understood, the ward sister or charge nurse, and had worked effectively with for many years, was removed.

What has been occurring at the nurse/service user interface is that the work conditions, in which nursing care is delivered, have changed and continue to change. Managers need to be alert to these changes, which can sometimes be on a daily basis. If nurses are not alert to and respond to the changes, problems are likely to emerge and/or worsen.

Mental health and intellectual disability nursing today is very different to what it has been in the past and charge nurses now have many more issues to consider. The mechanistic hierarchical model of management is no longer appropriate in the current health service or indeed the wider health and social care sector. Today, a very different model is needed, one which individualises care, is more autonomous, and one which aligns staff to service users rather than to tasks. As long ago as the 1980s, calls were made to enhance the role of the charge nurse, what was then termed ward sister (Pembury, 1980). However, until more recently, little coordinated help appears to have been available to support and educate people in this vital role.

The challenge of clinical nurse leadership has to be aligned to the charge nurse role but it has also been taken into the advance practitioner, nurse consultant and senior nurse manager roles. Leadership in the current and future health and social care climate needs to respond proactively to government initiatives. Clinical nurse managers and leaders must demonstrate personal qualities of, among others, resilience and political astuteness.

The reported apparent deterioration of health and social care work environments must be of concern to anyone but more so to the nurse leader or manager. A healthy work environment and workforce is necessary for improved quality of care for service users. One possible cause for this apparent deterioration, and there are others, such as the increase in unregulated healthcare assistants, could be that nurses are placed in leadership positions without being adequately prepared and without adequate support for their roles. It is therefore necessary to explore the concept of leadership and how it can help clinical nurses.

Leadership approaches

There is a vast body of knowledge on leadership. What has been seen to be central to good leadership has been the attributes of a good leader. Why is it a person is accepted as a leader within any group? Little or no agreement exists when it comes to attempting to answer this question. Areas often cited as being linked are:

- Tendency to possess the qualities expected in the group.
- Qualities/attributes of being a person.
- Significance or worth.
- Sustained enthusiasm.
- Integrity – trustworthy/loyal.
- Toughness – demanding and fair.
- Humility – lack of arrogance, open to being criticised.
- A willingness to learn.

What would appear to be essential are a person's position in the organisation, and his or her knowledge and charisma, with the latter two seen as most important.

Two styles of leadership have tended to dominate in recent years. Transactional leadership, which focuses on providing everyday care, and transformational leadership, which emphases processes that motivate colleagues to achieve their full potential through inducing change and providing direction. These are briefly described as:

- *Transactional leadership*: This involves the skills required for effective day-to-day running of a team.

- *Transformational leadership*: Involves how an integrated team works together and the innovativeness of their approach to the work.

(Adapted from Outhwaite, 2003).

While a transactional approach has its uses, transformational leadership is currently more appropriate to the health and social care sector. For instance, a leader can empower team members by allowing individuals to lead specific parts of a project, based on their expertise. By doing so, these individuals will be inspired to develop their leadership skills. Additionally, leaders must address barriers and identify conflicts as they arise, and then work in partnership with others to resolve them rather than letting them continue.

The ability of a leader to communicate a shared vision is an important aspect of transformational leadership. Transactional leadership is largely concerned with managing predictability, while transformational leaders identify and challenge the status quo (Faugier and Woolnough, 2002).

It is not the intention of this chapter to explore the styles of leadership in depth but it is important to understand these differences in the context of current care delivery.

Governance

The NHS developed clinical governance as the favoured approach to working, where staff became accountable for continuous quality improvement while simultaneously safeguarding standards of care and creating a setting for clinical excellence (Moiden, 2002). UK government policies have in recent years necessitated leadership which better reflects the diversity of the workforce and the community as a whole (Scott and Caress, 2005). However, leadership still needs to be strengthened and to involve all staff. Shared governance has been identified as one method of allowing for this. This method of leadership empowers all staff within the decision making process, and facilitates staff to work together to develop multi-professional care (Scott and Caress, 2005). Shared governance is a decentralised management (rather than leadership) approach which enables all team members to have responsibility. Managers are facilitative, rather than using a hierarchical management style where they are controlling and staff are not involved in decision making. Scott and Caress (2005) argue that this type of management will lead to increased morale and job satisfaction, increased motivation and staff contribution, encouragement of creativity, and increased sense of worth. However, management and leadership are two things and a good manager is not necessarily a good leader.

Practice leadership for inter-professional nursing

Ward sisters were originally seen as a central cog around which all care was delivered (Pembury, 1980). Health and social care have moved on considerably since this time, and inter-professional delivery of care has developed in importance, together with an increased emphasis on community-based care. The World Health Organization (2010) emphasised the importance of inter-professional working. Similarly the Nursing and Midwifery Council has a central theme within its code of practice emphasising the importance of collaborating with those in your care:

• You must listen to the people in your care and respond to their concerns and preferences.
• You must support people in caring for themselves to improve and maintain their health.
• You must recognise and respect the contribution that people make to their own care and well-being.
• You must make arrangements to meet people's language and communication needs.
• You must share with people, in a way they can understand, the information they want or need to know about their health.

(Nursing and Midwifery Council, 2008: 3)

Inter-professional learning for healthcare professionals became a government (Department of Health, 2000, 2001) and university objective (Coster et al, 2008: 668). The UK government encouraged universities to increase inter-professional education at pre-registration levels for health professionals. The pre-registration nurse education standards also stressed the requirement for inter-professional working and emphasised inter-professional learning which they defined as:

An interactive process of learning which is undertaken with students or registered professionals from a range of health and social care professions who learn with and from each other.

(Nursing and Midwifery Council, 2010)

Inter-professional education is now fairly well established throughout undergraduate nursing programmes within the UK. However, Begley (2009) stated that for it to be successful, educators need to commence inter-professional learning early in the programme, and that it needed to be both theoretical and involve practice placements to ensure it was both valued and assessed. This latter element is perhaps where this can fall down, given the large number of nurses working in practice and mentoring students, who have perhaps themselves had inadequate preparation to be leaders. Current nursing students need to see their mentors role modelling good leadership to enable them to develop the necessary attributes to become future leaders of nursing.

Since students of nursing spend a large proportion of their time working inter-professionally, they will experience good leadership qualities and should incorporate these in their own clinical practice.

Education for leadership

For nursing practice to improve and for nurses to be in a position to work more effectively inter-professionally there needs to be an investment in educating nurses to be effective leaders. Cook (2001) argued that leadership should be introduced in pre-registration nurse education, and that mentoring should also be available for nurse leaders. This would prepare them to have better understanding and be able to manage situations that may occur (Moiden, 2002). Successive changes to nursing curricula have enhanced learning about leadership and the inclusion of the above requirement to enhance leadership knowledge and skills within the pre-registration standards will assist in the longer term. The integration of the NHS Leadership Qualities Framework (NHS Leadership Academy, 2011), with its emphasis on personal qualities, setting direction and delivering the service into undergraduate nursing programmes, will also assist in enhancing nursing leadership.

As a further example, the Medical Leadership Competency Framework (NHS Institute for Innovation and Improvement, 2010), which has recently become the Leadership Framework for Clinicians, will also be of value. It will not only raise the awareness of leadership within medicine, but also how it impacts on nursing, other organisations and individual practitioners as they negotiate how such leadership attributes can promote an ethos of collaboration in such areas as:

- *Personal qualities*: Acting with integrity, self-development, self-management, self-awareness.
- *Working with others*: Working within teams, encouraging contribution, building and maintaining relationships, developing networks.
- *Managing services*: Managing performance, managing people, managing resources, planning.

- *Improving services*: Facilitating transformation, encouraging innovation, evaluating critically, ensuring patient safety.
- *Setting direction*: Evaluating impact, making decisions, applying knowledge and evidence, identifying the contexts for change.

As a caution, however, nurse educators need to avoid selecting contemporary management and leadership competencies and theories, and then expecting students to be able to apply these in practice settings. Such standards and competencies have to be applicable to current practice. With the remodelling of health and social care and greater inter-professional working, leadership is required which can bring about meaningful changes in practice.

Adair's Action-Centred Leadership Model has been seen to be very effective in bringing about change. Adair, who has been one of the most influential figures in leadership in the last 30 years, argued that for leadership to be truly effective the whole organisation has to buy in to a unified approach (Adair, 2012). The Action-Centred Leadership Model provides a method for leadership for any team, group or organisation. It comprises of three parts and is represented by three overlapping circles, see *Figure 17.1*.

The circles represent the three core responsibilities involved within a change.

- Achieving the task.
- Managing the team or group.
- Managing the individual.

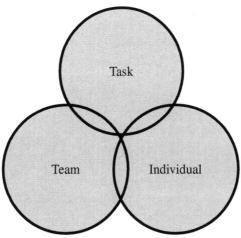

Figure 17.1. Adair's Action-Centred Leadership Model.

All three elements are mutually reliant upon one another and this requires a balance of attention not only to task and the individual, but also to the team (Swanwick and McKimm, 2011). The elements are also all separately essential for a leadership role. There are other core functions associated with the model which are essential for it to work effectively. The model does not stand alone and necessitates an integrated approach to management and leadership, hence the need for a whole organisation approach.

Adair (2012) argued that an organisation/group consists of a task (primary function), a team (which has forces holding it together while simultaneously trying to pull it apart) and an individual. All three are constantly working together, pulling and pushing. If one of these were to be removed it would have the effect of causing the organisation/group to fail. However, behind the three circles is a leader holding it together and ensuring that all three elements continue to work to the same goal. As you work within and across teams, look towards the extent these areas are addressed and how well they are looked after by those in leadership positions.

However, other skills and attributes are also needed. Who and what you are, what you know and what you do all define a good leader. Good leaders also have excellent communication skills and are able to deal with challenging individuals. Further, a good leader holds high-quality values that they need to be able to demonstrate to others. Leaders do not just control others, they act as visionaries, help colleagues to plan, and lead, control, and organise their activities (Jooste, 2004). If they do not they will not survive as the leader.

As health organisations begin to use such approaches as action-centred leadership, nurse education programmes need to incorporate them into their undergraduate and postgraduate programmes. The action-centred leadership approach can, itself, be taught. However, the principles, qualities, skills and values described above can be, and are already, taught in many nurse education programmes. What nurses need to do now is to have the confidence and desire to challenge the status quo and any changes that are felt to be counterproductive to achieving quality care for service users.

Conclusions

Leaders are change agents who are not at ease with the status quo of time-honoured organisational processes. They relish innovation and the challenge change brings. Leaders do not simply control staff, they act as visionaries and facilitators to assist employees to plan, lead, control, and organise their own activities (Jooste, 2004).

The 21st century has and will continue to demand different leadership approaches. A new kind of leader will materialise and lead in a new way. Nonetheless, the basic qualities of good leaders will continue to underpin effective leadership. Currently, mental health and intellectual disability nurse leaders are continually asked to do more with less and need to be innovative while relying on teamwork in all levels of care delivery. They develop and sustain a working environment that motivates rather than suppresses employees. Leaders must apportion equal priority to staff development as they do to finance to achieve the mission, values, and vision of the organisation they work in.

In the current health and social care sector, mental health and intellectual disability nurses need to work in ways that extol collaboration, sharing both the power and the responsibility that goes with it. Nurses have to be prepared for partnerships and further collaborative working and the shared leadership that is necessary for success. Shared leadership provides a framework that offers nurses maximum involvement in decision making about care and the work environment.

The National Leadership Framework gives a coordinated approach; the challenge will be to ensure engagement with all staff within healthcare and for that to be translated into inter-professional working not only within health services but also within social, voluntary and private sectors.

References

Adair J (2012) *Opening address: Action centred leadership launch event.* Sandwell & West Birmingham Hospitals NHS Trust, Birmingham

Begley CM (2009) Developing inter-professional learning: Tactics, teamwork and talk. *Nurse Education Today* **29**(3): 276–83

Cook M (2001) The renaissance of clinical leadership. *International Nursing Review* **48**(1): 38–46

Coster S, Norman I, Murrells T, Kitchen S, Meerabeau E, Sooboodoo E, d'Avray L (2008) Interprofessional attitudes amongst undergraduate students in the health professions: A longitudinal questionnaire survey. *International Journal of Nursing Studies* **45**: 1667–81

Department of Health (2000) *The NHS plan. A plan for investment, a plan for reform.* Department of Health, London

Department of Health (2001) *Investment and reform for NHS staff: Taking forward the NHS plan.* Department of Health, London

Department of Health and Social Security (1983) *The Griffiths Report. NHS Management Inquiry Report.* Department of Health and Social Security, London

Faugier J, Woolnough H (2002) National nursing leadership programme. *Mental Health*

Practice **6**(3): 28–34

Jooste K (2004). Leadership: A new perspective. *Journal of Nursing Management* **12**(3): 217–23

King's Fund (2011) *The future of leadership and management in the NHS: No more heroes.* The King's Fund, London. Available from: http://www.kingsfund.org.uk/ publications/nhs_leadership.html

Moiden M (2002) Evolution of leadership in nursing. *Nursing Management* **9**(7): 20–5

NHS Institute for Innovation and Improvement (2010) *Medical leadership competency framework.* NHS Institute for Innovation and Improvement, Coventry

NHS Leadership Academy (2011) *Leadership qualities framework.* Available from: www. leadershipacademy.nhs.uk

NHS Leadership Academy (2012) *National leadership framework.* Available from: http:// www.leadershipacademy.nhs.uk/discover/leadership-framework/

Nursing and Midwifery Council (2008) *The code: Standards of conduct, performance and ethics for nurses and midwives.* Nursing and Midwifery Council, London

Nursing and Midwifery Council (2010) *Standards of proficiency for pre-registration nurse education.* Nursing and Midwifery Council, London. Available from: http:// www.nmc-uk.org/Educators/Standards-for-education/Standards-of-proficiency-for-pre-registration-nursing-education/

Outhwaite S (2003) The importance of leadership in the development of an integrated team. *Journal of Nursing Management* **11**(6):3 71–6

Pembury S (1980) *The ward sister: Key to nursing.* Royal College of Nursing, London

Scott L, Caress A-L (2005) Shared governance and shared leadership: Meeting the challenges of implementation. *Journal of Nursing Management* **13**(1): 4–12

Swanwick T, McKimm J (2011) What is clinical leadership and why is it important? *The Clinical Teacher* **8**(1): 22–6

World Health Organization (2010) *Framework for action on interprofessional education and collaborative practice.* World Health Organization, Geneva

Chapter 18

Cultural diversity

Marion Johnson

The function of education is to teach one to think intensively and to think critically...Intelligence plus character, that is the goal of true education.
Martin Luther King Jnr (1929–1968)

If the NHS is to become fit for purpose for the 21st century it must acknowledge the diversity of the communities it wishes to serve and address the unique needs of individuals within these communities. NHS leaders have to interpret the law and address organisations and structures while focusing and implementing legislation, such as the Equality Act 2010, and other legislations relating to egalitarianism and discrimination. Within this agenda, the NHS needs to augment and enhance its willingness to be involved and work with communities (Weisbord and Janoff, 2010). Since it was set up in 1948 the NHS has championed the service of individuals, groups and communities.

The consumers of today's health service are empowered, they know their rights through legislation and information technology and request up-to-date information about their care and prognosis. They are no longer the passive recipients of care but rather work in partnership with care providers (Human Rights Act 1998; Equality Act 2010; Department of Health, 2006, 2010d, 2010b, 2011a). To continue advancement in this area, the government has created *Healthwatch England* (Department of Health, 2010c). This document will be used as a strategic part of the Care Quality Commission's (2011) aim to champion the rights of consumers.

The Winterbourne Inquiry (Department of Health, 2011b) found that health professionals ignored the guiding principles-based approach to ethical decisions of health autonomy, justice, beneficence and non-maleficence (Beauchamp and Childress, 1989). Lord Victor Adebowale, Chief Executive of Turning Point, has been commissioned to undertake an inquiry into deaths in police custody of mentally ill individuals. The information obtained will enhance understanding of the journey faced by mentally ill individuals in police custody prior to entering health services. This may lead to health improvements in this area through collaborative working within communities, including information sharing about health promotion and resources.

There have always been disparities and inequalities in health for certain groups in relation to access, care and appropriate discharge back into the community

(Department of Health, 1980). The Equality Act 2010 was implemented in an attempt to address these inequalities regarding sexuality, gender, age, physical disability, religion/beliefs and race.

It was suggested by MacPherson (1999) that public services should examine their practice and how they are used by ethnic communities, in order to measure their suitability for the communities they purport to serve. If rates of referrals or access to healthcare for certain ethnic minorities are low in comparison with better represented population groups in the same region, then there is *prima facia* evidence that the service is not appropriate, unless it can be shown that there are other reasons for reduced referrals and/or access.

The 2011 Census (Office for National Statistics, 2012) identified that the ethnic population in England and Wales is increasing. This trend is expected to continue for the future, hence the importance of collaboration and partnership working with ethnic communities. Ethnic professionals with appropriate skills and knowledge need to be acknowledged and promoted as leaders in the future, using legislation and positive action.

The needs of the identified protected groups are vast, similar in many ways but also different. Effective communication is the key to opening the door to all these groups. Communication is not just about verbal or non-verbal communication but about showing respect and listening actively while allowing groups to express their thoughts and feeling in ways with which they are comfortable. Maslow's (1999) hierarchy of needs identifies that groups and individuals all have basic needs that need to be fulfilled to enable them to reach their full potential. Following on from physiological needs is the necessity for groups and individuals to feel safe and valued. Members of communities need to become proactive as representatives in health organisations so they can influence any decisions for their communities or groups.

Leaders should have strong self-belief and positive coping skills, be approachable and self-aware, have knowledge of their limitations, be able to self-manage and have high personal integrity. At the same time, they should have the ability to foresee outcomes and the directions that need to be taken, and collaborate with the community and other health professionals. To achieve this may require intellectual flexibility, political assertiveness, networking, broad scanning and the drive to achieve results. However, the drive to achieve results can lead to issues the community feels strongly about being ignored, a situation that can at times lead to conflict. This is where personal characteristics are invaluable, as is the ability to use their skills. If professionals and communities become dissatisfied they may take their complaints to the public domain, using the media or social networks, thereby bringing NHS leaders and organisations into disrepute.

Leaders need to listen to their staff on a regular basis and allow time to challenge current practice. Such discussions may improve knowledge, skills and behaviour and lead to service redesign.

The National Leadership Council commissioned the NHS Leadership Framework (Institute for Innovation and Improvement, 2010a) to acquire knowledge of leadership skills required and also to identify talent for the benefit of the organisation and communities served. The Leadership Qualities Framework (Department of Health, 2010a) identified the qualities needed by 21st century NHS leaders to enable them to address all aspects of cultural diversity. The aim is to acquire leaders with knowledge, skills and characteristics that fit the post and communities they serve.

Broad scanning is useful for gathering information but it must be observed who is gathering such information, who is evaluating it, and whether he or she is knowledgeable and sensitive to the area concerned. A few years ago a trust embarked on addressing the in patient health needs of African Caribbean people. They undertook broad scanning and decided to employ African nurses to meet this particular need. However, this led to many problems:

- Verbal/non-verbal communication issues.
- Cultural differences/understanding.
- Societal misunderstanding by the patient and health practitioner.

It should be recognised that although the trust's aims were honourable in trying to address the identified situation, what it clearly demonstrated was that it did not understand the particular community it sought to serve. The trust's mistake was later rectified following discussions and collaborative partnership working with the African Caribbean communities to identify the right person, with the right knowledge, skills and personal characteristics, to work in this sensitive area.

Nature or nurture

Thomas and Ely (1996) do not believe that leaders are born but rather that people can be nurtured to become leaders. Therefore, recognising leadership talent from diverse groups should be encouraged, with legislation used to make it happen. Leaders from diverse groups will have different life experiences and will bring with them different perspectives on cultural issues, values and beliefs. Different perspectives encourage learning opportunities and challenge organisational structure, professionals and the community.

There are two types of leaders identified by Hampden-Turner and Trompenaars (2000): individual and community. Individual leaders are competitive, self-reliant and interested in their own personal growth and development. They exhibit the "selfish self" by not working collaboratively with the team and not acknowledging the team's skills, knowledge and ability. This particular leadership style eventually leads to disruption, failure of communication and the development of barriers that prevent success.

Community leaders are concerned with the social issues of the community and require the community's cooperation and involvement (Department of Health, 2006, 2010b, 2010d, 2011a). A "community NHS leader" actively seeks to form collaborative partnerships, with community and professionals working together. Community leaders augment and provide training for and promotion of culturally diverse individuals who have appropriate skills and knowledge within the organisation.

The NHS Leadership Framework (Department of Health, 2010a) and the Leadership Qualities Framework (Institute for Innovation and Improvement, 2010a) suggest that such qualities should be used when working in culturally diverse communities to identify the right person for the job. The Clinical Leadership Competency Framework (Institute for Innovation and Improvement, 2011) advocates:

- *Working collaboratively with others*: individuals, carers, groups, communities and other professionals.
- *Demonstrating personal qualities*: communication, active listening, reflection, flexibility, critical thinking, and emotional intelligence.
- *Setting directions* as per government plans, community feedback and up-to-date peer-reviewed research evidence.
- *Improving services* in line with the identified community's requirement which is evaluated and audited for satisfaction.
- *Managing services* to ensure they are effective, financially viable and well-resourced.

These five care leadership competency domains clearly identify the requirements essential for NHS leaders for the 21st century. Health educators should incorporate these features in all training curricula in conjunction with the essential professional code of conduct standards.

The Nursing and Midwifery Council (2008) Code states that you must:

- Make the care of people your first concern, treating them as individuals and respecting their dignity.
- Recognise and respect the contribution that people make to their own care and well-being.
- Work with colleagues to monitor the quality of your work and maintain the safety of those in your care.
- Work cooperatively with teams and respect the skills, expertise and contributions of your colleagues.
- Deliver care based on the best available evidence or best practice.
- Ensure any advice you give is evidence based if you are suggesting healthcare products or services.
- Demonstrate personal and professional commitment to equality and diversity.
- Adhere to the law of the country in which you are practising.

It should be acknowledged that there may be issues affecting leadership style, such as resistance to change. The questions to be asked are, why is there resistance to change, what is the issue, and is training required?

Leaders should be transparent and promote egalitarianism and a non-bureaucratic structure that will encourage exchange and promotion of ideas by all, and allow for constructive challenges that will lead to improvements, while also accepting differences.

Personal and organisational barriers to communication must be broken down. Personal barriers include self-doubt and past experiences that have been construed negatively. Individuals with the right skills should be identified and promoted and they should be made aware of their track record of positive contributions.

As an individual you can bring about change by appraising your current position within the organisation and identifying where you want to be in the future. Use your individual performance review to:

- Identify how the organisation can help you, e.g. shadowing a senior manager.
- Discuss the skills and expertise required for the role and ways to acquire such skills.
- Identify what additional information you will need for the position you would like to apply for in the future.

The more you learn and develop, the more valuable you are to any organisation.

Recruitment of diverse leaders

To address lack of diversity in the protected groups identified in the Equality Act 2010, NHS leaders and senior managers should make the process of promotion transparent and established on the following criteria:

- Is the candidate the best person for the job? Use a marking criteria in which the candidate clearly demonstrates, before the interview, a track record connecting clinical aptitude with knowledge and experiences.
- If there is in-house cover for the job advertised, how long has the individual been in post? A document should be attached which demonstrates the percentage of those providing cover who are promoted versus external candidates. Remove the belief that the interview process is a tick box exercise to conform to legislation.

Transparency at all stages would provide evidence that the best candidate has been chosen for the job.

- All members of the interview panel should acknowledge if there is a conflict of interest. Do they have previous knowledge of the candidate in a work capacity, as a family member, friend or any other capacity?

We live in a multicultural society and barriers are not as overtly obvious as they were in the past. This is due to legislation, including the Equality Act 2010. However, individuals from diverse communities are aware that such barriers exist and that they occur in all areas of their life.

Over the past few years various leadership and training courses have been set up for black minority ethnic groups to promote social mobility towards leadership and senior manager posts. However, this has failed for many reasons, including black minority ethnic people being put in positions to fill a "quota" rather than on merit. They are therefore set to fail because they lack the necessary knowledge and skills required for the role. This creates a self-fulfilling prophecy where such people are seen to fail and therefore it will be assumed that others will fail in the future. Colleagues in the same organisation will realise that such individuals are merely filling a quota and will resent and undermine them.

Individuals from black minority ethnic backgrounds who demonstrate natural leadership knowledge and abilities or potential leadership skills should be encouraged and recognised by their organisation (Betancourt et al, 2002).

A change of attitude and behaviour by human resources personnel is a pre-requisite for all NHS institutes to ensure black minority ethnic people applying for leadership positions are given equal opportunities for meaningful employment. Positions should be advertised in ethnic minorities' papers and an equality officer should check advertisements before publication.

Barriers to equality

Barriers can be internal or external. Internal barriers include candidates feeling unworthy, lacking in self-esteem and motivation, and possibly having had past negative experiences of promotion systems. External barriers could be political due to organisational structure, or could occur where individuals are not party to meetings and/or social gatherings due to their lower status in the organisation.

Diversity has been identified by Jehn et al (1999) to consist of three components:

- Demographic differences (social class status).
- Informational, which is concerned with knowledge, education and experiences.
- The effect of value, i.e. the individual's personality, attitudes and behaviour.

Most senior leaders in the NHS are white Anglo-Saxon males. Nursing, which has been and still is a female dominated profession, has few female senior managers and fewer still from black minority ethnic groups of either gender.

In 2009 only 15% of all NHS employees were from black minority ethnic communities (Institute for Innovation and Improvements, 2011). Although these communities are on the increase this is not reflected either in numbers of students in nursing courses in universities or in leadership positions.

Cultural competency will mean that individuals and groups, whether in the clinical area or in education, will be able challenge assumptions and verbal and non-verbal communication, and gain an understanding of individuals or groups different from their own cultural background (Ramden, 1992).

The following is adapted from Berlin and Fowkes' (1983):

- *Listen*: seek to understand the perspective of others for the benefit of all.
- *Explain your perceptions and strategies* to all involved in the task while seeking feedback and clarification of those involved.
- *Acknowledge and discuss* differences and similarities as to how to move forward.

- *Recommend a way forward* while remembering cultural parameters.
- *Negotiate an agreement* that respects prevailing cultural frameworks.

Conclusion

There are many requirements for NHS leaders if they are to be effective and fit for purpose for the 21st century. Communities are no longer passive recipients of services but rather are active participants in all aspects of care through legislation, technology and empowerment of the service user.

The world is changing and the recognition of a black minority ethnic person in a leadership role should be encouraged and promoted as a reflection of the diversity of any country. The importance of interpersonal skills and cultural knowledge and understanding by NHS leaders is paramount to improvement in health services. This will eventually have a positive effect on finance as the right care will be identified at an early stage. This will only be achieved through community and NHS leaders working collaboratively and in partnership. It is acknowledged that there are barriers but these can be addressed by transparency of promotion within organisations.

References

Beauchamp T, Childress J (1989) *Principles of biomedical ethics*. Oxford University Press, Oxford

Berlin EA, Fowkes WC (1983) A teaching framework for a cross-cultural care. *Western Journal of Medicine* 139: 934–8

Betancourt JR, Green AR, Carrillo JE (2002) *Cultural competence in health care: Emerging frameworks and practical approaches*. Available from: http://www.commomwealth.org/~media/Files/Publication

Department of Health (1980) *Black Report: Inequalities in health*. HMSO, London

Department of Health (2006) *Our health, our care, our say*. HMSO, London

Department of Health (2009) *Inspiring leaders: Leadership for quality*. HMSO, London

Department of Health (2010a) *The Leadership Qualities Framework (LQF)*. HMSO, London

Department of Health (2010b) *New horizon*. HMSO, London

Department of Health (2010c) *Health watch England*. HMSO, London

Department of Health (2010d) *Equality and excellence: Liberating the NHS*. HMSO, London

Department of Health (2011a) *No health without mental health*. HMSO, London

Department of Health (2011b) *Mid-Staffordshire Hospital NHS Foundation Trust Inquiry.* HMSO, London

Hampden-Turner C, Trompenaars F (2000) *Building cross-cultural competence.* Yale University Press, New Haven, CT

Institute for Innovation and Improvement (2010a) *National Health Service leadership framework.* HMSO, London

Institute for Innovation and Improvement (2010b) *Medical Leadership Competency Framework.* Available from: http://www.institute.nhs.uk/images/documents/ Shared%20Leadership%20Underpinning%20f%20MLCF.pdf.

Institute for Innovation and Improvement (2011) *Clinical Leadership Competency Framework project. Report on findings.* HMSO, London

Jehn KA, Northcraft GB, Neale MA (1999) Why differences make a difference: A field study of diversity, conflict and performance in work groups. *Administrative Science Quarterly* **44**(4): 741–63

MacPherson W (1999) *The Stephen Lawrence Inquiry.* HMSO, London

Maslows AH (1999) *Towards a psychology of being* (3rd Edn). John Wiley and Sons, New York

Nursing and Midwifery Council (2008) *The code: Standards of conduct, performance and ethics for nurses and midwives.* Nursing and Midwifery Council, London

Office for National Statistics (2012) *Census 2011.* HMSO, London

Ramsden IM (1992) *Cultural safety in nursing education in Aotearoa.* Paper presented at the Year of Indigenous Peoples Conference, Brisbane, Australia

Thomas D, Ely RJ (1996) Making differences matter: A new paradigm for managing diversity. *Harvard Business Review* **Sept/Oct**: 79–91

Weisbord M, Janoff S (2010) *Future search: An action guide to finding common ground in organizations and communities.* Berrett-Koehler, San Francisco, CA

Index

Symbols

Index

solution-focused
  approach 63
  coaching 57
  communication 39
  practice 62
staff training 155
standards
  Care Quality Commission 152
  development of 152
  setting 153
SWOT analysis 23

T

Ten Essential Shared Capabilities 2
Tidal Model 16
total quality management 151
training
  for mental health nurses 183
  for staff 155
transactional leadership 111, 194, 215
transformational
  change 124
  leadership 111, 119, 194, 206, 216
    matrons 206

V

values
  nursing 205
Valuing people 6, 27, 69–78, 139

W

Winterbourne Inquiry 7, 28, 109, 223

Y

Youth
  Advisory Panels 183
  Ambassadors 183